Atlantic City
& the
New Jersey Shore

FODOR'S TRAVEL PUBLICATIONS

are compiled, researched, and edited by an international team of travel writers, field correspondents, and editors. The series, which now almost covers the globe, was founded by Eugene Fodor in 1936.

OFFICES
New York & London

Fodor's Atlantic City & the New Jersey Shore

Editor: Kathy Ewald
Area Editors: Jerome Klein, Mike Schwanz
Maps: Mark Stein Studio, Pictograph
Illustrations: Ted Burwell
Cover Photograph: Joe Viesti/Viesti Associates Inc.

Cover Design: Vignelli Associates

SPECIAL SALES

Fodor's Travel Publications are available at special discounts for bulk purchases (100 copies or more) for sales promotions or premiums. Special editions, including personalized covers, excerpts of existing guides, and corporate imprints, can be created in large quantities for special needs. For more information, write to Special Marketing, Fodor's Travel Publications, 201 East 50th Street, New York, NY 10022. Enquiries from the United Kingdom should be sent to Merchandise Division, Random House UK Ltd, 30–32 Bedford Square, London WC1B 3SG.

Fodor's 89

Atlantic City & the New Jersey Shore

FODOR'S TRAVEL PUBLICATIONS, INC.
New York & London

ISBN 0-679-01597-3

MANUFACTURED IN THE UNITED STATES OF AMERICA
10 9 8 7 6 5 4 3 2 1

CONTENTS

FOREWORD

Atlantic City, the crown jewel of the New Jersey Shore, draws crowds from all over the country with its beachside casinos and top-name entertainment. And it's not the shore's only resort; each beach town attracts its own clientele with a distinct atmosphere and individual charm. There are big, noisy boardwalks and quiet stretches of sand; neon motels from the 50s and 60s and restored Victorian bed-and-breakfasts; rock and roll bars and elegant restaurants. As long as your tastes don't run to deserted beaches, you'll find a perfect summer sun spot at the Jersey Shore.

Fodor's Atlantic City and the New Jersey Shore is designed to help you plan your own trip here, based on your time, your budget, your likes and dislikes—your idea of what this trip should be. Perhaps having read this guide, you'll have some new ideas.

We have tried to offer you the widest range of activities and within that range selections that will be safe, worthwhile, and of good value. The descriptions we provide are designed to help you make your own intelligent choices from among our selections.

The first section of this book, Fact at Your Fingertips, consists of material designed to help you plan your trip to the shore and learn what sorts of amenities and activities are available.

Next is an introduction to help you with the background of the place: some history, the way of life, the feel of the region.

Following this, we break down the NJ Shore into areas. First we describe each area generally and tell you what there is to do and see. Then we give you the Practical Information: lists of accommodations and restaurants, details about the beaches, boardwalks, nightlife, historic sights, and more.

While every care has been taken to assure the accuracy of the information in this guide, the passage of time will always bring change, and consequently the publisher cannot accept responsibility for errors that may occur.

All prices and opening times quoted in this guide are based on information available to us at press time. Hours and admission fees may change, however, and the prudent traveler will avoid inconvenience by calling ahead.

Fodor's wants to hear about your travel experiences, both pleasant and unpleasant. When a hotel or restaurant fails to live up to its billing, let us know and we will investigate the complaint and revise our entries where the facts warrant it.

Send your letters to the editors of Fodor's Travel Publications, 201 E. 50th Street, New York, NY 10022, or 30–32 Bedford Square, London WC1B 3SG, England.

ATLANTIC CITY
AREA

FACTS AT YOUR FINGERTIPS

FACTS AT YOUR FINGERTIPS

DEFINING THE AREA. Few areas in North America are as naturally blessed as the New Jersey Shore, which encompasses a 127-mile stretch of land ranging from Sandy Hook on the north (the southern border of New York Harbor) to Cape May on the south (which touches Delaware Bay). With its moderate climate (caused by the warm waters of the nearby Gulf Stream) and its wide, white, sandy beaches, this region remains a mecca for lovers of the sea.

The epicenter of the shore is, of course, Atlantic City—about 85 miles south of Sandy Hook and 40 miles north of Cape May. In the late 1800s and early 1900s, this town was one of the major resorts of the East Coast. Today, it is the only city outside of Nevada that allows gambling, and some 30 million people a year visit here, easily making it the shore's number one tourist attraction.

However, some 60 other towns border the Atlantic, and each one of them has its own personality and character, as you will see later in this book. Some are "party" towns, catering to the young, and others are family towns, catering to the older set. A number are dominated primarily by one ethnic group (usually Italian, WASP, or Jewish) while others are a complete mixed bag. So no matter what type of seashore vacation experience you are seeking, it's likely that one of these towns will suit your needs.

TIPS FOR BRITISH VISITORS. Passports. You will need a valid passport (cost £15) and a U.S. Visa (which can be put only in a passport of the 10-year kind). You can obtain the visa either through your travel agent or directly from the *United States Embassy,* Visa and Immigration Department, 5 Upper Grosvenor St., London W1; 01–499 7010. Note that the embassy no longer accepts visa applications made by personal callers.

No vaccinations are required for entry into the U.S.

Customs. If you are 21 or over, you can take into the U.S.: 200 cigarettes, 50 cigars, or 3 lbs. of tobacco; 1 U.S. quart of alcohol; duty-free gifts to a value of $100. Be careful not to try to take in meat or meat products, seeds, plants, fruits, etc. And avoid narcotics like the plague. Returning to Britain, you may bring home (1) 200 cigarettes or 100 cigarillos or 50 cigars or 250 grams of tobacco; (2) two liters of table wine and, in addition, (a) one liter of alcohol over 22% by volume (most sparkling wine), (b) two liters of alcohol under 22% by volume (fortified or sparkling wine), or (c) two more liters of table wine; (3) 50 grams of perfume and 1/4 liter of toilet water; and (4) other goods up to a value of £32.

Insurance. We recommend that you insure yourself to cover health and motoring mishaps with *Europ Assistance,* 252 High St., Croydon CRO 1NF; 01–680 1234. Their excellent service is all the more valuable when you consider the possible costs of health care in the United States. Trip-cancellation and luggage insurance is another wise buy.

Air Fares. We suggest that you explore the current scene for budget flight possibilities. Check APEX and other fares at a considerable saving over the full price. Quite frankly, only business travelers who don't have

1

to watch the price of their tickets fly full-price these days—and find themselves sitting right beside APEX passengers! APEX roundtrip fares to Philadelphia cost from £336.

Electricity in the U.S. is 110 volts. You should take along an adapter since American razor and hair-dryer sockets require flat two-prong plugs.

TOURIST INFORMATION. The first step one should take when planning a trip to the shore is to contact several of the state's very efficient tourism bureaus. These include:

New Jersey Division of Travel and Tourism, CN 826, Trenton, NJ 08625 (609–292–2470).

Atlantic City Visitors Bureau, Department of Public Relations, Convention Center, 2310 Pacific Ave., Atlantic City, NJ 08401 (609–348–7044).

Monmouth County Department of Economic Development, Division of Tourism, Freehold, NJ 07728 (201–431–7476).

Ocean County Tourism Advisory Council, CN 2191, Administration Building, Toms River, NJ 08753 (201–929–2163).

Long Beach—Southern Ocean County Chamber of Commerce, 265 W. 9th St., Ship Bottom, NJ 08008 (609–494–7211).

The three major daily newspapers in this region are the *Atlantic City Press,* the *Asbury Park Press,* and the *Ocean County Observer.* Several local publications will also give you up-to-date information about special events, restaurants, nightlife, etc. *Atlantic City* magazine covers the southern shore region. Every June, *New Jersey Monthly* publishes a special shore issue that offers lots of useful information.

WHEN TO GO. Deciding when to visit this area is a bit of a catch 22. For a century now the summer season has been the lifeblood of the New Jersey Shore, since most visitors come here to enjoy the sand, the sea, the sun, and the recreational activities that go along with them—sunbathing, swimming, sailing, etc. The weather is usually excellent in the summer, and there are more things to do, by far, from Memorial Day to Labor Day. In addition, this is the one season when you are guaranteed that absolutely everything is open, from motels and restaurants to bars and shops. But keep in mind that summer is also the season when the hotel and motel rates are highest, and when the beaches, streets, restaurants, and stores are most crowded. Basically, things are just more of a hassle.

Temperatures are generally in the high 70s or low 80s during the day, dropping into the 60s at night, during the summer. By mid-July, the ocean temperature is at least 70°F in most spots.

Spring and fall are generally quite pleasant. And even the winters are relatively mild compared to the rest of the Northeast, due to the moderating effect of the Atlantic Ocean. However, many veteran travelers think the finest period to visit this area is right after Labor Day, when the weather is still warm and the water temperature of the ocean is the highest of the year—usually 70° to 75° in most places. Nearly every establishment (even the more seasonal ones) remains open at least until September 30, and best of all, the crowds are significantly reduced. For recreation lovers, it should also be noted that September is an excellent month for golf, tennis, sailing, and especially fishing.

By mid-September, most beach-oriented activities grind to a halt, as cool autumn temperatures dominate the area, and after September 30, many businesses close down for the season, although at least half the restaurants and motels stay open year-round.

In October, days on the shore are usually sunny and pleasant and cool. With fall foliage at its peak, this is a particularly nice time to do some hiking, bike riding, and automobile touring.

From November through April, things are pretty slow on the shore, and the people who want to have some time to themselves will really enjoy the easy, slower pace of the off-season. There is plenty of shopping, and one can stroll the beaches and boardwalks in virtual solitude. The weather is blustery and cold, but except for January and February, it seldom gets below 32° next to the Atlantic Ocean.

WHAT TO PACK. In general, things are very casual on the Jersey Shore, and visitors should dress to be practical, not to "be seen." Naturally, one should bring along plenty of suntan lotion, as well as a hat, lip balm, thongs, etc. It is wise to bring some insect repellent. Also bring beach chairs, beach umbrellas, etc.—although it is possible to rent these locally. A comfortable pair of tennis shoes is perfect for strolling along the boardwalks.

Even in mid-July, it can get cool in the evenings, so always pack a sweater and windbreaker. Daytime high temperatures are usually in the 75°-to-85° range. Sometimes restaurants and motel rooms have too much air-conditioning, and if you are sunburned, you'll freeze. Sweatpants and a sweatshirt may not be a bad idea.

Evening dress codes in restaurants and night spots are usually quite casual. Even the Atlantic City casinos, which once required coats and ties on men, have relaxed their dress restrictions. Only the fanciest restaurants in the casino-hotels, and perhaps a few restaurants in luxury hotels in other shore towns, now require formal attire.

COSTS. As one might expect, the Jersey Shore is most expensive during the summer, or high season. Prices go down about 25 percent in the fringe seasons of spring and fall and a further 25 percent during the winter.

Compared to other seaside spots on the East Coast, the shore is quite reasonable. Two couples, for example, can rent a very nice house right on the sea for about $1,000 a week in some towns: with two couples sharing the cost, that's only $500 per couple. Motel rooms during peak season average about $85 a night. Restaurants can cost as much as you're willing to spend—there is such good variety and competition that most menus are fairly reasonably priced.

The 12 Atlantic City casino-hotels are, by far, the most expensive places for lodging and dining. They can cost $160 a night or more. Gambling is also expensive; many games require a minimum bet of $5. Slot machines are 25¢, 50¢, and $1.

Most towns now require a beach pass, which can range from $3 to $8 a day. Weekly passes can run from $8 to $15, however, many hotels and inns provide guests with complimentary passes.

SENIOR CITIZEN DISCOUNTS AND STUDENT DISCOUNTS. Because it caters to a large percentage of older people, Atlantic City does offer a few select opportunities and discounts to the elderly. For complete information on which discounts might be available to you, contact the *Atlantic County Office of the Aging and the Disabled,* 1133 Atlantic Ave., Atlantic City, NJ 08401 (609–345–6700).

Several major bus companies servicing senior citizens offer discounts, upon proof of age. Just ask the driver if you are eligible when you board the bus. Also, several stores in Atlantic City participate in a senior-citizen discount program, so be sure to always carry a driver's license and/or Medicare card.

As for other shore towns, the best way to get a senior-citizen discount is to ask the individual proprietor of the restaurant or motel you are visiting. There is no official policy up and down the shore. Generally, though, the established stores and restaurants do offer slight discounts.

Since there are no sizable universities in the immediate area of the shore, there are few students and therefore few student discounts. It is possible that a few local movie houses may offer breaks.

HOW TO GET THERE. The vast majority of visitors drive to the shore. In many ways, it's the most efficient way to get to this area. In addition, except possibly for Atlantic City, you will need a car to get from one place to another, once you are settled in your particular seaside town.

People visiting here from other parts of the country can fly to New York or Philadelphia, rent a car, and then make the one- to two-hour drive to their exact shore destination.

The Garden State Parkway is the main north-south artery leading to the shore. Virtually every exit leads to an eastbound road, and then it's another 10 to 15 miles or so to the ocean. Once you get off the Parkway, it usually takes less than 20 minutes to drive to most shore points.

Several bus companies from New York City and Philadelphia also service this region. A train line runs from New York to as far south as Bay Head (about halfway down the shore). In addition, a sparkling new train station is scheduled to open in the spring of 1989, providing service from New York and Philadelphia.

See the How to Get There and How to Get Around sections in the Practical Information for each chapter.

ACCOMMODATIONS. The variety in housing opportunities here is enormous. Most lodging on the shore is comprised of small, functional motels that cater to tourists. Few places are luxurious, but most of them are certainly respectable. Most people staying here spend 12 to 16 hours a day outside of the motel rooms anyway.

A few towns, such as Spring Lake and Bay Head, have wonderful bed-and-breakfast establishments. These places are usually grand old Victorian homes with 10 to 20 bedrooms, one master dining room, and one master living room. These houses are usually tastefully decorated, and their hosts provide a nice personal touch.

Houses can be rented for a week or longer in many areas. This can be an excellent, even inexpensive housing alternative, especially for a group of people. All costs are shared, and many meals can be prepared right on the premises. Summer houses, however, are much in demand, and most of them must be reserved several months in advance.

Costs can vary widely, but a few factors will strongly affect price: The season—some establishments even have two or three seasons within the peak summer season. (June is always the least expensive month.) Any place right on the ocean will cost more and if your room has an ocean view, its cost will certainly be greater. Atlantic City casino-hotels cost much more than other accommodations along the shore.

It's always wise to write to several places far in advance, asking for their brochures and complete rate structure, and then try to confirm your reservations as far in advance as possible. You can always get some sort of lodging at the last minute, but if you want to get the exact type of lodging you want, try to have everything lined up by May first. A deposit is usually required.

To start obtaining information about renting a house, contact the municipality which you intend to visit. For complete addresses, see "Rentals" in the *Practical Information* chapter of this book. The towns will then send you a list of licensed real-estate agents, and you can contact them directly.

For information about bed-and-breakfast establishments, there is a statewide reservation service, *Bed and Breakfast of New Jersey, Inc.* (201–444–7409). For more information about those guest houses in Spring Lake, contact *Spring Lake Chamber of Commerce,* Box 694, Spring Lake, NJ 07762 (201–449–0577). In the Point Pleasant and Bay Head area, contact *Greater Point Pleasant Chamber of Commerce,* 517A Arnold Ave., Point Pleasant Beach, NJ 08742 (201–899–2424).

Also see the individual listings in the "Bed-and-Breakfast" section in *Practical Information.*

CAMPING. There are many good campgrounds on the shore. Unfortunately, because of the incredible value of land, none of these are right on the sea. Those people who like to camp out on the beach and have the crashing surf lull them to sleep will be disappointed.

Generally speaking, there are more camping opportunities at the southern end of the shore than at the northern end. Many are concentrated near Atlantic City. Some campgrounds are located only on an open parcel of land, and offer nothing but the ground itself, while others feature swimming pools, video arcades, tennis courts, general stores, and other niceties. Costs vary widely, generally from $5 to $20 a night.

A few campgrounds take reservations; others don't—it's first come, first served. Since the shore gets so crowded in the summer, it may be less stressful to find one where you can reserve in advance, so you will be ensured of a spot.

The tourism bureau of each shore county (see Tourist Information, above) has a brochure that lists various camping facilities. Specific campgrounds are listed later in this book in the Practical Information sections.

DINING OUT. Thousands of eating establishments dot the New Jersey Shore. It's safe to say that no matter where you are staying, you will be less than a five-minute walk or drive from a good restaurant. The variety of eating places is so staggering that no matter what cuisine you feel like, it should be easy to find.

In nearly every town, there are coffee shops, diners, or fast-food places where one can get a quick breakfast or lunch. And most towns have two or three premier restaurants that offer sumptuous dinners. In addition—

for those towns that have boardwalks—innumerable places sell snacks, ice cream, candy, etc. You'll also find many types of ethnic food available, although the longtime specialties of the shore are Italian and seafood. Mexican restaurants and standard Continental fare are also well represented.

Dress is casual in most of the restaurants. During the busy summer season, a dinner reservation may be needed, especially on Friday and Saturday nights. Some places, even top-notch restaurants, won't accept reservations, so be prepared to wait in line.

Although every restaurant is open in summer, many are closed in the off-season. If you're on the shore between October first and May first, it's wise to call ahead to verify that a place is open.

BEACHES. Probably the shore's greatest assets are its great beaches. Nearly the entire shoreline is covered with wide, white beaches filled with soft, rock-free sand, and swimmers love the gradual declines into the surf. Although a few beaches were briefly closed in 1987 due to pollution, the problem was not as severe in the summer of 1988.

With the exception of Atlantic City and Wildwood, all shore towns now require a beach pass for access. These can usually be purchased right on the boardwalk, or they can be purchased in advance at a town's police station or city hall. Daily fees range from $3 to $8. Weekly and season passes are sometimes offered as well. Some motels and hotels offer their guests free beach passes, so feel free to ask about this perk.

The majority of towns provide lifeguards and changing rooms with toilets and showers. For a complete listing of individual towns' beach services look under the Beaches section in Practical Information for each area.

BOARDWALKS AND AMUSEMENTS. One of the unique and most fun attractions of the New Jersey Shore is its free, great boardwalks that parallel the sea. These wide wooden sidewalks are often the epicenter of activity for each shore town.

The most famous one, of course, is Atlantic City's, upon which 10 of the city's 12 casinos are located. Here, one can stroll from one end of town to the other, seeing the ocean on one side, and the great, brilliantly lit casinos on the other. The Ocean One shopping mall is here, as are hundreds of small souvenir stores and snack shops. Musicians, jugglers, and other street performers are everywhere. Best of all, the beach is free, and there are public bathhouses.

Several other towns north of Atlantic City also feature boardwalks. In some of them, such as Sea Bright, Spring Lake, and Ocean Grove, the boardwalks are very peaceful and tranquil; no amusement parks are allowed, and only a very limited number of food places and convenience shops. In other towns, like Point Pleasant, Asbury Park, and especially Seaside Heights, the boardwalks offer giant amusement parks, complete with roller coasters, log flumes, and ferris wheels. During the day, parents with small children populate these areas; at night, thousands of junior-high and high-school kids cruise these pedestrian highways.

For a guide of which towns have boardwalks and/or amusements, write to the *New Jersey Division of Travel and Tourism,* CN 826, Trenton, NJ 08625, and ask for its brochure, *New Jersey's Shore Region.*

CASINOS. The chief reason why 30 million people visit Atlantic City each year is its gambling casinos. Currently, there are 12 casino-hotels operating in Atlantic City. A new facility, the Taj Mahal, is under construction and will open sometime in 1989.

Ten of the casinos are located right next to the Boardwalk. Two—Trump's Castle and Harrah's Marina—are found near Farley State Marina, a couple of miles away.

Gambling is limited to anyone 21 years of age or older, and this is very strictly enforced. The casinos themselves are huge, and offer virtually every gambling game one can think of. Each casino has scores of blackjack and roulette tables, and hundreds of slot machines, which take quarters, fifty-cent pieces, or silver dollars.

The *minimum* bet for blackjack, roulette, and other table games is a $5 chip. Naturally, there are tables with $25, $50, and $100 minimums for the really high rollers. (Budget-conscious gamblers may want to consider the Atlantis, which has a few, select $2 blackjack and roulette tables.)

Besides its casino, each casino-hotel has several high-quality restaurants featuring different ethnic cuisines, one or two cocktail lounges (often with live entertainment), and an official showroom, where the big-name entertainers perform (Frank Sinatra, Bill Cosby, etc.).

All these casino-hotels are huge, each offering at least 500 rooms. Many of them also provide lavish health clubs and other athletic facilities to their guests. See the Atlantic City chapter for details.

How to Play the Games

Baccarat. Wagers made in baccarat invariably are the highest in the casino, which adds to the excitement of this international "Game of James Bond." The game is played with eight decks of cards dealt from a "shoe." The object of the game is to have your cards total as close to 9 as possible. Face cards count as 10, and all others count at face value. Participants wager on one of two hands, either the player's or the bank's, each of which is initially dealt two cards. The hand finally totaling 9 or the next closest to it is the winner. The last digit of the card total determines the hand value. For instance, two 9s total 18, so the value of the hand is 8. Two cards are dealt to the player having the largest wager against the bank, and two cards to the person acting as banker. The player acts first. In case of a tie, the hand is played over.

Rules stipulate that when a third card is dealt, if the banker wins, he retains the shoe. When the banker loses, the shoe moves to the right, giving each player a chance to handle or pass the shoe. Many players like baccarat because it is a game where no real skill is involved; it's all pure luck. If you're feeling lucky that night, have a good bankroll, and like to sit next to well-dressed, often beautiful people, then go for it.

Blackjack. The object of the game is to draw cards that total as close to 21 as possible without exceeding it. Face cards count as 10, and the ace can count as either 1 or 11. The dealer gives each player two cards face down and gives himself two, one face up. The player may stand (take no more cards) or draw additional cards to try to get close to 21. If you "bust" (go over 21), you lose, even if the dealer also loses. If your total is closer to 21 than the dealer's, you win. If there is a tie, no one wins. Any ace with a ten, jack, queen, or king is automatically a blackjack (21). If both the player and the dealer have a blackjack, it's a tie.

Split bets: If the player's first two cards are of the same value, he may split them into two hands, betting the same amount on each.

Double down: A player can double his bet on any two cards and then draw one card only.

Insurance: If the dealer has an ace showing, a player may take insurance (bet up to one half of his original bet). If the dealer's down card is a ten, jack, queen, or king, the player wins two for one. If it is any other card, the dealer wins.

Craps. The most exciting and the noisiest game in the casino. Just look at all that action! Craps is a dice game in which every player has an opportunity to place a bet on *every* roll of the dice. If you bet the "pass line," you win on 7 or 11, and lose on 2, 3, or 12 on the first roll. If any other number comes up, it's your "point." If your point comes up again before 7 is thrown, you win; otherwise, you lose. If you bet on the "don't pass" line, you lose on 7 or 11 and win on 2 or 3 on the first roll. You also lose if the point comes up again before 7.

Come bet: A come bet may be made at any time after the first roll. You win on 7 or 11; you lose on 2, 3, or 12. Any other number is your point. If your point comes up again before 7, you win.

Don't come: The reverse of a come bet. You lose on 7 or 11 and win on 2 or 3 (12 is a standoff). You win if 7 comes up before the point is made.

Field: A bet for one roll only. You bet on 2, 3, 4, 9, 10, 11, and 12. If any of these numbers is thrown on the next roll, you win even money, except on 2 or 12, on which you win two-to-one.

Big 6 and 8: You win even money if 6 or 8 is rolled before 7.

Any 7: You win five-for-one if 7 is thrown on the first roll after your bet.

Hard ways: You win at odds quoted on the table layout if the exact combination of the numbers you bet comes up. You lose if the number is rolled any other way—or if 7 comes up.

Any craps: You win eight-for-one if 2, 3, or 12 is thrown on the first roll after your bet.

Eleven: You win fifteen-for-one if 11 is thrown on the first roll after your bet.

The odds: Once a point is established, either a shooter's point on the first roll or a come point on the succeeding roll, you can get odds with the dice or give odds against the dice. You get two-to-one on 10 and 4; three-to-one on 5 and 9; six-to-five on 8 and 6. You lay the same odds when you bet against the point.

Place bets: You may make a place bet on the following numbers: 4, 5, 6, 8, 9, and 10. The number you place must be made by the shooter before 7 is thrown.

Roulette is a relatively easy game to learn. Take a look at the felt in front of you: You can place a bet on a single number (which pays the highest odds), on two numbers, by straddling the line, on three numbers, on four numbers, on the red or the black, on six numbers, etc. The more numbers you are covering with a single chip (or a stack of chips), the less you will win, of course, if you hit. When all the bets are down, as you have seen countless times in movies, the dealer will spin the little white ball in the roulette wheel, and where it stops is the winner. As we said, just study the felt for a few minutes, and that should tell you everything.

Slots. The slots are simplicity itself. Most of them are quite self-explanatory. Gamblers feel that you should bet the maximum number of coins each time. Your coins may be gone faster that way, but if you do win, you will win the maximum. A relatively recent innovation is the introduction of the video slot machine and the progressive carousel slots.

In these, a number of slot machines are linked together in a circle by computer so that each time someone plays one and loses, the total goes higher . . . and higher . . . and higher. You can win as much as a million dollars on one of the progressive dollar slot machines—and people have done it!

SPORTS. Sports enthusiasts, especially those who enjoy water sports, will love this region. It offers virtually every type of activity available.

Swimming can be done anywhere. Sailing and boardsailing are easy to do; in virtually every town there is a marina where one can rent a sailboat or boardsail. In some marinas, jet-skis can be rented. The mild surf and windy conditions are perfect for these sports. Water-skiing boats also can be rented, and there are many launch ramps for those who have their own boats.

Surfing is generally poor, since the surf itself is so mild and calm. However, on occasion, a good, strong easterly wind can cause excellent surfing conditions.

Some great fishing can be enjoyed in the Atlantic, especially in spring and fall. Many charter boats can be hired for the day at the major marinas along the coast. In addition, the larger marinas have party boats, which take approximately 30 or 40 fishermen. These can be a much cheaper alternative—$20 a day as opposed to $400. No reservations are necessary for party boats; just show up. The local weekly paper in each town usually has listings of charter-boat captains.

Public tennis courts can be found in most towns, probably within a few minutes' drive of your motel. The larger Atlantic City casino-hotels have their own courts. There are several golf courses a few miles from the sea, and there are several good horseback-riding operations, also further inland.

And, of course, the boardwalks are the perfect places for bicyclists (often allowed mornings only) and joggers.

BARS AND DRINKING LAWS. One of the major activities on the shore during the evening hours is to visit one of the hundreds of bars, lounges, taverns, and dance clubs that dot the shoreline.

Virtually every type of drinking establishment can be found on the shore, from romantic cocktail lounges overlooking the sea to wild, raucous rock and roll bars. (New Jersey–born rock superstar Bruce Springsteen got his start playing with a band in Asbury Park.)

The drinking age in New Jersey is now 21 and each town has its own regulations and closing times for bars and taverns. Ocean Grove and Ocean City, for example, prohibit liquor entirely. But in Atlantic City, some local establishments stay open until 6 A.M., in order to cater to local casino employees who work through the night. Those towns with a lot of rock and roll bars (Asbury Park, Seaside Heights, Belmar) are open much later than the quiet, sedate family towns (Spring Lake, Ocean

Grove, Avon). *A word of warning:* police often park outside these bars, looking for speeders or drunk drivers.

For specific listings, consult the "Nightlife" sections found in the Practical Information of each chapter.

TELEPHONES. The area code from Island Beach State Park north is 201. From Barnegat south it is 609. In most areas, the cost of a pay-phone call is 25 cents. For local information, call 411. If you are calling for assistance out of your area code, dial 1 plus area code plus 555–1212. To dial long distance, dial 1 before the area code. Dial 0 before the area code for operator assistance on credit-card, collect, and person-to-person long-distance calls. Dial 911 for emergencies.

HINTS TO HANDICAPPED TRAVELERS. With a little homework, it should be fairly easy to determine whether an area you are interested in visiting offers decent facilities for people with disabilities.

You can start by writing to the *Division of Tourism,* CN 826, Trenton, NJ 08625 (609–984–2308), asking for copies of their tourism brochures, specifying your area of interest. These publications all indicate whether a given attraction has facilities for handicapped people. You may then want to call the facility for more specific details.

As a general rule, the newer hotels in the state have the best facilities. All the Atlantic City casino-hotels, for example, have excellent facilities.

One advantage of boardwalks is that they are a lot easier to navigate in a wheelchair than plain old sand. Therefore, you may want to stay in a town with a boardwalk. In addition, Island Beach State Park, Long Branch, and Atlantic City all have ramps leading right down to the ocean.

For additional information, contact these fine organizations: *Governor's Committee on the Disabled,* Labor and Industry Building, Room 200, Trenton, NJ 08625 (609–633–6959). *Atlantic County Office for the Disabled,* 1333 Atlantic Ave., Atlantic City, NJ 08401 (609–345–6700, ext. 2831). *Monmouth County Office of the Handicapped,* 29 Main St., Freehold, NJ 07728 (201–431–7399). *Ocean County Office for the Disabled,* 34 Hadley Ave., CN 2191, Toms River, NJ 08754 (201–244–6804).

THE JERSEY SHORE

An Introduction

by
DEBRA BERNARDI

Bruce Springsteen was far from the first to recognize the pleasures of the Jersey Shore. He may have popularized the place for music fans of the 1980s, but before the New World was even a gleam in the eyes of Europeans, the Lenni-Lenape Indians were making summer pilgrimages to the beaches that line New Jersey's Atlantic coast.

"The shore" is loosely defined as the 127-mile stretch of beach that runs from Sandy Hook, New Jersey, south to the state's southern tip, Cape May Point, including the barrier islands that dot the coastline. In the seventeenth century the Dutch settled here, followed by the English. New Englanders came south for the whaling opportunities, eventually depleted the whale population, and returned home. Pirates, too, saw the attractions of the area; legends claim that Captain Kidd left buried treasure at Cape May Point and Brigantine.

Steamboats, then railroads, and eventually highways brought people from the cities to the beach resorts. Cape May, which claims to be America's oldest seaside resort, advertised rooms for seven cents in an 1801 Philadelphia paper. (Prices have increased substantially. One thing about the Jersey Shore—it's not cheap. Expect to pay upwards of $70 a night for a double room with private bath in the summer season. Dinner for two at a nicer restaurant can easily run about $40.)

The Methodists founded two resort towns: Ocean Grove and Ocean City. Both are still dry today, but liquor is in abundance in neighboring communities.

Of course, there have always been some who seem immune to the charms of the Jersey Shore. Thomas Budd, a land speculator, who eventually was to buy Atlantic City, looked over that barrier island in 1695 and said, "I don't want that swampland at any price. It will never be good for anything but seagull nests."

Today there are people who are similarly short sighted and who can't understand why hordes of people will sit in the famous summer-weekend traffic of the Garden State Parkway to reach the shore towns of their choice. The truth is that the towns are so different from one another, each person on the Parkway is heading toward his or her ideal vacation spot. As long as you're not looking for a deserted beach, you can find your perfect shore town here, too.

It's hard to generalize about the shore towns; they're all wonderfully unique. All the beaches are open to the public, though there is usually a charge, and you may have trouble finding public access to a beach lined with private homes, as in Deal or Harvey Cedars. (There is currently a move to improve this situation.) Beach passes vary widely in price—from about $2 a day at, say, Seaside Heights, to $8 a day at Spring Lake. Many beaches have bathhouses with changing areas and rest rooms.

In every town you'll find good restaurants (especially seafood and Italian), probably a good diner (with at least one waitress who will call you "hon"), miniature golf, and a very active nightlife.

The brassy rock and roll that the NJ Shore is famous for can be found in a number of bars. Usually they're large (with room for dancing), crowded, and dumpy looking in the cold light of day. The crowd is mostly young, but there are rock and roll fans of all ages who come to listen to the sounds, dance, drink, and sweat. The Stone Pony in Atlantic City is the most famous—Springsteen got his start here, and you can still find musicians who have played with the Boss (or with friends of the Boss) or who make great rock and roll in their own right. There are plenty of other music clubs—in Long Branch, Asbury Park, Belmar, Long Beach Island—all along the shore.

For those who want something besides rock in the evenings, the shore offers a great selection of sing-along bars. The evening bar at Crane's Hotel, in Surf City (on Long Beach Island), might be the standard. The bar room is huge, with about three separate bars. During the evening, the room is packed with people of all ages, from seniors to those just this side of the drinking age. A local band (it consisted of two people the night I was there) plays ethnic songs, patriotic songs (people hold money over their heads during "America the Beautiful," though the significance of this remains a mystery to me), show tunes, and standard hits like "New York, New York." Through it all everyone sings their hearts out and sways back and forth. It's an experience that must truly be felt to be believed. Carney's Other Room, in Cape May, has a sing-along atmosphere much like Crane's, though I've never seen people holding dollars over their heads there.

And, of course, for a completely different brand of nightlife, there are the stars and casinos of Atlantic City.

ATLANTIC CITY

Atlantic City is in a category by itself. Opened as a bathing resort in the 1850s, the town was soon attracting an upscale crowd of people who stayed in elegant boarding houses. When the owners of the boarding houses discovered that guests tracked in sand and ruined upholstery, it was suggested that a walkway of boards be built on the sand. The boardwalk was born, which is part of the unique attraction of many NJ Shore towns today.

The opening of casino nightclubs was not the first time top stars came to Atlantic City: Sarah Bernhardt, W. C. Fields, George M. Cohan, John Philip Sousa all performed here in theaters on the seashore.

And there have always been the beauty queens. The pageants were originally thought up to prolong the summer season: The first Miss America received her crown in 1921.

In the 1960s and 1970s, though, it became clear that AC was far from the glamorous resort it once was. The businesses along the boardwalk were run-down, the city's economy severely depressed. There can be no doubt that the advent of the casinos (gambling was legalized in 1976) changed the face of the resort. Whether or not gambling has improved life for the residents of the town is a matter of some controversy. Many local people claim that the casinos have only hurt AC's already troubled economy by keeping all the tourist dollars in the casino hotels; these critics claim that gambling has brought no jobs to residents and no dollars to local businesses. There is a profound difference between life on and off the boardwalk today.

Still, whether you stay in AC or visit from a nearby shore town, you'll find a real excitement here. As you cross the bridge from the mainland, the skyline rises ahead like the Emerald City; with all the money flying around, green is an appropriate color for this place. The high rollers arrive in the casinos' complimentary limousines; senior citizens pour off buses with their complimentary rolls of change for the slot machines; the buildings are large and glittering (there's even a huge statue of Julius Caesar facing the ocean—outside Caesar's Palace, of course). Strollers along the boardwalk carry more than the usual ice-cream cones; here they are holding casino cups containing their slot-machine winnings (or maybe they're just carrying what they haven't lost yet).

NORTH OF ATLANTIC CITY

The towns from Sandy Hook State Park south to AC are as different from each other as they are from AC itself.

Down-to-Earth

Long Branch, one of the northernmost shore towns, offers a nice beach (with changing rooms and toilets), a shortish boardwalk with the requisite wheels of chance and stuffed-animal prizes, a special amusement area with an impressive haunted house for children, rock-'n'-roll bars, and probably the best hot dogs (with hot relish) anywhere (at Max's near the south end of the boardwalk, a block from the ocean).

Though new condos hint at gentrification, Long Branch is still run-down enough to let you feel perfectly comfortable, perfectly relaxed. You never need to worry about feeling out of place or not having the right resort wear. It's this down-to-earth feeling that makes this the perfect place to expose a not-quite-perfect body in a swimsuit to the world. You can be yourself and simply enjoy yourself.

Just south of Long Branch, Asbury Park holds forth. Thanks to Bruce Springsteen, the town and its rock 'n' roll clubs are now the stuff of legends. Like Long Branch, Asbury is also somewhat run-down; but developers already have plans underway to change all this. The beach is big and often very crowded. The boardwalk is magnificent. Once considered the best on the shore, it still has two beautiful old carousels, a convention hall from 1928, fudge and taffy, waffles and ice cream, games, and T-shirt stores.

Teen Favorites

Asbury has always been a favorite with families, and like all shore towns, beloved by teens. A little farther south is Belmar, famed as a young "party animal's" dream. Group rentals of summer houses cram this town with kids from Memorial Day to Labor Day. In 1986, Belmar cracked down on summer shares, which have actually been illegal for years. This has raised quite a bit of disagreement between those who want to discourage the young visitors and those (especially local merchants) who want their business. The turn Belmar will take in the future remains to be seen. But traditionally it's been a town where kids are off the beach by 4 P.M. and in the nearest bar dancing and singing along to (you guessed it) Springsteen's music. Evenings find lots of parties at the shared houses, and it's not uncommon for party-goers to tramp through each others' houses on their way to the festivities.

Farther south is Seaside Heights. Here the boardwalk is two-and-a-half miles long with rides at either end, pastel benches lining the stretch, and countless stands selling frozen custard, raw clams, pizza, corn on the cob, Italian sausage, and, naturally, the ubiquitous T-shirts. When I was in high school, the annual trip to Seaside was the beginning of many a romance, and there still seem to be plenty of 16-year-olds in love (or something similar) walking close together on the boardwalk or lying close together on the sand. With the crowds this beach gets, though, everyone lies close together.

Peaceful and Pretty

Between Belmar and Seaside, Spring Lake is an abrupt change from its frenetic neighbors. An old resort town, called the Irish Riviera, Spring Lake has large hotels, which have been attracting regular guests for years, and lovely Victorian homes (some are now bed-and-breakfasts). There are swans on the lake that gives the town its name; a boardwalk just for strolling, with no amusements in sight; and a beach that at $8 a day, is less crowded than others. Spring Lake has nice restaurants (many are BYOB), a pleasant bar called the Beach House, which overlooks the ocean, and lots of places perfect for the peaceful contemplation of the sea.

Island Beach State Park, just south of Seaside, is just for enjoying the ocean. You'll have to arrive early, though (often before 9 A.M.), because once the parking lot fills to its limit of 2,200 cars, the park closes to traffic. You can spend your days at this relatively un-crowded beach and your nights at action-packed Seaside.

From the south end of Island Beach State Park, you can see one of the shore's famous landmarks, Barnegat Lighthouse. The lighthouse is at the northern end of the long skinny island, called (appropriately enough) Long Beach Island. (The residents of Long Beach Island actually levied a tax on themselves to save the lighthouse, built in 1858 and affectionately called "Old Barney.") The island was popular with whalers in the eighteenth century, and in the nineteenth century began to attract travelers—mostly fishermen.

Today the island still offers party boats for fishing enthusiasts, opportunities for divers, and miles of beautiful, clean, wide beaches. There are no boardwalks here—and the beaches stay clean by rigorous enforcement of a no-food-or-beverage-on-the-beach restriction. Not to worry, refreshments are available one block from the beach. After you've had enough sun, stop at Shuck's Clam Bar in Crane's Hotel, Surf City, for beer and raw clams; the bartender remembers the clientele from one season to the next. Harvey Cedars and Loveladies are the towns on Long Beach Island with the mansions; Surf City, Ship Bottom, and Beach Haven have smaller rental houses. There are many good restaurants (often crowded, so be prepared to wait), the usual rock and roll bars (Joe Pop's Shore Bar is a popular one), and we've already discussed the evening activities at Crane's.

SOUTH OF ATLANTIC CITY

South of Atlantic City, two communities, the Wildwoods and Cape May, show the full diversity of the shore. Wildwood is famous for having the wildest ride of any boardwalk (the Sea Serpent), the wildest bars (open until 5 A.M.), the wildest kids, and the widest beaches. It's filled with neon—spectacularly colored motels from the '50s and '60s—that couldn't be farther from the types of accommodations available in Cape May, just down the coast.

Cape May is omnipresent Victoriana: the restored bed-and-breakfast inns that are so popular here, the many fine restaurants, the shops—sometimes its feels like a Victorian theme park. Yet it's tasteful, quiet, pretty, and unlike any other shore town.

The Jersey Shore is all of these towns—and many more—but mostly it's people having fun. Gambling, swimming, beauty contests, rock and roll, Italian food, Frank Sinatra, peace and quiet, roller coasters, T-shirts, raw clams, Victorian architecture, walks along the beach at night, miniature golf, families, teenagers, senior citizens—if any (or all) of these appeal to you, you'll love it here.

ATLANTIC CITY

Queen of the Shore Towns

by
MIKE SCHWANZ

Mike Schwanz, a writer based in New York City, specializes in travel, sports, and outdoor recreation. He has written extensively about the New Jersey Shore.

Atlantic City is the crown jewel of the Jersey Shore, and by far its biggest attraction. Whereas most visitors to other parts of the shore are, for the most part, from nearby Eastern states (Pennsylvania, New Jersey, New York, etc.), Atlantic City draws a national—and international—mix of visitors. In the last few years, an average of 30 million people a year poured into this small city, which has a population of only 40,000 or so. It is one of the most heavily visited pure vacation spots in the country. In 1987, 31.8 million visitors came here.

The reason for this, of course, is the fact that Atlantic City is the only seaside community in the country that allows gambling. (For that matter, it is the only East Coast gambling city within 2,000 miles of Nevada.)

17

Twelve spectacular casino-hotels dominate the skyline—and the town itself. It's probably safe to say that 95 percent of the 30 million visitors at least *enter* a casino to either gamble or catch the great entertainment acts found in casino showrooms. Certainly all visitors to this area owe it to themselves to at least walk into a casino to observe the frenzied activity. There is nothing like it anywhere! But keep in mind that there is more to Atlantic City than gambling.

Atlantic City encompasses about 16 square miles. It is located on Absecon Island, about two thirds of the way down the Jersey Shore. It shares the island with the small towns of Ventnor, Margate, and Longport, which are southwest of it.

If ever a city had the perfect geographical location for attracting tourists, this is it. Atlantic City is close to all of the East Coast's major population centers. It is just an hour's drive from Philadelphia; $2\frac{1}{2}$ hours from New York; $2\frac{1}{2}$ hours from Baltimore; and $3\frac{1}{2}$ hours from Washington, D.C. In fact, 25 percent of all Americans (about 60 million people) live within 300 miles of the city.

The main drag in town is Pacific Avenue, which runs from the northeast to the southwest, and parallels the Atlantic Ocean. (Absecon Island juts out into the Atlantic at an odd angle, so the shoreline itself does not run straight north-south, as one might think.) On Pacific Avenue, 10 of the 12 casino-hotels are located within $1\frac{1}{2}$ miles of one another. Behind the casinos lies Atlantic City's great boardwalk, and then the ocean itself.

The major avenues in town, which run parallel to Pacific Avenue, are named after major world oceans—Pacific Avenue, Atlantic Avenue, Arctic Avenue, Baltic Avenue. Many of the cross streets are named after states.

The most northeastern casino-hotel on Pacific Avenue is the Showboat, on Delaware Avenue. Bally's Grand, off of Providence Avenue, is the southwesternmost casino-hotel. Between these two buildings are eight other casinos, the Convention Hall, and many other major shopping areas and tourist attractions.

The two other casino-hotels, Trump's Castle and Harrah's Marina, are found near Farley State Marina at the northern end of town, about $1\frac{1}{2}$ miles away from the other casinos.

History

The first people on Absecon Island were the Lenni-Lenape Indians. The Dutch explorers were the first white men here; they first appeared in the early 1600s. The English took over control of the Jersey Shore from the Dutch in the late 1600s, and began to settle the area sporadically. English landowners were seasonal residents of the island in the 1700s; these early settlers were primarily fishermen and hunters. Later generations established salt works and bog-iron foundries. Still, as late as the Revolutionary War, only three families were in the vicinity, and they were only seasonal inhabitants. In 1788, Jeremiah Leeds became the first permanent settler in this area, and soon more and more families moved in for good.

In 1852, a group of Philadelphia and South Jersey businessmen decided to put in a railroad that would run from Camden, New Jersey, to a proposed "bathing village" on Absecon Island. In 1854, Atlantic City was incorporated. By the late 1800s, it had become a well-known vacation resort for wealthy Philadelphians.

During the period from the late 1800s to the early 1900s, Atlantic City flourished. Many mainstays of Americana were born here. The first boardwalk was built here in 1870. The first ferris wheel was introduced in 1872. The first Easter Parade was held in 1876. The first saltwater taffy was sold in 1883. The golf term "birdie" was coined at the Atlantic City Country Club in 1899. The first Miss America Pageant was held in 1921. In the 1930s, the town's streets became the inspiration for the classic board game Monopoly.

After World War II, the city's fortunes started to decline. With the advent of air travel, tourism dropped, since tourists started to fly to more exotic lands. The city's buildings started decaying; young people moved out; and suddenly the bulk of the population was comprised of the elderly and the poor. Unemployment was high. As a result, in their desperation to improve their lot, Atlantic City residents begged state officials to allow gambling. On November 2, 1976, New Jersey residents passed a referendum that legalized casino gambling in Atlantic City.

The first casino to open was Resorts International, in May 1978. Others quickly followed suit.

It was hoped that the casino-hotels would spark a real boom in the city's economy. In one way they did, since they created thousands of new jobs. But many residents claim that most jobs went to out-of-towners, and areas of town are still in decay. For the most part, the areas in the immediate vicinity of the casino-hotels are thriving, and that is where most of the tourists are based.

The Boardwalk

Atlantic City's boardwalk is the most famous in the world. More than five miles long, and approximately 60 feet wide, it is the focal point of all activity. Everything "happening" in town is usually either on, or near, the boardwalk. It's populated by every type of person imaginable: millionaires, beggars, teenagers, senior citizens, runners, bikers, kite flyers, families. In nice weather, jugglers, dancers, musicians, and other street entertainers are usually performing. On one side of the boardwalk are hundreds of small stores and arcades selling fast-food, souvenirs, postcards, T-shirts, ice cream, fudge, pizza, saltwater taffy, and more. On the other side of the wooden planks is the very wide, white sandy beach . . . and the ocean.

Atlantic City is one of the very few Jersey towns with a "free" beach, meaning that anyone can use it without a beach tag or pass. Although it is patrolled by lifeguards, there are no public bathhouses.

The best thing about the boardwalk is that it is free. It costs nothing to walk, run, fly a kite, or just sit down and watch the parade of people go by. Bicycling can be done in early morning (from 6 A.M. to 10 A.M.). This can be especially delightful, since the boardwalk is virtually deserted then. During the summer, there are many free concerts, craft fairs, parades, and other events. Casino-hotels are continually sponsoring special events. To find out what is going on, simply consult the daily newspaper.

Besides walking up and down the boardwalk, visitors can also take motorized trams, which cost $1 (75¢ for senior citizens and children under 12).They run every 15 minutes or so, and are a very pleasant way to sit back, relax, and take in all the sights. In addition, rolling chairs were reintroduced to the boardwalk a few years ago. (They date back to 1887.) These carts, which seat two large adults or three skinny adults, are powered by the strong legs of the drivers who push them. They cost $5 per mile or $25 an hour, and, if you ask (and sometimes if you don't), you can get personal tips and insights from the driver about Atlantic City.

Boardwalk Attractions

Many of the town's foremost attractions are based along the boardwalk, and can be seen in a one-hour stroll. If you start at the far northeastern end of town, the first attraction worth seeing is Absecon Lighthouse, at Rhode Island. This 167-foot-high lighthouse was built in 1857, to warn ships of tricky rocks and reefs. It is a New Jersey State Park.

About four blocks west is Garden Pier, which contains two noteworthy attractions. The Atlantic City Historical Museum has displays on theaters, nightlife, piers, the beach and boardwalk, and exhibits highlighting the town's heritage. The Atlantic City Art Center, in the same building, has numerous rotating exhibits. The pier is open from 9 A.M. to 4 P.M., seven days a week.

Continuing in a southwestern direction, one comes to the Steel Pier, once used for high-diving acts; in its heyday, young women would ride on horses that dove into a large pool. It's now in decay, and the only thing left is a heliport that's used to bring in high rollers. However, plans are in the works to restore the pier about the time the Taj Mahal opens in 1989.

About a block away from the Steel Pier, on Atlantic Avenue, is Gordon's Alley, a classy pedestrian mall patterned after Ghirar-

POINTS OF INTEREST

1. Absecon Lighthouse
2. Atlantis Casino
3. Bader Field Airport
4. To Pomona Airport
5. Bally's Park Place Casino
6. Caesar's Casino
7. Central Pier
8. City Hall
9. Claridge Casino
10. Convention Hall and Visitor's Bureau
11. Garden Pier
12. Bally's Grand Casino
13. Gordon's Alley
14. Harrah's Marina Casino
15. Historic Gardner's Basin
16. Million Dollar Pier
17. Ocean One Shopping Mall
18. Resorts International Casino
19. Sands Casino
20. Showboat Casino
21. Steel Pier
22. Steeplechase Pier
23. TropWorld Casino
24. Trump Plaza Casino
25. Trump's Castle Casino

ATLANTIC CITY

SCALE

0   .25   .5 Mi.

0   .25   .5   .75 Km.

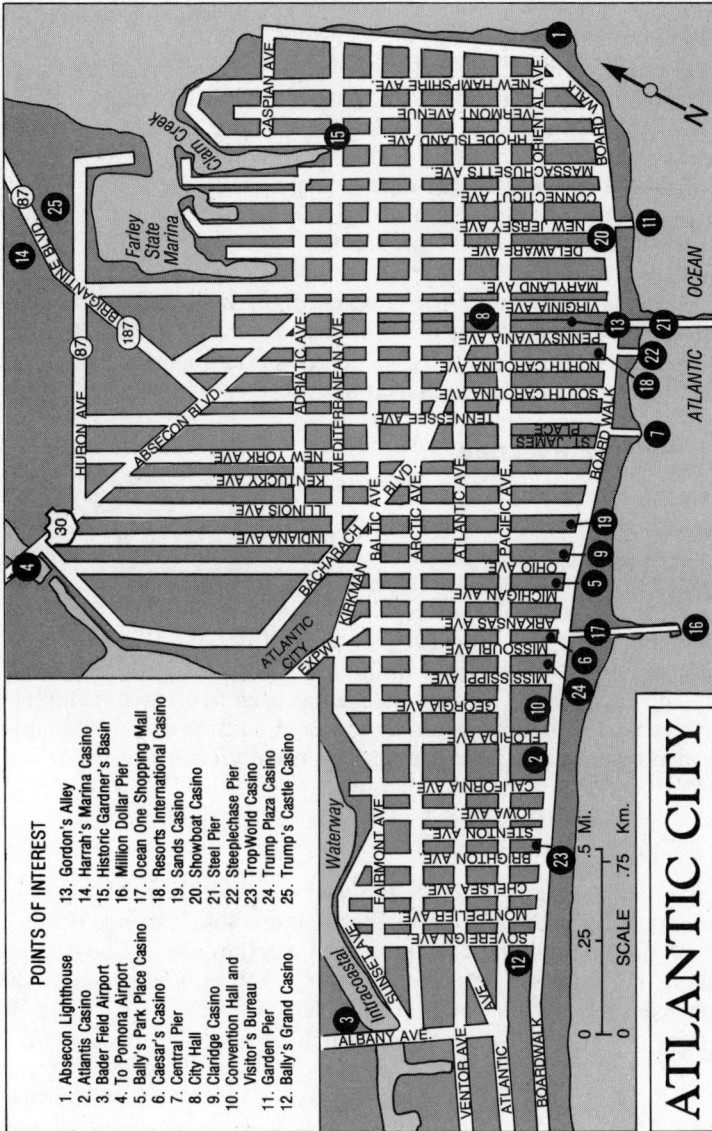

delli Square and Cannery Row in San Francisco. It features a nice assortment of classy shops, boutiques, and restaurants.

Walking down Pennsylvania Avenue back to Pacific Avenue and the boardwalk, one can't miss the Showboat, the first of a string of casino-hotels. As one continues southwest for the next 1½ miles or so, one encounters the Sands, Claridge, Bally's, Caesars, Trump Plaza, Atlantis, TropWorld, and finally Bally's Grand.

Along this stretch of boardwalk are two other major attractions: Ocean One and Convention Hall. Ocean One, located at the end of Missouri Avenue on the ocean, is a large, three-story, indoor mall. Its shape resembles an ocean liner from the outside; inside are about 150 stores and restaurants.

At the corner of Mississippi Avenue and the boardwalk is Convention Hall—the site of the famous Miss America Pageant. It is sometimes open to the general public, depending on what trade show is in town. Call 609–348–7000 for more information on whether it is open the week you are there.

Farley State Marina

One of the most picturesque parts of town is the Farley State Marina. Harrah's Marina and Trump's Castle are based here, within easy walking distance of the water. The marina is filled with hundreds of sailboats and yachts; it is also the main fishing area of town. Boat lovers will thoroughly enjoy strolling up and down the dock. For information, call 609–441–3600.

Be sure to visit Gardner's Basin, at N. New Hampshire Avenue and the bay. Here, a seaport village has been re-created, complete with coastal museum, historic shops and boutiques, and a couple of nice restaurants. The grounds are usually open from dawn to dusk.

A Typical Casino

Everyone, at least once, should visit a casino-hotel. The ones in Atlantic City, while having their own individual "themed decor," are all pretty much the same in the features they offer. (The Roman theme of Caesar's is actually quite remarkable: *Where* else would you see a giant statue of Julius Caesar on a beach boardwalk or a copy of Michelangelo's *David* watching over slot machines.)

The main attraction in a typical casino-hotel is, of course, the gambling casino itself, which is always easily found on the first floor. The din is deafening, as hundreds of slot machines whir, and an occasional bell goes off when as someone hits the jackpot. Expert slot-machine players play several machines at a time and never seem to show any excitement when quarters (or dollars or whatever) come tumbling down. During the day the slot machines are occupied by the many senior citizens who have come to AC by the hundreds on buses that come into town every day, providing riders with coins and after meal vouchers. Dress is usually quite casual. Grim-faced gamblers are sitting over the blackjack and roulette tables, paying rapt attention. (You have never seen concentration until you've seen a big-stakes gambler watching the ball spin around the roulette wheel!) Craps dealers can be heard loudly calling the bets on their tables.

The casinos are huge, stretching almost as far as the eye can see. Most are plushly decorated with expensive carpets, many mirrors, and brilliant chandeliers. Waitresses are everywhere, dressed in little outfits that reflect the theme of the casino (the uniform in Caesar's is, of course, an abbreviated toga). They carry sustenance to the gamblers. There are no clocks and no windows: time passes unnoticed.

The hotel usually has at least five extravagant restaurants. There is probably a 24-hour coffee shop, a deli, and maybe an ice-cream parlor. There are also at least two lounges: The larger one offers nightly entertainment (usually a lone singer, or a two- or three-piece band). The other lounge is simply for relaxing, having a cocktail, and resting your feet. Finally, there is the large showroom (often with 500 to 1,000 seats), where you can sit at long tables, order drinks, and watch some of the most famous performers in the world do their thing.

All casino-hotels have very up-to-date health clubs, with swimming pools, saunas, Nautilus machines, racquetball courts, massage areas—just about anything a fitness-conscious guest may need. The lobbies have shops and boutiques. All casino-hotels in Atlantic City have more than 500 guest rooms, which cost *at least* $160 a night on a summer weekend.

The concept is simple: A casino-hotel takes care of every need or desire; you never have a reason to leave.

Miss America Pageant

You may want to do more than gamble if you come to Atlantic City during its most famous event—the Miss America Pageant—held during the second week in September. The annual Boardwalk Parade is usually held on the Tuesday night of Miss America Week. The contestants stroll from Garden Pier to Montpelier Avenue, and can be observed from either bleacher seats or from grandstand seats near Convention Hall. Visitors can also purchase tickets for the preliminary swimsuit and talent competitions held at Convention Hall during the week. Tickets for the grand finale—held on Saturday night and nationally televised—range from about $8 to $20. For more information, call 609–345–7571.

Nightlife

Atlantic City's world-class nightlife is probably the town's second major attraction (after gambling), as well it should be. The 12 casino-hotels compete vigorously for the top names in show business. In any given year, Bill Cosby, Joan Rivers, Frank Sinatra, and Rodney Dangerfield will all play here. Instead of individual stars, some casino-hotels elect to put on lavish musicals, such as "An Evening at La Cage" or "Bodacious." Still others feature comedy acts. From Bobby Vinton, the Polish Prince, to Pudgy, the female Don Rickles, whatever your preference, you'll find some act that will please you.

Night owls can really let loose here. Casino bars stay open 24 hours a day. Outside the casino-hotels, scores of other cocktail lounges and night clubs offer a myriad of entertainment possibilities, and many of these clubs are open all night long.

Sports Activities

Although gambling is still the number-one form of recreation, sports enthusiasts will find a surprisingly wide variety of activities. Of course, swimming and running along the boardwalk are two favorites. Boardwalk bike riding can be done in the early morning, from 6 A.M. to 10 A.M. Frisbee throwing and kite flying can be done on the beach anytime. Many casino-hotels have their own racquetball courts, tennis courts, and swimming pools. In addition, public tennis courts and golf courses are only short drives away from Pacific Avenue. Farley State Marina is a major hub of deep-sea fishing, boating, and sailing.

Neighboring Towns

Atlantic City's immediate neighbor on Absecon Island is Ventnor (population 14,000). There are a few motels in this village, and a lot of condos and summer houses. Southwest of Ventnor is Margate (population 11,000), which is mostly residential with upperclass homes and high-rise condominiums. Margate is most famous for a six-story cement elephant named Lucy; children can walk through her. At the far southwestern tip of the island is the exclusive town of Longport (1,250 full-time residents). It is populated mostly by wealthy people from Philadelphia's Main Line suburbs.

Other Attractions Outside Town

If you have the luxury of staying in the Atlantic City area for several days, there are many sights within a 45-minute drive from town that are worth seeing.

The Edwin B. Forsythe Wildlife Refuge in Oceanville is only about a 20-minute drive north of town. The pleasant, eight-mile drive through the wetlands is a nice, quiet diversion from the ringing slot machines.

Another nice drive is along Ocean Drive—the 40-mile-long road that weaves from Atlantic City south to Cape May. It offers many beautiful vistas of the sea; some of the shoreline here is still undeveloped.

The Towne of Historic Smithville is 12 miles north of Atlantic City on Route 9. This beautiful little village is a replica of an 1800s Colonial Village, with cobblestone paths, a little pond, and about 30 specialty shops.

About 15 minutes out of town in Absecon Highlands is the Bernard D'Arcy Wine Cellars. There are free self-conducted tours of winemaking facilities, plus free samples.

Central Square (Central Ave. and New Road, Linwood) is a charming shopping mall with a "country village" atmosphere. There are more than 60 shops, as well as a restaurant. It's open daily.

Leamings Run Botanical Gardens and Colonial Farm (Route 9, Swainton) boasts 24 different gardens. The farm itself has farm animals and a whaling museum. Kids will also love Storybook Land, Black Horse Pike, Cardiff, which features characters and scenes from nursery rhymes and fairy tales.

PRACTICAL INFORMATION FOR ATLANTIC CITY

HOW TO GET THERE AND HOW TO GET AROUND. Perhaps Atlantic City's chief advantage over its archrival, Las Vegas, is the fact that it is extremely easy to get to by car—especially if you live on the East Coast. Roughly 25% of the population of the United States lives within 300 miles (or a six-hour drive) of Atlantic City.

For those who don't want to drive, all the major cities in the East have special casino bus tours, in which a rider gets a round-trip ticket, a roll of quarters, and even a meal voucher. These casino buses leave every major Eastern city many times a day.

Visitors can fly into Philadelphia or Newark airports from any big city in the country, and then either rent a car or take public transportation down to Atlantic City. Driving time is about one hour from Philadelphia, and about 1½ hours from Newark.

Two big recent developments will make it easier to get here by train or plane. In April, 1989, a new $14 million train station will open. New Jersey Transit and Amtrak will offer service between New York City, Philadelphia, and other large cities. In addition, more airlines are negotiating to begin service to Pomona International Airport from several large eastern cities. USAir has already started nonstop service from Pittsburgh.

Once you get to Atlantic City, getting around is a snap. The local jitneys cruise up and down Pacific Avenue 24 hours a day. In addition, a tram runs up and down the boardwalk continually. If you want to go elsewhere to see a local tourist attraction, local taxis are found in front of every casino. And a new "people mover" moving sidewalk, located right off the boardwalk, takes people between the Sands and the Claridge.

Best of all, though, many of the main sites (Ocean One Mall, Convention Hall, and all the Pacific Avenue casinos) are within 1½ miles of each other on the boardwalk. Walking the boardwalk is by far the most enjoyable way of taking in the sights.

By car: When driving to Atlantic City from the north, take any one of the many major highways that eventually connect to the Garden State Parkway. (The New Jersey Turnpike, or Interstate 95, connects with the Parkway shortly south of Newark Airport.) Take the Parkway to one of two exits: Route 30 or the Atlantic City Expressway. Drivers from Philadelphia can take the Atlantic City Expressway directly to Atlantic City. From the south, take I–95 or US 40 from Washington, D.C.; then connect to the Expressway. Atlantic City is about a 2½-hour drive from New York, and a 4½-hour drive from Washington.

By bus: An incredible 1,000 buses pour into Atlantic City every day from all points along the East Coast. From major cities such as New York, Philadelphia, Baltimore, Trenton, Newark, and Washington, buses leave many times a day. (The Sunday Travel section of your local daily paper usually is filled with ads from the major carriers.)

These bus companies often offer package deals. For $20–$25, you get at least $10 in quarters, a meal discount coupon worth $5 or so, and a round-trip ticket. It's one of the best bargains you'll find *anywhere.* Of course, the bus companies are partially reimbursed by the casinos, who know that the average bus rider is going to spend far more than that!

Some of the major bus carriers are: *Atlantic City Transportation Company* (609–345–3201); *Domenico Bus Company* (201–339–6000); *Greyhound* (201–642–8205 or 212–971–6363); *New Jersey Transit* (800–772–2222 in 201 area code; 800–582–5946 in 609 area code or 201–762–5100); *Short Line* (201–529–3666); *Trailways* (201–642–0505); and *Transport of New Jersey* (800–772–2222). Some buses go directly to casino-hotels; others go to the Municipal Bus Terminal, about two blocks from Pacific Avenue.

By plane. The closest major airports to Atlantic City are those in Philadelphia and Newark. From there, one can rent a car for a one- or two-hour drive to the Atlantic City area. Or, transfer to *Allegheny Commuter Airlines* (609–344–7104), which services Atlantic City's Bader Field. Prices from major U.S. eastern cities, such as Philadelphia, New York, and Washington, D.C., range from $50 to $100, one-way. *Bader Express* (800–351–0033, or 609–348–4990) operates between Bader Field and New York's La Guardia Airport. *Eastern Express* (212–986–5000) operates daily nonstop service to Bader Field from New York, Philadelphia, and Washington, D.C. In 1988, *U.S. Air* started nonstop flights to Pomona from major U.S. cities. Call 412–922–7500, or 800–428–4322. The International Air Terminal in Pomona, about 12 miles away, handles mostly charter passenger lines.

Taxis serve both airports. Some visitors prefer to fly into Philadelphia, and then take a shuttle limousine to Atlantic City. For information about limousines, call the following companies: *AA Limousine Service*

(609–344–2444); *Airport Limousine Service* (609–345–3244); *B&M Transportation* (609–344–6161); *Blue and White Airport Service* (609–848–0770); *Casino Limousine Service* (609–646–5555); *May's Call-a-Cab* (609–646–7600); or *Rapid Rover Airport Shuttle* (609–344–0100).

By rental car. If you don't have your own car, you can rent one at Bader Field, just on the outskirts of Atlantic City. Be sure to make arrangements in advance, since the airport doesn't have that many rental cars. The major companies here are: *Budget* (609–345–0600 or 800–527–0700); *Avis* (609–345–3350 or 800–331–1212); and *Hertz* (609–646–1212 or 800–654–3131). The "800" numbers listed above can also be used to inquire about renting a car at Newark or Philadelphia airports. *Snappy* will deliver cars directly to all the casino-hotels (800–321–7159).

By taxi. Getting a cab generally isn't too difficult in Atlantic City. They are usually lined up in front of the casino-hotels, and most companies respond quickly to calls. Some of the major cab companies include: *Mutual Cab* (609–345–6111); *Radio Cab* (609–345–1105); *Red Top Cab* (609–344–4104); *Yellow Cab* (609–344–1221); *City Cab Service*, Pleasantville (609–641–0762); and *Dial Cab* (609–822–9422).

All service Atlantic City, Ventnor, Margate, Longport, and nearby cities on the mainland. A typical two-mile trip (say from the Convention Center to the Farley State Marina) is about $4.

By jitney. The jitneys are a fun—and very practical—way to get up and down Pacific Avenue, the main strip. They run about every five minutes during the day . . . and they operate 24 hours a day. These minibuses seat 13 people; the fare is $1. The jitneys also run from Park Place to Harrah's Marina and Trump's Castle (Farley State Marina).

By tram. A great way to tour the boardwalk, especially when your feet are sore, is to take the tram. It runs along the boardwalk from Garden Pier to Albany Avenue. Cost is $1 for adults; 75¢, senior citizens and children under 12. Hours are: 10 A.M.–9 P.M. Sun.–Thurs.; 10 A.M.–midnight Fri.–Sat.

Driving and Parking

It should be mentioned that all routes into Atlantic City are extremely crowded on Friday afternoons and Sunday evenings, especially during the summer. Try to avoid traveling during those times.

If you are staying in a casino-hotel or a large motor inn, it will probably offer free parking. If you are just visiting a casino-hotel, you can still park for free, if you get your parking ticket validated inside the casino.

On-street parking is very difficult on weekdays, and almost impossible during weekends in summer. If you want to see the boardwalk without visiting a casino, try parking your car at either of the far ends of the Pacific Avenue jitney route. Then take the jitney to the main casino strip. Or use a parking lot—there are several up and down Pacific Avenue. Expect to pay $12–$18 a day, though.

USEFUL ADDRESSES. The major source of tourist information for this region is the *Atlantic City Visitors Bureau,* Department of Public Relations, Convention Hall, Atlantic City, NJ 08401 (609–348–7044). A second excellent source of information is the state's official tourism bureau—*New Jersey Division of Travel and Tourism,* CN 826, Trenton, NJ 08625

(609–292–2470). This office will mail, upon request, several good brochures about tourism opportunities in southern New Jersey.

Handicapped travelers should definitely write for some of the state's tourism brochures. Each brochure and pamphlet describes whether a given attraction has facilities for the handicapped. The casino-hotels in Atlantic City have excellent facilities for the handicapped; the older motels do not. Two good sources for handicapped travelers are: *Atlantic County Office for the Disabled,* 1333 Atlantic Ave., Atlantic City, NJ 08401 (609–345–6700, ext. 2831); and *Governor's Committee on the Disabled,* Labor & Industry Building, Room 200, Trenton, NJ 08625 (609–633–6959).

As soon as you get to town, pick up a copy of the daily newspaper, the *Atlantic City Press.* It does a very good job of listing sports events, nightlife opportunities, and special events along the boardwalk.

Senior citizens should contact the *Atlantic County Office of Aging and Disabled,* 1133 Atlantic Ave., Atlantic City, NJ 08401 (609–345–6700). This agency offers a book of discount coupons if you visit the office personally and can prove you are 65 or older. Senior citizens can also purchase discount tickets for the jitneys at many full-service banks in town. They cost only 30 cents instead of the usual $1.

For information about shows in the casino showrooms, contact *Teletron,* at 609–344–1770, 201–343–4200, or 800–233–4050 (in NJ, NY, and PA).

Those having problems getting room reservations might want to call *Atlantic City Reserve-A-Room,* a reservation service. Its numbers are: 609–347–1900 or 800–227–6667 (outside of New Jersey).

ACCOMMODATIONS. Atlantic City offers some of the most extravagant hotel lodging in the country—and some of the sleaziest. Fortunately, there is a nice middle road; there are a lot of fine motels and motor lodges within a block or two of the casino-hotels. However, know this at the outset—the lodging in town is very expensive during the summer, especially on weekends.

The casino-hotels are awash in luxury. Most have five or six restaurants, two or three cocktail lounges, modern health clubs and athletic facilities, and several fancy boutiques. For the most part, the guest rooms are equally posh, with wall-to-wall carpeting, expensive hardwood furniture, large bathrooms, changing rooms, in-room movies, etc. All hotels are dominated, of course, by the casinos, which are huge, usually 60,000 square feet or more.

If you plan to stay at a casino-hotel in peak season, you can expect to pay at least $160 a night for a room on a weekend. However, if you decide to take a package deal, you can reduce this cost considerably. Most packages, though, are offered only during weekdays or during the off-season. A typical package might include a double room for two people for two nights, at least one dinner per person, admission to a show, use of a health club, a free cocktail, and other souvenirs and amenities. The cost might be $100–$150 per person, based on double occupancy. By Atlantic City standards, this is a decent bargain. Winter packages are half the price.

There are scores of motels, however, located within a block or two of the big casinos on Pacific Avenue. If you expect to spend most of your time at a casino, and only want a place to sleep, these might be worth considering. Most of them offer clean, modern rooms . . . and few other amenities. They will cost between $70 and $120 a night in high season, with weekend prices always much higher. Even the most basic motel will charge $65–$75 during the week, and $85–$95 during the weekends. The best bargains are found in motels three or four miles from the ocean. Travelers also might be better off staying in towns south of the city, such as Wildwood, where they would get much more for their money. You can save $50 a night, but you will have to drive a half-hour to get to the casinos. It may be worth it to you. (See the Southern Shore chapter.)

Reservations should be made several months in advance for the casino-hotels, which get a lot of convention business and are therefore frequently sold out. Even for a motel, book at least a month in advance during the summer. A deposit is almost always required. There is an official room-reservation service in Atlantic City—*Atlantic City Reserve-A-Room.* Call 800–227–6667 or 609–347–1900.

Since most people want to visit Atlantic City in summer, the room rates listed below pertain to the *in-season* (highest) prices for a standard double room, per night. Rates are significantly lower—often half the price—at other times of the year, especially winter. A room that might cost $85 on a July Friday, can cost $35 on a winter weekday. The price categories are as follows: *Super Deluxe:* $160 and higher; *Deluxe:* $120–$160; *Expensive:* $85–$120; *Moderate:* $60–$85. Very few establishments cost less than $60 during peak season.

Casino-Hotels

Super Deluxe

Atlantis. Florida Ave. and the boardwalk, Atlantic City, 08401; 609–344–4000. Formerly the Playboy, this casino-hotel's black, glassy tower dominates the boardwalk. It offers 500 rooms, three restaurants, and two lounges. There are several shops, and some excellent athletic facilities on the top (22nd) floor, including a swimming pool, exercise room, hot tub, and racquetball courts. One can view the boardwalk and ocean right from the pool windows.

Bally's Park Place. Park Pl. and the boardwalk, Atlantic City, 08401; 609–340–2000. Has 800 guest rooms, 300 of which are in the new hotel tower scheduled to open in early 1989. 42 suites. Nine restaurants and four lounges. Large casino's escalator is surrounded by a 100-foot-high waterfall. Spa and an indoor and outdoor pool. Guests have access to 40,000-square-foot health spa.

Caesars. Arkansas Ave. and the boardwalk, Atlantic City, 08401; 609–348–4411. The statue of Julius Caesar on the boardwalk is your first clue that you've arrived at this casino-hotel. Offers 645 rooms, 15 shops, two swimming pools, health spa, beach club, platform tennis. There are eight restaurants, a 24-hour deli, three cocktail lounges, and an amusement arcade. Shops.

Claridge. Indiana Ave. and the boardwalk, Atlantic City, 08401; 609–340–3400. A major renovation on this hotel was just completed. It has 504 rooms, a split-level casino, a cabaret theater, glass-enclosed swimming pool, health spa, indoor gardens, five restaurants, three lounges, and an ice-cream parlor. Free valet parking for guests.

Bally's Grand. Boston and Pacific aves., at the boardwalk, Atlantic City, 08401; 609–347–7111. Most of the 520 rooms offer a view of the sea. Casino has a Victorian decor. Health club with indoor pool, Opera House Theatre, eight restaurants, three cocktail lounges, arcade. The eight restaurants are reached by riding an escalator surrounded by a waterfall. Parking includes 620 valet spaces, and about 900 self-park spots.

Harrah's Marina. 1725 Brigantine Blvd., Atlantic City, 08401; 609–441–5000. Located away from other casinos, on Absecon Inlet near the Inland Waterway and Farley State Marina. There are 750 guest rooms, three shops, a beauty salon, seven restaurants, five cocktail lounges, a newly renovated show room, paddle tennis, table tennis, shuffleboard courts, a game room, an enclosed pool, and an exercise room with Nautilus gear. There are also more than 100 slips next to hotel for those who want to bring their boats.

Resorts International. North Carolina Ave. and the boardwalk, Atlantic City, 08401; 609–344–6000. The first casino-hotel in Atlantic City now has 710 rooms, eight restaurants, six cocktail lounges (two with live entertainment), a musical revue show, and a new health club with sauna, steamroom, hot tubs, glass-enclosed swimming pool, and a sundeck.

Sands. Indiana Ave. at Brighton Park, Atlantic City, 08401; 609–441–4000. Facilities include 500 rooms, 14 restaurants, four cocktail lounges, indoor and outdoor pool, Nautilus fitness center, five racquetball courts. Only casino with its own golf course—the Sands Country Club. Copa Room is used as a show room and as a disco on weekends.

Showboat. Delaware Ave. and the boardwalk, Atlantic City, 08401; 609–343–4100. Newest casino-hotel in town, built to resemble a giant cruise ship. It stands 24 stories high, and contains 516 rooms. Seven shops, eight restaurants, five lounges. Unique feature is 60-lane bowling center. Also contains miniature golf course and fitness center.

TropWorld. Iowa Ave. at the boardwalk, Atlantic City, 08401; 609–340–4000. A recently completed expansion added 500 more rooms (to the original 515), as well as an adult entertainment center. 17 restaurants, four lounges, outdoor pool, two outdoor tennis courts, paddle tennis, and health club. Eight shops on premises. Newly completed Transportation Center has room for 1,000 cars (all parking is free). TropWorld Showroom has top entertainment. Top of the Trop lounge offers one of the best views in town.

Trump's Castle. Brigantine Blvd. and Huron Ave., Atlantic City, 08401; 609–441–2000. Opened in the summer of 1985, this is one of the newest casino-hotels in town. There are 586 rooms, each with a waterfront view. Shoppers can browse through three gift shops and a children's toy store. There are eight restaurants and two lounges, and some excellent athletic facilities (health club, shuffleboard courts, jogging track, pool, five tennis courts). The hotel's marina was expanded in 1988.

Trump Plaza. Mississippi Ave. and the boardwalk, Atlantic City, 08401; 609–441–6000. Features include 614 rooms, eight restaurants, three lounges. There are several shops, a swimming pool, health club, racquetball courts, two outdoor tennis courts and a shuffleboard court. This is the tallest building in town.

Deluxe

Admiral's Quarters. 655 Absecon Blvd., Atlantic City, 08401; 609–344–2201. Located near marina, and the Trump's Castle and Harrah's Marina casino-hotels. Has 52 rooms and suites, each with full kitchen. Some rooms have balconies. Complimentary breakfast served. Free parking.

Best Western Inn. Indiana and Pacific aves., P.O. Box 5309, Atlantic City, 08401; 609–348–9175. Features 107 modern, refurbished rooms. Good central location. All-weather heated pool, sauna, small game room, sundeck. Free parking.

Comfort Inn North. 405 E. Absecon Blvd., Rte. 30, Absecon, 08201; 609–646–5000 or 800–228–5150. Relatively new facility, offering quiet atmosphere, away from traffic congestion of Pacific Avenue. On one of main roads leading into town. 200 rooms. Restaurant, pool, cable TV with in-room movies, shuttle service to casinos.

Comfort Inn West. Black Horse Pike, Rte. 40, West Atlantic City, 08232; 609–645–1818. Modern, classy facility with restaurant, pool, in-room movies, shuttle service to casinos.

International Motel. The boardwalk at Chelsea, P.O. Box 1904, Atlantic City, 08401; 609–344–7071. Has 125 rooms, three dining rooms, coffee shop, cocktail lounge, all-year pool, health spa, and game room.

Madison House. 123 S. Illinois Ave., Atlantic City, 08401; 609–345–1400. 206 guest rooms, restaurant, lounge, golf privileges at nearby course. Everything here is first-class.

Midtown Motor Inn. Indiana at Pacific Ave., Atlantic City, 08401; 609–348–3031. One of largest motels in town, with 300 rooms. Just completed $2 million renovation project. Indoor and outdoor pool, restaurant, lounge, nightly entertainment in summer.

Quality Inn. Beach block, South Carolina and Pacific Aves., Atlantic City, 08401; 609–646–5000 or 800–228–5151. One of the newest hotels in town, with 200 luxury rooms, restaurant, health club, free parking.

World International. 110 S. Pennsylvania Ave., Atlantic City, 08401; 609–344–1151. A large, 11-story hotel, with pool and solarium, dining room and lounge. Next to Resorts International.

Expensive

Brigantine Inn. 1400 Ocean Ave., Brigantine, 08203; 609–266–2266. Open year-round, with 85 comfortable rooms. Outdoor pool; 24-hour restaurant; Nautilus fitness center. Located about 15 minutes from Atlantic City boardwalk.

Dunes Motel. 2819 Pacific Ave., Atlantic City, 08401; 609–344–5271. Centrally located, with 35 modern rooms. Wall-to-wall carpeting, color TV, individual room air conditioning, free parking, sundeck, outdoor swimming pool. Some efficiencies available.

EconoLodge Boardwalk. 117 S. Kentucky Ave., Box 7128, Atlantic City, 08401; 609–344–9093. Has pool, restaurant that serves breakfast and lunch in summer. Located near Sands Casino. Free parking. *Moderate* prices weekdays.

El Greco. 3200 Pacific Ave., Atlantic City, 08401; 609–345–6195. Located next to Bally's Grand. Has 38 modernly appointed rooms.

Flamingo Motel. Chelsea and Pacific aves., Atlantic City, 08401; 609–344–3061. Dining room and cocktail lounge open 24 hours. Air conditioning, color TV, wall-to-wall carpeting, full-tile bath, free parking, three sundecks. Located between TropWorld and Bally's Grand casino-hotels.

Oceanaire. 5300 Boardwalk, Ventnor, 08406; 609–823–2785. Located right on Ventnor's quiet, pleasant boardwalk. Features about 35 rooms; outdoor pool. Open year-round.

Royal Inn. Park Pl. near the boardwalk, Atlantic City, 08401; 609–344–7021. Next to Claridge. Features outdoor pool, restaurant, 150 guest rooms, and use of Claridge's athletic facilities for guests. Free parking.

Scottish Inn. 3001 Pacific Ave., Atlantic City, 08401; 609–344–2925. Free parking, air-conditioned rooms, sundeck, free cable TV, open year-round. 68 newly furnished rooms.

Whittier Inn. Black Horse Pike, Pleasantville, NJ 08232; 800–237–9682 or 609–484–1500. New luxury hotel with 200 rooms. Features continental breakfast and shuttle service to casinos. Remote cable TV/HBO. Pool.

World Tower. 109 S. North Carolina Ave., Atlantic City, 08401; 609–347–8000. Restaurant, cocktail lounge, coffee shop, rooftop swimming pool, and 200 modern rooms. Free parking.

Moderate

Ascot. Ocean end of Iowa Ave. on the boardwalk, Atlantic City, 08401; 609–344–5163. Directly across street from TropWorld. Free parking, pool, cable TV. Children free.

Days Inn. 1150 Tilton Rd., Pleasantville, 08232; 609–641–4500. Open year-round; part of national chain. 118 rooms; outdoor pool, 24-hour restaurant. Shuttle bus runs over to Atlantic City boardwalk, about 15-minute drive away.

EconoLodge. Black Horse Pike, West Atlantic City, 08232; 609–646–5220. Has 141 rooms, with outdoor pool. Dining room serves breakfast only; larger restaurant located across street. Located only two miles from Boardwalk.

Golden East Motel. 169 S. Kentucky Ave., Atlantic City, 08401; 609–344–7001. Ideal location; one block away from three casinos. Free parking, modern guest rooms.

Hi-Ho Motel. 2300 Black Horse Pike, Atlantic City, 08232; 609–641–1500. Offers 20 rooms, all with color cable TV. Free parking. Only five minutes from boardwalk.

Inn at Golf and Tennis World. 4005 Black Horse Pike, West Atlantic City, 08232; 800–528–1234 or 609–641–3546. A Best Western Inn, ideal for sports enthusiasts. Features indoor and outdoor tennis, health spa, full-service restaurant. Golf course nearby.

Martinique Motel. 3029 Pacific Ave., Atlantic City, 08401; 609–348–2599. 42 rooms; open year-round. Near TropWorld and Bally's Grand.

Trinidad Motel. Tennessee Ave. near boardwalk, Atlantic City, 08401; 609–344–8956. 74 rooms, cocktail lounge, swimming pool. Some kitchen efficiencies available. Free parking. Near Resorts International. Open year-round.

Village Motel. Boardwalk at Kentucky Ave., Atlantic City, 08401; 609–345–8500. Large facility, with 134 rooms; free parking, color cable TV.

RENTALS. Opportunities for renting houses in Atlantic City and its surrounding communities, Margate, Ventnor, and Longport, are somewhat scarce. Many of the homes in this area are second homes owned by Philadelphians. Since the Atlantic City casinos are such an attraction— and since this area is only an hour away from Philadelphia—these home-owners use their homes throughout the year, as opposed to renting them out.

There are some seasonal rental houses in Atlantic City itself, but these are not considered really desirable, due to the congestion and noise. Hous-es in Margate, Ventnor, and Longport are in better residential areas . . . and cost more.

A typical three-bedroom, two-bath beach-block house in Margate, Ven-tnor, or Longport costs $15,000 and up a season. A house right *on* the beach can cost $25,000 to $40,000 a season.

A few blocks from the beaches in these towns, the prices drop dramati-cally. A three-bedroom, two-bath house in good condition might cost $8,000 to $9,000. And in the little hamlet of Ventnor Heights—about seven blocks from the beach—houses can be rented for as little as $3,000 a season. Unfortunately, there just aren't that many rentals available in Ventnor Heights.

Unlike other areas of the shore, Margate, Ventnor, and Longport re-quire rentals for either a full or half-season. (The first half of the season runs from Memorial Day to late July, the second half runs from late July to Labor Day.) Houses are rented to groups and families in Ventnor and Margate, to families only in Longport.

The best place to find group housing in this area is in the southwestern part of Margate, near Longport. Here, near Margate's strip of bars and restaurants, houses are rented to groups, often singles in their 20s. Here, houses three or four blocks away from the Atlantic Ocean rent in the $5,000-to-$10,000 range for the season.

The best places to find one-week or two-week rentals in this area are those towns south of Ocean City (see the Southern Shore chapter).

More information about summer rental opportunities in the greater At-lantic City area can be found by contacting the following:

Cara Realtors, 9600 Ventnor Ave., Margate, 08402; 609–822–4355.

Grace Realty, 3400 Central Ave., Ocean City, 08226; 609–398–6200.

Jean Farley Realty, 5312 Atlantic Ave., Ventnor, 08406; 609–822–1836.

Ocean Club Realty, 3109 Boardwalk, Atlantic City, 08401; 609–345–3101.

Philip Guber, 3900 Ventnor Ave., Atlantic City, 08401; 609–344–2811.

Silk Associates, 2210 Atlantic Ave., Atlantic City, 08401; 609–348–8888.

Stephen Frankel Real Estate, 14 S. Tennessee Ave., Atlantic City, 08401; 609–344–0800.

Ventnor City Clerk, 6201 Atlantic Ave., Ventnor, 08406; 609–823–7904.

Women's Realty, 7802 Ventnor Ave., Margate, 08402; 609–823–4300.

CAMPING. Camping out in this region is an extremely viable alterna-tive to staying in an expensive motel or hotel. There are approximately 20 very good campgrounds within a half-hour drive of the Atlantic City casinos and boardwalk. Besides the usual amenities found in every camp-ground (electrical hookups, water, restrooms, etc.), many campsites offer such features as grocery stores, fireplaces, picnic tables, laundry facilities, swimming pools, boating and fishing, playgrounds, even clubhouses with ping-pong tables, pool tables, or both.

The costs usually fall between $7.50 and $15 a night, which is about average for the East Coast.

Many campsites can be reserved in advance, with a deposit. This is a wise thing to do, due to the heavy crowds that pour down here during the summer. See also Parks, Gardens, and Forests, below.

Atlantic City Blueberry Hill Campground. Clarks Landing, Dept. S–80, Port Republic, 08241; 609–652–1644. 30 acres, 160 sites, flush toilets, sewer hookups, dumping stations, showers, hot water, electric and water hookups, groceries, refreshments, fireplaces, picnic tables, ice, pets, laundry, swimming, boating (nearby), fishing (nearby), playground, and clubhouse. Feb. 1–Dec. 15.

Atlantic City West KOA. R.D. 2, Box 60B, Heidelberg Ave., Egg Harbor City, 08215; 609–965–1944. 42 acres, 151 sites, flush toilets, sewer hookups, dumping stations, showers, hot water, electric and water hookups, groceries, refreshments, fire rings, picnic tables, ice, pets, laundry, swimming, boating (nearby), fishing (nearby), playground, and clubhouse. Apr. 1–Oct. 1.

Chestnut Lake Campground. Old New York Rd., Rte. 575, Port Republic, 08241; 609–652–7251. 30 acres, 250 sites, flush toilets, sewer hookups, dumping stations, showers, hot water, electric and water hookups, groceries, refreshments, fire rings, picnic tables, ice, pets, laundry, swimming, boating, fishing, playground, and clubhouse. Apr. 15–Oct. 15.

Colonial Meadows Family Campgrounds. 557 Somers Point Rd., Mays Landing, 08330; 609–653–8449. 22 acres, 112 sites, flush toilets, sewer hookups, dumping stations, showers, hot water, electric and water hookups, groceries, refreshments, fire rings, picnic tables, ice, pets, laundry, swimming, boating (nearby), fishing (nearby), playground, and clubhouse. May 15–Oct. 15.

Country Mouse Campgrounds. R.D. 4, Box 373, Dorothy, 08317; 609–476–2143. 17 acres, 115 sites, flush toilets, sewer hookups, dumping stations, showers, hot water, electric and water hookups, groceries, refreshments, fireplaces, picnic tables, ice, pets, laundry, swimming, boating (nearby), fishing (nearby), playground, and clubhouse. Year-round.

Egg Harbor River Campground. 181 Thompson Lane, English Creek, Mays Landing, 08330; 609–927–6841. 27 acres, 130 sites, flush toilets, sewer hookups, dumping stations, showers, hot water, electric and water hookups, groceries, refreshments, fire rings, picnic tables, ice, pets, laundry, swimming, boating, fishing, playground, and clubhouse. Apr. 15–Oct. 1.

Holiday Haven Campground. P.O. Box 271, Mays Landing, 08330; 609–476–2963. 90 acres, 170 sites, flush toilets, dumping stations, showers, hot water, electric and water hookups, groceries, refreshments, fireplaces, picnic tables, ice, pets, laundry, swimming, fishing (nearby), playground, and clubhouse. Apr.–Oct.

Holly Acres Campground. 218 S. Frankfurt Ave., Egg Harbor City, 08215; 609–965–2287. 60 acres, 150 sites, flush toilets, sewer hookups, dumping stations, showers, hot water, electric and water hookups, groceries, refreshments, fireplaces, picnic tables, ice, pets, laundry, swimming, fishing, playground, and clubhouse. Apr. 15–Oct. 15.

ATLANTIC CITY

Lazy River Campground. Cumberland Ave., Box 136, Estell Manor, 08319; 609–476–2155. 600 acres, 100 sites, flush toilets, sewer hookups, dumping stations, showers, hot water, electric and water hookups, groceries (nearby), refreshments, fireplaces, picnic tables, ice, pets, laundry, swimming, boating, fishing, playground, and clubhouse. Apr. 15–Oct. 15.

Pomona Campground. Oak Dr., P.O. Box 675, Pomona, 08240; 609–965–2123. 6.5 acres, 125 sites, flush toilets, sewer hookups, dumping stations, showers, hot water, electric and water hookups, groceries (nearby), refreshments, fireplaces, picnic tables, ice, pets, laundry, swimming, boating (nearby), fishing (nearby), and playground. Apr. 15–Oct. 15.

Red Wing Lakes Campground. Sooy's Landing Rd., Port Republic, 08241; 609–652–1939. 2,300 acres, 200 sites, flush toilets, sewer hookups, dumping stations, showers, hot water, electric and water hookups, groceries, refreshments, fireplaces, picnic tables, ice, pets, laundry, swimming, boating, fishing, playground, and clubhouse. Apr.–Oct.

River Beach Camp II. Somers Point Rd., Box 89, Mays Landing, 08330; 609–625–8611. 30 acres, 141 sites, flush toilets, sewer hookups, dumping stations, showers, hot water, electric and water hookups, groceries, refreshments, fireplaces, picnic tables, ice, pets, laundry, swimming, boating, fishing, and clubhouse. May 1–Oct. 1.

Winding River Campground. R.D. 2, Box 246, Mays Landing, 08330; 609–625–3191. 74 acres, 132 sites, flush toilets, sewer hookups, dumping stations, showers, hot water, electric and water hookups, groceries, refreshments, fireplaces, picnic tables, ice, pets, laundry, swimming, boating, fishing, playground, and clubhouse. Apr. 1–Oct. 1.

State Forest

Wharton State Forest. Batsto R.D. 4, Hammonton, 08037; 609–561–3262. 108,499 acres, accommodates 1,600 visitors, picnic tables, swimming, boating, fishing, and playground. Year-round.

DINING OUT. No other section of the New Jersey Shore boasts the variety in restaurants that Atlantic City does. This is the one area where you are almost guaranteed to find: 1) a restaurant that serves the type of food you like; 2) the right price range and the atmosphere you seek; and 3) the opportunity to eat anytime in a 24-hour period.

If you want to really live it up, you can go to one of the candlelit, romantic ultra-plush casino-hotel restaurants, which serve, on expensive china and silver, dishes prepared by world-class chefs. (Casinos compete very heavily among themselves to hire the best chefs, in order to offer the best four-star restaurant in town.)

Each of the casinos has between five and ten different restaurants, so if you're staying in one, chances are good you can find something you like. But if you want to escape from the casino atmosphere, it might be worth it to make a quick, five-minute drive to some of the other good eating establishments, both in Atlantic City and in Margate and Ventnor. In these places, you will probably get more personal service and less expensive meals than you would in the fanciest restaurants in each casino.

Virtually every type of ethnic dish can be found here—American, French, Mexican, Chinese, Italian, and seafood being the primary styles of cuisine. You can pay $30 for a Mexican dinner, or $6—depending on where you want to go, and what type of atmosphere you want to eat in.

ATLANTIC CITY

Many restaurants stay open as late as 6 A.M. in order to attract the thousands of casino workers who get off at this time, when the casinos close for a few hours. If you need to eat at that hour for one reason or another, you will find a surprising number of places open then.

Hundreds of fast-food places are scattered right along the boardwalk. If you want to grab a quick bite for breakfast or lunch, and then stay out on the beach, it's easy to leave your beach blanket, walk about 100 feet, and find some sort of a snack shop. When you get right down to it, eating in your bathing suit on the beach for $2 may offer you a better view than if you had just forked out $100 to eat.

Some of the better restaurants in Atlantic City casinos require at least a jacket for men, and sometimes a tie as well. Since these same places are the ones in which you are most likely to need a reservation, always ask about their dress code. During summer especially, a reservation at the better restaurants is highly recommended. Unlike other shore towns, nearly every restaurant in Atlantic City and vicinity stays open year-round.

The price categories for restaurants in Atlantic City and neighboring towns is as follows: *Super Deluxe:* $25 and higher; *Deluxe:* $18–$25; *Expensive:* $12–$18; *Moderate:* $8–$12; and *Inexpensive:* below $8. This covers the price of a typical three-course meal for one person. (Drinks, tax, and tip not included.) Credit card symbols are abbreviated as follows: AE—American Express; CB—Carte Blanche; DC—Diners Club; MC—Master Card; V—Visa. D means dinner; L, lunch; B, breakfast.

All telephone numbers listed below are in the 609 area code.

Super Deluxe

By the Sea. Bally's. Park Place and Boardwalk, Atlantic City; 340–2000. Features terrific view and dining by candlelight. Seafood entrees. Dinner only; 6 P.M.–midnight. AE, CB, DC, MC, V.

Delfino's. Trump's Castle. Huron Ave. and Brigantine Blvd., Atlantic City; 441–2000. Continental dining in a Mediterranean decor. Dinner only, served 6 P.M.–midnight. AE, CB, DC, MC, V.

Jeanne's. Atlantis. Florida Ave. and Boardwalk, Atlantic City; 344–4000. Continental and American food served in a quiet, fashionable setting. D, 6–11 P.M. Fri.–Tues. AE, CB, DC, MC, V.

Le Palais. Resorts International. North Carolina Ave. and Boardwalk, Atlantic City; 344–6000. French cuisine served in a romantic setting of red velvet and crystal chandeliers. Piano and violin music; vintage wines. D, 6 P.M.–midnight. Closed Sun. and Mon. AE, CB, DC, MC, V.

Les Paris. TropWorld. Iowa Ave. and Boardwalk, Atlantic City; 340–4000. Old-style French cuisine, served in superb sauces. Guests dine off fine china and French crystal. D, 6–11 P.M. Dress code. AE, CB, DC, MC, V.

Maximillian's. Trump Plaza. Mississippi Ave. and Boardwalk, Atlantic City; 441–6000. Specialties of the house are prime rib and lobster, served in an elegant decor of mahogany and marble. D, 6–11 P.M. AE, CB, DC, MC, V.

Meadows. Harrah's Marina. Brigantine Blvd. and the Bay, Atlantic City; 441–5000. Offers beautiful view of harbor and marina. French specialties, such as veal maison and entrecôte, are served. D, 6 P.M.–midnight. AE, CB, DC, MC, V.

Mes Amis. Sands. Indiana Ave. and Brighton Park, Atlantic City; 441–4000. Romantic atmosphere, with candlelight and lace tablecloths. Gourmet French cuisine, and extensive wine list. D, 6 P.M.–midnight Thurs.–Sun. AE, CB, DC, MC, V.

Mr. Kelley's. Showboat. Delaware Ave. and the boardwalk, Atlantic City; 343–4000. House specialties include filet mignon stuffed with oysters, and lobster mousse. Decor includes beveled mirrors, marble floor, and a beautiful gold glass canopy. AE, CB, DC, MC, V.

Oriental Palace. Caesars. Arkansas Ave. and Boardwalk, Atlantic City; 348–4411. Set in a plush, romantic atmosphere, this restaurant features many types of Chinese cuisine: Cantonese, Szechuan, and Mongolian. Dinner only. AE, CB, DC, MC, V.

Pavilion. Claridge. Indiana Ave. at Brighton Park, Atlantic City; 340–3400. A French restaurant with a distinct California influence—fresh fruit is added to traditional French sauces. D, 6–11:30 P.M. Sun.–Thurs.; 6 P.M.–midnight Fri. and Sat. AE, CB, DC, MC, V.

Victoria's. Bally's Grand. Boston and Pacific Avenues, Atlantic City; 347–7111. Features Victorian atmosphere, French food. Veal and filet mignon are specialties. D, 6 P.M.–1 A.M. AE, CB, DC, MC, V.

Deluxe

Cafe Orleans. Lincoln Place and Boardwalk, Atlantic City; 347–0400. Serves authentic French Continental cuisine, such as cornish game hen, fresh salmon, and prime rib. B, 8 A.M.–noon; L, noon–3 P.M.; D, 5–10 P.M. AE, DC, MC, V.

International Restaurant. International Hotel. Chelsea Ave., Atlantic City; 344–7071. One of few kosher dining establishments in area. Features both a meat and dairy restaurant, with the meat restaurant being the fancier. Reservations suggested for meat restaurant, which is only open for dinner (6–8 P.M.). Dairy restaurant open from 8 A.M.–9 P.M. Sat.–Thurs.; 8 A.M.–6 P.M. Fri. AE, MC, V.

Johan's Zelande. 3209 Fairmount Ave., Atlantic City; 344–5733. The master chef here is Dutch, trained in Lausanne. The menu changes nightly. Fixed prices. Mostly French and Flemish food. Reservations are a necessity. D, from 6 P.M. AE, MC, V.

Knife and Fork Inn. Albany and Pacific Aves., Atlantic City; 344–1133. In business since 1927, this restaurant offers excellent seafood, great steaks, fresh vegetables (many from locally grown gardens), and an extensive wine list. Reservations are accepted every day, except Saturday. Jackets required for men. D, 5:30–10:30 P.M. AE only.

Ram's Head Inn. 9 W. White Horse Pike, Absecon; 652–1700. This Colonial inn is a favorite of celebrities working at nearby Atlantic City. Superb all-around menu; four-star rated. Has four dining rooms; one with skylight. L, 11:30A.M.–3 P.M. Mon.–Fri. D, 5–10 P.M. Mon.–Sat.; 5–10 P.M. Sat. Open 3:30–9:30 P.M. Sun. Reservations recommended. AE, DC, MC, V.

Ristorante Alberto. Mississippi and Pacific Aves., Atlantic City; 344–7000. Features sumptuous northern Italian dishes, with veal being the specialty. D, 4 P.M.–midnight. Reservations advised. AE, DC, MC, V.

Savoia. 2233 Atlantic Ave., Atlantic City; 348–5080. A classy, romantic, intimate restaurant. Specialty is northern Italian nouvelle cuisine.

(Less expensive Brajole Cafe next door.) D, 4 P.M.–midnight, Tues.–Sun. Dress code. AE, DC, MC, V.

Expensive

Dock's Oyster House. 2405 Atlantic Ave., Atlantic City; 345–0092. One of the best seafood places in town, and a local institution—it's been around since the turn of the century. Specializes in lobster and salmon. D, 5 P.M. to closing, Tues.–Sun. Closed Mon. Reservations advised. AE, MC, V.

Harbour Lights. Bay Ave. and Longport Blvd., Somers Point; 653–0900. Beautiful view of bay, from two decks. Specializes in seafood, steaks, and fettucine. L, 11:30 A.M.–5 P.M. Mon.–Sat.; D, 5 P.M.–2 A.M.; Sunday Brunch, 11 A.M.–2 P.M. AE, DC, MC, V.

McGee's. 1615 Pacific Ave., Atlantic City; 344–7521. Steaks, chops, prime rib, and seafood (lobster thermidor is the specialty of the house). Open 11 A.M.–10 P.M. Mon.–Fri.; 4–11 P.M. Sat.; 4–10 P.M. Sun. AE, DC, MC, V.

Oceanfront Restaurant. Brigantine Inn, 14th St. and the beach, Brigantine; 266–7731. Relatively new restaurant is right on sea, with great views. Art deco atmosphere. Seafood, veal, Cajun, chicken, and beef are all served. B, 8 A.M.–11:30 A.M. Mon.–Fri.; 8 A.M.–noon Sat. and Sun.; L, 11 A.M.–4 P.M., D, 5–11 P.M. Sun.–Thurs., 5–midnight Fri., and Sat. Late snacks after midnight. AE, DC, MC, V.

Old Waterway Inn. 1700 W. Riverside Drive, Atlantic City; 347–1793. Located off Route 30 in Atlantic City, the Inn offers dining right on Absecon Inlet. Many features include seafood, poultry, and meat dishes. L, 11:30 A.M.–2:30 P.M. Tues.–Fri.; D, 5–10 P.M. Thurs.–Sat.; D, 4–9 P.M. Sun. Dress code. DC, V.

Orsatti's. 24 S. North Carolina Ave., Atlantic City; 347–7667. Beautiful Italian restaurant; one of the newest and most popular in town. Features veal dishes, seafood, and pasta. Piano bar. D, 4–11:30 P.M. Tues.–Sat. AE, CB, DC, MC, V.

Scannicchio's. 119 S. California Ave., Atlantic City; 348–6378. Newly renovated. Serves outstanding dishes of both Italian seafood and pasta. D, 4–11 P.M. Mon.–Sat.; 3–11 P.M. Sun. Late snacks also served. Espresso, cappuccino, and fresh pastries also available. Reservations advised. AE, DC, MC, V.

Moderate

Abe's Oyster House. 2031 Atlantic Ave., Atlantic City; 344–7701. One of oldest restaurants in town; has been serving fresh seafood for more than 50 years. Specialties are lobster and clams. Steaks and chops also available. L, noon–4 P.M.; D, 6 P.M. until closing. Open. Tues.–Sun. AE, MC, V.

Angelo's Fairmount Tavern. 2300 Fairmount Ave., Atlantic City; 344–2439. Known for its outstanding Sicilian and mainland Italian cuisine. Specialties are ravioli and meatballs. L, 11:30 A.M.–2 P.M.; D, 5–10:30 P.M. No credit cards.

Aubrey's. Arkansas and Pacific aves., Atlantic City; 344–1632. Features an outdoor cafe on patio. Seafood and salads are excellent. Delicious pastries for desserts. D, from 4 P.M. on. Late snacks until 6 A.M. AE, CB, DC, MC, V.

Brajole Cafe. 2233 Atlantic Ave., Atlantic City; 344–1733. Italian dishes are specialty; also serves steaks and seafood. Open from 4 P.M.–9 A.M.;

D, 4 P.M.–6 A.M. Late-night menu includes sandwiches, omelettes, etc. More expensive Savoia next door. AE, DC, MC, V.

Dear's Place. Two locations. 9400 Atlantic Ave., Margate; 822–8830. 101 S. Plaza Place, Atlantic City; 348–8833. Famous for homemade specialties, ranging from French toast to corned beef to pudding. Also known for excellent desserts. Open 7:30 A.M.–9 P.M. Closed Tues. No credit cards.

Little Rock Cafe. 5214 Atlantic Ave., Ventnor; 823–4411. A European-style, quiet cafe, featuring light food such as omelettes, quiches, croissants, salads, soups, and French toast. L, 10A..M.–3 P.M.; D, 5:30–9 P.M. Mon.–Thurs.; 5:30–10 P.M. Fri., Sat. Sunday brunch, 10 A.M.–3 P.M. No credit cards.

Lobster Shack. 230 N. Adams Ave., Margate; 823–8847. Delicious fresh seafood is the norm here. Restaurant is located right on a bay, so diners get an outstanding waterfront view. Reservations suggested. D, 4–10 P.M. AE, DC, MC, V.

Palladian Restaurant. Located in Madison House Hotel, 123 S. Illinois Ave.; 345–1400, Ext. 431. Pleasant, first-class restaurant with good variety of Continental cuisine. D, 6–10 P.M.; Sunday brunch, 7 A.M.– 1 P.M. Valet parking. AE, MC, V.

Peking Duck House. Iowa and Atlantic aves., Atlantic City; 344–9090. One of the best Chinese restaurants in area. Peking duck is carved right at your table, served with green scallions, cucumbers julienne. Extensive Szechuan, Mandarin, and Cantonese menu. Reservations advised. L, noon–3 P.M. Mon.–Sat.; D, 3–11 P.M. Sun.–Thurs., 3–midnight Fri. and Sat. Jackets and ties for men. AE, DC, MC, V.

Sabatini's. 2210–14 Pacific Ave., Atlantic City; 345–4816. Specialty is assortment of pasta dishes, such as manicotti and lasagna. Also serves seafood, steaks, chops, and prime rib. Open noon–8 A.M. AE, MC, V.

Sailfish Cafe. 7805 Ventnor Ave., Margate; 822–6311. Pleasing variety, ranging from chicken to steak to prime rib to seafood. Just opened new sports bar. L, 11 A.M.–5 P.M.; D, 5–11 P.M. Sun.–Thurs., 5 P.M.–midnight Fri. and Sat. Late snacks until 3 A.M. AE, MC, V.

Inexpensive

A. W. Shucks Oyster Bar and Beer. Ocean One, Arkansas Ave. and Boardwalk; 344–3321. Conveniently located in the big shopping mall at center of boardwalk, this pleasant restaurant serves fresh oysters as well as clams, shrimp, mussels, crabs, and homemade chowders. Open daily, 10 A.M.–10 P.M.; 10 A.M.–11 P.M. on Sat. No credit cards.

Carnegie Deli. Sands Hotel, Indiana Ave. and Brighton Park, Atlantic City; 344–0900. Patterned after the famous New York deli of the same name. Huge sandwiches, plus fish and prime rib. Open 24 hours a day. AE, CB, DC, MC, V.

Downbeach Deli. 7720 Ventnor Ave., Margate; 823–7310. Features pleasant all-wood decor with attractive Tiffany lamps; specializes in tasty deli sandwiches; salads; smoked fish. B, L, 7:30 A.M.–4 P.M. No credit cards.

Hunan Restaurant. 2323 Atlantic Ave., Atlantic City; 348–5946. Inexpensive but good Chinese food—features Hunan, Szechuan, and Cantonese cuisines. L, 11:30 A.M.–3 P.M.; D, 3–11 P.M. Open until midnight Fri. and Sat. AE, MC, V.

Los Amigos. 1926 Atlantic Ave., Atlantic City; 344–2293. Pleasant, informal restaurant, specializing in Mexican fare. Tacos, burritos, and Mexican pizza are specialties of the house. Great margaritas, and many types of Mexican beer. L, 11:30 A.M.–4 P.M. Mon.–Fri.; D, 4 P.M.–2 A.M. every day. Late snacks: 2–6:30 A.M. AE, DC, MC, V.

Silver Dollar Saloon. 1719 Pacific Ave., Atlantic City; 344–2202. Friendly pub atmosphere. Best choices on menu: burgers, cheesesteaks, homemade chili, omelettes, salads. Boasts largest jukebox in town. Open 24 hours. No credit cards.

White House Sub Shop. 2301 Arctic Ave., Atlantic City; 345–1564. Currently performing show-business celebrities often dash in here; it's known as one of the best submarine sandwich shops on the East Coast. If you are in the vicinity, it's definitely worth a visit. No credit cards.

PARKS, GARDENS, AND FORESTS. Atlantic City itself offers few great parks within walking distance of the casino-hotels. Its greatest parks, of course, are the beach and the Atlantic Ocean. There are, however, several nice county and state parks within a 30-minute drive of downtown.

Absecon Wildlife Management Area. Route 9, Absecon. Hiking is done year-round; fishing and hunting is permitted in season. Picnic areas.

Bass River State Forest. Route 9, New Gretna; 296–1114. Encompasses more than 17,000 acres of the Pine Barrens. Many types of camping options are offered: plain sites, lean-tos, shelters, and even cabins. Canoes can be rented here, and there are many hiking trails.

Birch Grove Park. Route 9 and Zion Road, Northfield; 641–3778. Open year-round for camping. Has 280 acres of woods, fields, and lakes, and offers camping, hiking, fishing, and birdwatching. There are picnic areas and playground facilities, including softball and soccer fields.

Bridgeton City Park. Besides housing the Cohanzick Zoo, this park offers picnic facilities, ball fields, canoe rentals, nature trails, and Indian burial sites. Encompasses 1,000 acres. Entrance on Commerce St., Bridgeton.

Estell Manor County Park. Route 50, Estell Manor; 625–1897. This is the largest park in Atlantic County, and has fishing, canoeing, picnicking, hiking, and a nature center. Also ball fields. Open 9 A.M. to dusk.

Leamings Run Botanical Gardens. Route 9 in Swainton; 465–5871. Visitors can stroll through some 24 different gardens. A whaling museum and colonial farm are also on premises.

McNamara Wildlife Management Area. Route 50 in Estell Manor. Several hiking trails slice through this park's 6,739 acres. There is also fishing, and a kids' playground.

Stillwater Park. New Road and Dolphin Ave., Northfield. A small (only 45 acres) but very pleasant little park; its chief advantage is that it is only 10 miles from Atlantic City.

Wharton State Forest. Batsto R.D.4, Hammonton; 561–3262. There are 150 square miles of wilderness for hiking, camping, and canoeing.

BEACHES AND BOARDWALKS. The towns of Atlantic City, Ventnor, Margate, and Longport all have wonderful, wide beaches, with fine, soft, white sand and gentle slopes into the sea. A boardwalk bisects the beaches of both Atlantic City (for about five miles) and Ventnor (for about two miles). Margate and Longport don't have boardwalks.

As opposed to many other shore towns, there are very few amusements—and no rides—in this region. There are a few video arcades along the Atlantic City boardwalk, as well as many souvenir stores and snack shops.

There is nothing in Margate and Longport but the beach itself.

Here's a summary of the beach facilities in each of these four towns, and a number to call for more information.

Atlantic City (609–347–5309 for information). Free beach, no tags required. Lifeguard on duty: 9:30 A.M.–5:30 P.M. Surfing permitted before and after lifeguard hours. Cabanas and lounges can be rented from the casinos. Five-mile-long boardwalk, with hundreds of small stores and food shops. Bike riding allowed 6–10 A.M. No carnival rides; some video arcades.

Ventnor and **Margate** (609–823–7904). Same regulations for both towns. Beach badges, which are good for either town, cost $10 for the season, or $3.50 daily or weekly. Can be purchased either at City Hall before the season, or at the beach during the season at Suffolk Avenue tennis courts. Lifeguard hours: 10 A.M.–6 P.M. Surfing is allowed at Cambridge Avenue. Fishing is done at Cambridge Avenue pier; call 609–823–3083 for information. There is a two-mile boardwalk in Ventnor; none in Margate. Bike riding allowed on Ventnor boardwalk from 6:30–10 A.M. and from 4:30–6:30 P.M. Two playground areas on this beach (at Suffolk Avenue and Newport Avenue) allow volleyball, cookouts, and beach parties with a permit (Ventnor beach only). No bathhouses.

Longport. (609–823–2371). Beach badges cost $10 for the season, or $3.50 daily or weekly. They can be purchased at Borough Hall before the season, or from beach inspectors during the season. Surfing is allowed at 32nd Avenue. Fishing is done at 11th Avenue jetty and at Atlantic Avenue and the bay. No boardwalk or other amusements. No bathhouses.

PARTICIPANT SPORTS. Although there is little doubt that gambling is the number one participant sport in Atlantic City, there are far healthier activities available for those who wish to take advantage of them. As a matter of fact, the opportunities for sports enthusiasts here are truly excellent, especially during the summer. One can swim or jog anywhere along the five-mile-long beach. Farley State Marina is a center for boating, sailing, and fishing; a new $17-million renovation has improved it considerably. It's dominated by Donald Trump's 300-foot-long yacht, *Trump Princess*. Nearly all of the casino-hotels have some sort of health facilities, usually swimming pools, saunas, racquetball courts, tennis courts, etc.

Public tennis courts and public golf courses are fairly accessible; most are only a short drive away. Biking enthusiasts will love the sights and sounds of the boardwalks of Atlantic City and Ventnor in early morning, when they are open to peddlers.

Most facilities are not that crowded, since so many of the town's 30 million visitors are here strictly to gamble. If you want to charter a fishing boat, or reserve a tee time for golf, it can usually be done within a day or two of when you call. See also Parks, Gardens, and Forests and Beaches and Boardwalks, above.

Bicycling

Atlantic City's boardwalk is open for bike riding from 6 A.M. until 10 A.M. Those diligent enough to get up early can see the sun rise out of the sea. In addition, Ventnor's boardwalk is open from 6:30 A.M. to 10 A.M., and from 4:30 P.M. to 6:30 P.M.

A few stores along the boardwalk in Ventnor and Atlantic City rent bikes at very reasonable rates.

AAAA Bike Shop. 5223 Ventnor Ave., Ventnor; 487–0808. Open 9 A.M.–5 P.M., Mon.–Sat.

Margate Bike Shop. 4 S. Douglas Ave., Margate; 822–9415. $3.50 per hour. Open 9 A.M.–5 ge 00022 v Mon.–Sat.; 9 A.M.–1 P.M., Sun.

Boardsailing

Bayview Sailboats. 312 Bay Ave., Ocean City; 398–3049.

Brigantine Sailboards. 406 West Shore Drive, Brigantine; 266–2727. Boards can be rented by the hour, and instruction is also offered.

Boat Rentals

All Seasons Marina. Roosevelt Blvd., Marmora; 390–1850.

Angler's Roost-Pier IV. 9401 Amherst Ave., Margate; 822–2272.

Bayview Sailboats. 312 Bay Ave., Ocean City; 398–3049.

Capt. Andy's Marina. 9317 Amherst Ave., Margate; 822–0916.

Canoe Rentals

Bel Haven Lake Canoe. State Highway 542, Green Bank; 965–2205 or 965–2031. Trips through Wharton State Forest.

Bridgeton City Park. Entrance on Commerce St.

Mick's Canoe Rental. Route 563, Jenkins; 726–1380. Organized canoe trips through the Wading River, with some overnight trips.

Pine Barrens Canoe Rental. Chatsworth Road, Chatsworth; 726–1515. Offers both day or overnight trips through Wharton State Forest.

Deep-Sea Fishing

Brick 'n' Sticks. Atlantic City Marina; 266–0056 or 266–9118. Specializes in bluefishing, and tuna and marlin. Leaves every day at 7 A.M. $300 half day; $450 full day.

Captain Andy's Marina. 9317 Amherst Ave., Margate; 822–0916. Has fleet of party boats, which carry up to 100 people. Rates vary.

Captain Allen's Fishing Center. 432 N. Rhode Island Ave., Atlantic City; 345–0075. Charter-boat service for private parties.

Captain Applegate. Farley State Marina, South Carolina and Brigantine Blvd.; 345–4077 or 652–8184. Offers half-day fishing: 8:15 A.M.–12:15 P.M.; or 1 P.M.–5 P.M. Cost is $13, adults; $8, children. Rod rentals on board.

Horizon Sport Fishing. Farley State Marina, 600 Huron Ave.; 645–1214. Charter boats for up to 10 people; half day or full day.

Fishing From Land

Sea wall on Penrose Avenue. Near Gardner's Basin, Atlantic City, free.

Marine Avenue Jetty. Atlantic City, free.

11th Street Jetty. Longport, free.

Ventnor Fishing Pier. S. Cornwall Ave. and Boardwalk. Nonmembers can fish 8 A.M.–4 P.M. daily. Fee is $5. Call 823-7944 for more information.

Golf

Courses open to the public within a 45-minute drive of Atlantic City include: *Brigantine Country Club.* Roosevelt Blvd. and the Bay, Brigantine (266–1388).

Mays Landing Country Club, Cates Road, McKee City (641–4411).

Pomona Golf and Country Club. Moss Mill and Odessa rds., Pomona (965–3232).

Call ahead for a tee time and information. Green fees vary, but are within the $10–$15 range.

The *Seaview Golf Resort,* Route 9 in Absecon, is scheduled to open in 1989 a new $850,000 golf school, run by John Jacobs Golf School. For more information, contact the Jacobs home office: 602–991–8587 or 800–472–5007.

Horseback Riding

Bill's Lazy B Riding Stables and Tack Shop. Route 9, Oceanville; 652–1973. $7 horse per hour, or $12 horse, two hours. Open every day from 10 A.M. to 5 P.M. Guided tours on several trails. Night rides from 6 P.M. to 8 P.M. in summer. Reservation advised.

Hidden Valley Ranch. 4070 Bay Shore Road, Cold Spring; 884–8205. Guided rides through wooded trails costs $8.50 per 45-minute session. A 1½-hour ride costs $16. Open 9 A.M. until dusk, Mon.–Sat. All instruction.

Scuba Diving

East Coast Diving. Route 9, two blocks north of Tilton Road, Northfield; 646–5090. Runs organized trips for certified divers.

Surfing

Heritage Surf Shop. 3700 Landis Ave., Sea Isle City; 263–3033. Rents boards by the hour.

Tennis

There are five good outdoor tennis courts open to the general public. Each has its own policy concerning reservations. On some, you simply show up and wait your turn. On others, you should call ahead to find out about that court's rules.

Bader Field. Albany Ave., Atlantic City; 347–5348.
N. Huntington and Fremont avenues, Margate; 822–8650.
Jerome Avenue, near Margate Bridge, Margate.
Surrey and Ventnor avenues, Ventnor Heights.
Suffolk and Atlantic avenues, Ventnor; 823–7946.

There are also two good indoor tennis centers within a half-hour drive of the casinos. *Atlantic Indoor Tennis.* 1225 W. Mill Rd., Northfield; 641–0372. Court is $24 an hour. Open 9 A.M. to 9 P.M. *Golf and Tennis World.* Black Horse Pike, West Atlantic City; 641–3546. Three indoor courts. Open early morning to late evening. Court fees are $16 to $22 per hour.

SPECTATOR SPORTS. Because of its small size (population, 40,000) Atlantic City can't support a pro or college team in a major team sport. Therefore, the opportunities for spectators are not that extensive. However, Atlantic City is the boxing capital of the East Coast, and some of the top fighters in the world fight here from time to time. In addition, the polo and horse racing here is top-notch.

Boxing

Throughout the year, at least half of the Atlantic City casino-hotels host championship fights in one of the major divisions of boxing. The Michael Spinks/Mike Tyson heavyweight fight of June, 1988 firmly established Atlantic City as the boxing capital of America. Unfortunately, there is no clearing-house number where one can get advance information on these. The best thing to do is to simply look at the Atlantic City newspaper once you arrive, to see if any fights are scheduled during the week you are there. Or, you can call each casino-hotel directly and inquire about its boxing schedule. The fights are usually held in the main show room of a given casino.

Casino-hotels that hosted major fights in 1988 included: *TropWorld* (609–340–4000); *Resorts International* (609–344–6000); *Trump Plaza* (609–441–6000); *Caesars* (609–348–4411); *Harrah's Marina* (609–441–5000); *Sands* (609–441–4000).

Horse Racing

The *Atlantic City Race Course,* Routes 322 and 40, McKee City, Hamilton Township (609–641–2190). Located 14 miles from town, it attracts some of the best race horses in the East, during its season (late June through August). Post time is 7:15 P.M. Grandstand fee is $2; $3 for clubhouse. Closed Tues. and Sun.

Polo

Harrah's Marina sponsors one of the best polo teams in New Jersey. All matches are played at 1:30 P.M. at the Mattix Run Equestrian Center, Moss Mill Road, Smithville. Admission is $3. Call 609–441–5000 for information. Most matches are usually on Sundays.

CASINOS. The lifeblood of Atlantic City is the 12 casino-hotels. Since casino gambling was initiated in 1978, approximately 60 billion dollars have been wagered. And this doesn't even include income from rooms, restaurants, cocktail lounges, and show rooms.

The stakes are enormous, and competition for the gambling dollar is fierce. This is a blessing for the visitor, because each hotel is continually adding features that will give it a competitive edge. In this aspect, at least, *every* visitor to Atlantic City wins.

You must be 21 years of age to gamble in Atlantic City. This is strictly enforced; at every entrance leading into the casino of every hotel, security men carefully watch every person coming in. Anyone even close to 21 years of age is usually carded.

Most casinos offer the same games: blackjack, craps, roulette, Big Six (or Wheel of Fortune), and Baccarat. Blackjack is, by far, the most popular game, and there are far more blackjack tables than anything else. At Caesars, for example, there are 72 blackjack tables, 24 craps tables, 11 roulette tables, three Big Six tables, and four baccarat tables, not to mention about 1,600 slot machines.

Novice gamblers can probably get the hang of roulette, Big Six, or blackjack simply by watching the action awhile. Craps is difficult to learn, and the craps tables are so crowded and noisy that the dealers won't have time to teach you. If you really want to learn craps, show up at 10 A.M., when the casinos first open and the dealers have some time to spend with you. If you come during the off-season, the casinos are somewhat less crowded.

There is a minimum bet of $5 at all table games in Atlantic City, with the exception of the Atlantis, which has a few $2 blackjack and roulette tables in addition to the usual $5 tables. Slot machines are in the nickel (infrequently), quarter, 50¢ and $1 categories.

For a complete description of each of the 12 casino-hotels, see the Accommodations section. For information about the entertainment offered by each casino-hotel, see the Nightlife section.

MUSEUMS AND GALLERIES. Only a few art galleries and museums can be found in Atlantic City and its neighboring towns. The ones there are, however, have a relatively good, interesting selection of exhibits.

If you are going to be in town for several days, try to visit the Garden Pier, which houses both the Atlantic City Art Center and the Atlantic City Historical Museum. The Pier is located right on the boardwalk, at New Jersey Avenue, about three blocks from Resorts International.

The other places mentioned below are within a 15- to 30-minute drive of Atlantic City. All phone numbers are in the 609 area code.

A. M. R. Yesterday and Today Gallery. 100 S. Weymouth Ave., Ventnor; 823–2404. Features handmade leather, brass, silver, and gold accessories, as well as sculpture, pottery, and jewelry. Hours vary, call for information.

Arthur Clauson's Fine Art Gallery. 2213–15 Arctic Ave., Atlantic City; 345–8878. Posters, graphics, oriental art prints. 8 A.M.–5 P.M., Mon.–Fri.; to 2 P.M. Sat.

Atlantic City Art Center. Garden Pier, Boardwalk and New Jersey Ave., Atlantic City; 347–5844. Rotating special exhibits, plus photography, paintings, sculpture. Open 9 A.M.–4 P.M. daily.

Atlantic City Historical Museum. Garden Pier, Boardwalk and New Jersey Ave., Atlantic City; 347–5844. Offers displays on theaters, nightlife, piers, the beach, and Boardwalk—everything that made Atlantic City's history so unique, including a special exhibition of the Miss America Pageant. Open 9 A.M.–4 P.M. daily.

Central Square Gallery. 10 Central Square, Linwood; 653–1080. Features original prints, posters, and graphics by artists. Open 10 A.M.–5 P.M. Mon.–Sat.

Circle Gallery. Park Place and the boardwalk, Atlantic City; 348–4800 or 800–257–0491. Open 9 A.M.–7 P.M. Mon.–Fri.; 9 A.M.–8 P.M. Sat.; 9 A.M.–7

P.M. Sun. One of the city's most diverse collections of paintings, sculpture, jewelry, and graphics works.

Noyes Museum. Lily Lake Road, Oceanville; 652–8848. One of better museums in the area. Has good rotating exhibits, as well as a collection of American art from Fred Noyes. There are working decoys, and decoy-carving demonstrations. Open 11 A.M.–4 P.M. Wed.–Sun. Admission: $1.50, adults; $1, senior citizens; 50¢, children and students.

HISTORIC SITES, ZOOS, THINGS TO SEE AND DO. Visitors to this region shouldn't miss the chance to visit some of the major attractions that do *not* revolve around gambling. Some, such as Absecon Lighthouse, Ocean One Shopping Mall, the Convention Hall, and the Art Center, are right along the boardwalk in the middle part of town.

A wide variety of other sites are 15 to 20 miles away, and will require a half-hour drive or so. These out-of-town attractions include a winery, a national wildlife refuge, and some historical villages and houses.

If you get a rainy day, or simply want a change of pace from the craziness of the casinos, the attractions listed below might all be worth visiting for a few hours.

All telephone numbers listed below are in the 609 area code.

Absecon Lighthouse. Rhode Island and Pacific Avenues, Atlantic City. This 167-foot-high lighthouse was built in 1857, to warn ships of tricky rocks and reefs. It is a New Jersey State Park.

Atlantic City Convention Hall. 2300 Boardwalk; 348–7044 or 348–7000. Centrally located in the middle of town, this huge hall is the site of both the Miss America Pageant and the world's largest pipe organ. Some conventions here (which are booked almost continually) are open to the general public.

Atlantic City Free Public Library. Tennessee & Atlantic aves.; 345–2269. Sponsors wide variety of children's activities, including a "story hour" for small children. Crafts classes also scheduled. Call for specific schedules.

Cohanzick Zoo. Mayor Aitken Drive, Bridgeton; 455–3230. This is the only municipal zoo in New Jersey, with 50 mammals and 100 birds. Open dawn to dusk. Donations suggested.

Edwin B. Forsythe National Wildlife Refuge. Great Oak Road, off Route 9, Oceanville; 652–1665. Has more than 20,000 acres of coastal marshland and woodlands. Some 200 bird species live here. Motorists can enjoy a free eight-mile self-guided tour for bird-watching and wildlife photography. There are two walking trails about a half-mile long. Open year-round. Office auditorium is open 8 A.M.–4:30 P.M. Plan two hours for a tour. There is a birding hotline (884–2626).

Elevator Rides: Atlantic City Casinos. It's quick and it's cheap—both the Tropicana and the Trump Plaza have outdoor elevators that offer a terrific panorama of the sea and "Casino Row."

Historic Gardner's Basin. 800 N. New Hampshire Ave., at the Inlet; 348–2880. This replica of a maritime village features historic vessels, coastal museum, marine mammal museum, a small aquarium, and a gift shop. There are films, boat rides, and a good restaurant. Admission is free. Open from May to Sept., 11 A.M.–4 P.M.

Lucy the Margate Elephant. 9200 Atlantic Ave., Margate; 823–6473. This huge elephant, built as a real-estate promotion a century ago, is six stories high, and weighs 90 tons. Children can walk through it. Lucy is open from May to Oct., on weekends, from 10 A.M.–5 P.M. From late June to Labor Day, it is open daily, from 10 A.M.–8:30 P.M. Admission is $1.50, adults; $1, children. Museum and gift shop.

Miss America Pageant. If you want to be a part of this famed annual event, held during the second week of September, you have a number of options. Watch the contestants stroll from Garden Pier to Montpelier Ave. during the Boardwalk Parade, usually the Tues. night of Miss America Week. Bleacher seats cost about $3.50, grandstand seats, about $6.50. You can also watch the swimsuit and talent competitions during the week at Convention Hall. Cost for these tickets is between $6 and $8. If you want to attend the final event of the pageant—the nationally televised Sat. night extravaganza—tickets will range from $6 to $16. Call 345–7571 for more information.

Ocean Drive. This 40-mile-long route, from Atlantic City to Cape May, may be the most beautiful drive along the entire southern shore. Along the way, one can stop and visit several marinas, and enjoy many beautiful views of the sea.

Ocean One. Boardwalk at Arkansas Ave., Atlantic City. This 900-foot-long mall resembles an actual oceanliner. It contains more than 150 shops, selling virtually anything you could possibly think of. There are also several fine restaurants here.

Renault Winery. 72 N. Bremen Ave., Egg Harbor City; 609–965–2111. Famous for sparkling champagnes. 45-minute tours, $1, offered from 10 A.M.–5 P.M. Sundays. Restaurant open noon–5 P.M. Mon.–Sat.

Towne of Historic Smithville. Route 9, 12 miles north of Atlantic City; 652–7775. This beautiful little lakeside village is a replica of an 1800s Colonial Village. It has cobblestone paths, a little pond, and about 30 specialty shops. Open daily. Free.

Storybook Land. Black Horse Pike, Cardiff; 641–7847. Characters and scenes from fairytales and nursery rhymes enchant children here. There are rides, a petting zoo, playground, picnic area, snack bar, and souvenir shop. Open daily. 11 A.M.–9 P.M. (summer hours).

SHOPPING. The selection of stores available to shoppers in Atlantic City is quite good; virtually every type of store you would possibly want to visit can be found here. Although you won't find any real bargains, the prices are not exorbitantly expensive, either.

If you have kids, be sure to take them to the boardwalk, where there are countless little stores that sell T-shirts, saltwater taffy, souvenir mugs, etc.

Clothing items are not taxed in New Jersey, and that will come as a pleasant surprise to clothes shoppers. The regular state sales tax is 6 percent.

The main shopping district runs along Atlantic and Pacific avenues, especially between Tennessee and Indiana avenues. Nearly every type of retail store is found there.

Central Square. New Road and Central Ave., Linwood; 926–1000. A charming, Early American village-style mall, with more than 40 specialty shops. Stores sell clothing, fine gifts, glassware, and more. Free parking.

Gordon's Alley. 1000 block of Atlantic Ave.; 344–5000. This quaint pedestrian mall is patterned after Ghirardelli Square in San Francisco. It features a nice assortment of classy shops, boutiques, and restaurants.

Ocean One. Boardwalk at Arkansas Avenue; 347–8082. This large, three-story indoor mall resembles an ocean liner from the outside. There are about 150 stores, as well as nearly every type of fast-food restaurant you can think of. Some of the restaurants have outdoor terraces, where you can sit at tables and watch the ocean.

Shore Mall. Black Horse Pike, Pleasantville. This enclosed mall contains such well-known stores as J. C. Penney and Sears, as well as more than 75 other small stores and restaurants.

A few discount clothing stores are located on Tilton Road in Northfield. Shoppers can sometimes find bargains at these spots.

ENTERTAINMENT. Visitors interested in the fine arts will not find a huge selection of things to do in Atlantic City and its neighboring towns. Local colleges present operas, symphonies, string quartets, and other types of classical music. These schools—Glassboro State College and Stockton State College—also produce plays from time to time, and dance companies and symphonies sometimes perform at these same facilities.

The South Jersey Regional Theater puts on some first-class productions, and is probably the best place to go if you're interested in seeing a play.

Unfortunately, there are no movie houses left in Atlantic City itself; you have to drive a few miles out of town to see either a current-run or revival film.

Some casino-hotels, notably the Claridge, put on Broadway musicals several times a year. These shows, for the most part, feature name performers, and are quite professionally done—often as well as in New York.

A complete list of film, theater, music, and dance opportunities follows below. All phone numbers are in the 609 area code.

Film

Atlantic City has limited opportunities for film buffs. There aren't any movie theaters left in Atlantic City, but there a few first-run movie houses in neighboring towns. In addition, a couple of places sponsor film festivals and show old movies.

Atlantic Film Society. Located in Little Art Theatre, Harbor Village Square, Zion Road and Ocean Heights Ave., Bargaintown (653–1626). Specializes in foreign and revival movies. Admission: $4.50. Discounts for senior citizens. Call 24 hours a day for schedule.

Performing Arts Center. Stockton State College, Jimmie Leeds Road, Pomona (652–9000). Sponsors occasional film festivals. Call for schedule.

There are several first-run movie houses within a 20-minute drive of downtown Atlantic City. They are: *Margate Twin,* 7712 Ventnor Ave., Margate (822–3817). *Point 4,* MacArthur Blvd., Somers Point (927–0131). *Towne 4,* Shore Mall, Black Horse Pike, Pleasantville (646–4799). *Twin Plaza,* 5002 Wellington Ave., Ventnor Heights (823–6641). *Twin Tilton 1 and 2,* Tilton Shopping Center, Northfield (646–3147), *Ventnor Twin,* 521 Ventnor Ave., Ventnor (822–4422).

Music

If you love rock and roll, you'll love Atlantic City, which has a lot of exciting dance clubs. People who like jazz and country music will probably find at least one or two clubs that cater to their tastes. (See Nightlife, below.)

If you like opera, symphonies, string quartets, chamber music, etc., you will probably have to drive out of town to find it. Neighboring high schools and community colleges put on performances throughout the summer. When you get to town, simply check the entertainment section of the *Atlantic City Press*. Or call the numbers listed below for more information.

Atlantic City Community Concerts Association (822–7927). Sponsors operas, symphonies, string quartets, etc. at local high schools and other facilities. Call for admission prices, schedule, etc.

Atlantic Community College. Route 322, Mays Landing (625–1111). Sponsors string quartets and other classical performers. Call for information.

Glassboro State College. Route 322, Glassboro (823–5000). Occasionally produces both contemporary and chamber music. Call for admission prices, schedule.

Pinelands Cultural Society Weekly Concert Series. Route 9, Waretown Mall, Waretown (971–1593 or 542–9485). Country and old-time musicians play every Saturday night. Sing-alongs are encouraged. The action begins at 8 P.M. Admission fee: $2.50, adults; 50¢, children under 12.

Theater

Theater buffs will find a decent selection of shows in this area, both near Atlantic City's boardwalk and in outlying community colleges. Occasionally, a casino-hotel will present a famous Broadway musical, featuring a big-name star, or a lavish musical revue show. For example, the Claridge's Palace Theatre often presents musicals.

The South Jersey Regional Theatre has been acclaimed frequently for its professionally produced shows, and for its fine actors.

Atlantic Community College. Off Route 322, Mays Landing (625–1111). Presents various plays and operas throughout the year. Tickets are usually between $5 and $7.50.

Palace Theatre. Claridge Hotel and Casino, Indiana Avenue and Brighton Park (340–3700). Often sponsors well-known Broadway plays. Call for monthly schedule. Tickets are in the $15–$20 range.

South Jersey Regional Theatre. Gateway Playhouse, Bay and Higbee Avenues, Somers Point (653–0553). This is the only Equity theatre in Atlantic County, and offers some high-quality acting. It presents a continual assortment of dramatic plays and musicals. Tickets cost from $13 to $17. Curtain time is 8 P.M. weekdays; 8:30 P.M. on Fri. and Sat. Matinees are presented on Wed. (1 P.M.) and Sun. (2 P.M.). There is a 10% discount for senior citizens; 50% discount for students. Open from Oct.–Dec., and from Apr.–Jun.

Performing Arts Center. Stockton State College, Jimmie Leeds Road, Pomona (652–9000). Occasionally presents plays produced by theater companies from both this region and from other parts of the country.

Dance

Ballet fans will be disappointed by the limited opportunities available to them in this region. However, visiting dance companies occasionally perform at Glassboro State College and Stockton State College. Their addresses and telephone numbers are listed above.

NIGHTLIFE. Atlantic City is arguably the second most exciting city on the entire East Coast, behind only New York City. Few cities anywhere offer such an exciting variety of nightlife. All 12 of the great casino-hotels have huge show rooms (usually with between 350–1,000 seats) that attract the biggest names in show business: Bob Hope, Joan Rivers, Bill Cosby, Frank Sinatra, and so on. Others stage lavish musicals, either original revues or revivals of famous Broadway shows.

In addition, all casino-hotels have at least one large lounge, and often two or three, where more informal live entertainment (perhaps a piano player and singer) is offered.

Tickets for almost any show can be reserved or purchased the same day you want to see it. For the megastars such as Bill Cosby, however, one may have to reserve several weeks in advance. Casino-hotels usually have their schedules of big-name entertainers set up at least six months in advance, so when you have finalized your plans to go to Atlantic City, call up the casino-hotels to see what they're offering that month.

The *Atlantic City Press* lists all casino acts. Another good source of information is *Atlantic City Magazine,* which lists various events in each of the major casino-hotels. If you live on the East Coast, the entertainment section of your daily paper will probably have ads from some of the casinos, hyping their shows.

Atlantic City's casinos are only a small part of the town's total nightlife picture, however. There are scores of taverns, pubs, discos, and lounges. Some of these establishments are open throughout the night, closing at 6 A.M. If you really want to kick up your heels and "go for it," this is the place to do it. You can eat a late dinner, go dancing till 4 A.M., then go to a romantic lounge until dawn, and watch the sun come up.

In this section are listed the major entertainment opportunities in each of the casino-hotels, as well as some of the more popular clubs and night spots in both Atlantic City and its satellite communities.

The Casino-Hotels

It is pretty easy to get tickets to casino acts. First of all, you don't have to be a guest at a casino-hotel. Tickets for big, headline engagements can be purchased at individual casino box offices, local Ticketron outlets, or charged, via credit cards, through Teletron. (Teletron numbers are: North Jersey: 201–343–4200; New York: 212–947–5850; Pennsylvania: 215–627–0532.) In all cases, try to reserve as early as possible. Locally in AC call 344–1770.

Ticketron outlets can be found at the Atlantis, Florida Ave., and Boardwalk, 344–4000; Bally's Grand, Boston and Pacific aves., 347–7111; Resorts International, North Carolina Avenue and Boardwalk, 344–6830; and TropWorld Hotel and Casino, Iowa Avenue and Boardwalk, 344–4000.

Atlantis. Florida Avenue at Boardwalk, 344–4000. The Cabaret Theatre offers big-name stars. There is also entertainment in the Shangri-La and Le Club lounges.

Bally's Grand. Boston and Pacific avenues, 347–7111. Opera House Theatre showcases big-name stars. Gatsby's lounge has nightly entertainment. Opened new "Grandstand Under the Stars"—an outdoor amphitheater—in June, 1988.

Bally's Park Place. Park Place and Boardwalk, 340–2700. The Park Place Cabaret features a musical revue. Billy's Pub offers nightly entertainment, as does Upstairs in the Park.

Caesars. Arkansas Avenue at Boardwalk, 348–4411. Circus Maximus has continual headliners. Other performers are found in Arena and Forum lounges.

Claridge. Indiana Avenue at Brighton Park, 340–3400. Palace Theatre has old Broadway musicals, plus occasional headliners. There is continuous music and entertainment at the Celebrity Cabaret.

Harrah's Marina. 1725 Brigantine Boulevard, 441–5000. Broadway-by-the-Bay Theatre offers first-rate performers during most of the year. The Atrium Lounge, a beautiful garden bar with waterfalls, trees, and skylights, is a great place for late-night drinks. Bay Cabaret Theatre has live music.

Resorts International. North Carolina Avenue at Boardwalk, 344–6000. Top-name performers entertain in the Superstar Theatre. Carousel Lounge offers musical revues. Other nightly entertainment is found in the Rendezvous lounge.

Sands. Indiana Avenue and Brighton Park, 441–4000. Copa Room features nationally known stars. Punch Bowl and Players lounges offer continual music. The Copa Room is converted into a disco every Friday and Saturday nights, and stays open until 5 A.M.

TropWorld. Iowa Avenue at Boardwalk, 340–4000. TropWorld Showroom features major show-business headliners. Top of the Trop lounge, which was newly renovated in the summer of 1988, offers great view of the ocean from the 21st floor, and guests can stare at the sea and boardwalk while listening to jazz. Sizzles lounge features various musical groups.

Trump's Castle. Huron Avenue and Brigantine Boulevard, 441–2000. King's Court Showroom is major show room. Nightly entertainment in Viva's and the Casino Lounge. DJ's is a fine piano bar.

Trump Plaza. Mississippi Avenue at Boardwalk, 441–6000. Trump Plaza Theatre has headliners. Jezebel's is a nice piano bar. Swizzle's—a two-level bar—overlooks casino.

Other Night Spots

Aubrey's. 2024 Pacific Avenue, Atlantic City; 344–1632. Next to Caesars, this bright, cheerful restaurant and bar has a very nice enclosed sidewalk patio. Open 3 P.M.–7 A.M.

Chez Paree. New York Ave. and Boardwalk, Atlantic City; 348–4313. One of the largest discos in town, with one of the most sophisticated light and sound systems in Atlantic City. Opens at midnight on weekends. Dress code.

Club Ancoppa. Mississippi and Atlantic aves., Atlantic City; 344–1733. Newly renovated two-level dance club, with gigantic aquarium, suspended dance floors. Open from 11 P.M. Fri.–Sun.; 4 P.M.–midnight Mon.–Thurs.; noon–7 A.M. Fri.–Sun.

Dolley's Lounge. Madison House Hotel, 123 S. Illinois Avenue, Atlantic City; 345–1400. Cozy atmosphere in newly renovated hotel. Features

Happy Hour with free hors d'oeuvres from 5–7 P.M. Mon.–Fri. Open noon–2 A.M. daily.

Friar Tuck's Tavern. 2323 S. New Road, Northfield; 345–9400. Found on the mainland a few miles away, this is worth the drive. It has a medieval decor and good food and drinks. Open 11 A.M.–3 A.M.

Gilhooley's. 9314 Amherst Ave., Margate; 823–2800. An upscale club, filled with greenery. A DJ plays music every night. Open from 4 P.M.–4 A.M. for drinking and dancing. Comedians every Wednesday night.

Grabel's. 3901 Atlantic Ave., Atlantic City; 344–9263. Favorite hangout of locals. Club is dominated by black starlit walls. Live entertainment nightly. Open 3 P.M.–8 A.M. weekdays; from 5 P.M. Sat., Sun.

Irish Pub. St. James Place at Boardwalk, Atlantic City; 345–9613. Live entertainment featuring Irish music; light meals served 24 hours. Burgers and sandwiches are good.

Le Club. The Enclave condominiums, Lincoln Place and Boardwalk, Atlantic City; 347–0400. Offers excellent jazz. Highlights include a great view of the ocean, and a nice clam bar. Open 5 P.M.–2 A.M.

Longport Inn. 31st and Atlantic aves., Longport; 822–5435. An elegant little bar that provides a great place for a quiet drink. Open 3 P.M.–2 A.M. Mon.–Fri.; 11 A.M.–2 A.M. Sat.; noon–2 A.M. Sun.

Memories. Madison and Amherst aves., Atlantic City; 823–2196. DJ spins tunes every night. Newly renovated. Open 9 P.M.–4 A.M.

Red's. 9217 Atlantic Avenue, Margate; 822–1539. Features three different sections: a pub, a dance club, and a video lounge. Live bands play or a DJ spins tunes. Hours vary.

Touché. 9300 Amherst Avenue, Margate; 923–2144. A sophisticated nightclub, complete with live dance revue, dancing bartenders and waitresses, and special nightly events. Happy Hour buffets with unlimited free shrimp. Open daily, 4:30 P.M.–4 A.M. Mon.–Fri.; 4 P.M.–4 A.M. Sat. and Sun.

Waterfront. 998 Bay Ave., Somers Point; 653–0099. Pleasant setting, with a beautiful view of the bay; favorite spot of local businessmen. Open 11:30 A.M.–3 A.M. daily. Free parking.

THE NORTH SHORE

North of Atlantic City

by
MIKE SCHWANZ

The northern New Jersey Shore has been enjoyed by mankind for centuries. Indian relics have been found that date back as far as A.D. 300. In the late 1400s, the Lenni-Lenape, or Delaware, Indians moved into the region. This tribe enjoyed a nice, peaceful existence for about 150 years, and thrived on the abundance of shellfish, waterfowl, and game. They cultivated crops and used seaweed as a fertilizer.

In the early 1600s, the Dutch, led by explorer Henry Hudson, began settling the shore. During this century, many of the first white settlers were whalers. Then, as the whaling industry declined, people moved inland and started farming.

In the 1700s, other industries thrived in the shore region, especially glassworks, charcoal manufacturers, bog iron furnaces, lumbering, and shipbuilding. Tuckerton, on Little Egg Harbor, became one of the major ports on the entire East Coast.

During the Revolutionary War, the shore area and immediate vicinity played an important role. The Battle of Monmouth on

June 28, 1778, was an important turning point of the war; General George Washington won an important victory here. Elsewhere on the shore, pro-Revolution privateers attacked British trading vessels up and down the shore, trying to intercept ships bringing troops and arms to the soldiers. The pirates would use lanterns to lure ships onto the dangerous, rocky shoals. One of the more notorious pirates was Captain Kidd. His treasure is said to be still hidden somewhere on Long Beach Island.

By the late 1800s, with the development of railroad lines, the shore towns became respectable places to live, and families set up residences.

In the early 1900s, as the automobile gradually became a fixture in American society, the shore area became extremely popular. Many of the hotels still in use today were built during this period. More and more towns began to cater to tourists, and by the 1930s this region was one of the most popular vacation spots in the United States. Over 50 years later, the New Jersey Shore remains one of the great seaside resort areas in the country.

The millions of people who flock to this area every year do so for a reason. Simply put, the shore has many attractions that can't be found anywhere else in the country.

The boardwalks that run parallel to the sea in many communities are a distinct New Jersey feature. Atlantic City built the first boardwalk in 1870; other towns followed suit shortly after. More than a century after the first one was built, these wooden walkways are still the epicenter of activity in each town that has one. They provide wonderful promenades for strolling beside the sea. For people who want more action, they have innumerable fast-food shops, souvenir stands, carnival rides, and arcades. People from every walk of life, and of every age, can be found here. Above all, the boardwalks are never boring.

The beaches themselves are special here—smooth, white, sandy, and soft. During the summer, the ocean is warm and fairly calm, so it's easy for swimming. Despite the bad press New Jersey often gets, many people who have visited both areas prefer the Jersey Shore beaches to those in southern California, where the Pacific Ocean is much colder and rougher. And even though a few isolated spots of the shore were despoiled by pollution spills in the last two years, 99 percent of the shore beaches remain clean and attractive.

The public beaches in each town usually have excellent facilities, including lifeguards and changing rooms. Some have snack bars and beach-goods souvenir stands; some don't.

Budget-conscious families will really appreciate the shore. The cost of a beach pass is usually minimal, and many towns sponsor special events and free concerts in the evenings. Most snack bars are relatively inexpensive, so breakfast and lunch cost little.

A BRIEF TOUR

The North Shore encompasses about 80 miles of shoreline, from Sandy Hook at the far northern point to Brigantine, just north of Atlantic City. Although most people head directly to their favorite shore town, let's assume for a moment that you have a lot of time and the luxury of being able to casually tour this entire stretch of land. Many sights are worth seeing.

Sandy Hook and Long Branch

At the far northern tip of the shore lies one of the most underrated attractions of this area: the Gateway National Recreation Area. This large urban park, off Route 36 in Sandy Hook, contains a series of forts and artifacts that date back to the Revolution, as well as the famous Sandy Hook Lighthouse. First used in 1764, this 85-foot-high lighthouse is the oldest operating lighthouse in New Jersey, originally used by the British during the Revolutionary War. You can walk through old Fort Hancock, and see the gun emplacements that defended the entrance of New York harbor. There are several public beaches for swimming, with restrooms and snack shops, and opportunities for hiking, biking, and surf fishing. On clear days, you can see the World Trade Center towers in lower Manhattan, about 18 miles away.

South on Route 36—the main highway that runs parallel to the ocean at this section of the Northern Shore—is Sea Bright. Ocean Avenue (Route 36) in Sea Bright has a number of good restaurants and bars with views of the sea.

Long Branch, a few miles south of Sandy Hook, was once one of the most prestigious beach resorts in the country. Six different presidents—Hayes, Arthur, McKinley, Grant, Garfield, and Wilson—belonged to the same Long Branch Church, now called the Church of the Presidents. Though much of this town is now somewhat run-down, a new 250-room Hilton Hotel opened here in 1988.

One of the biggest attractions here is Kids' World, once the Long Branch Pier. This amusement park specializes in "soft play"—with such features as air trampolines, tunnels, slides, and arcade games. There are also a swimming pool and water slides, as well as changing rooms with showers. Admission is about $5.

Long Branch has some great rock-and-roll clubs that will give visitors a good taste of brassy New Jersey rock—the kind that Bruce Springsteen made famous.

Whereas the Atlantic City casino-hotels are the center of big-time entertainment, the Garden State Arts Center also gets its share of big-name performers. (In 1988, Bob Dylan, Debbie Gibson, John Denver, and the Beach Boys were among the performers to play here.) There is a 5,000-seat amphitheater, and room for

SCALE

0   4   8   Mi
0   4   8   12   Km

Sandy Hook Lighthouse △
Gateway N.R.A.
Sandy Hook Unit

Sandy
Hook
Bay

36

Matawan

Garden State Parkway

35

Red Bank

△ Navesink
Lighthouse

Highlands

520

Monmouth
Beach

9

71

Long Branch

Freehold

34

547

Deal

195

Allaire
S.P.

35

Asbury Park

33

Ocean Grove

Farmingdale

Neptune

Bradley Beach
Avon
Belmar
Spring Lake

Butterfly Bogs
Wildlife Management
Area (WMA)

34

Sea Girt
Manasquan

528

Lakewood

Brielle

88

Point Pleasant
Bay Head

539

Mantoloking

70

Bass
Forest
WMA

Normandy Beach
Chadwick
Ocean Beach
Lavallette
Ortley Beach
Seaside Heights
Seaside Park

Toms River

37

72

Greenwood Forest WMA

Garden State Parkway

Barnegat Bay

ATLANTIC OCEAN

9

Sedge
Islands
WMA

Barnegat
Lighthouse
△

N

Barnegat

Stafford Forge WMA

Barnegat
National
Wildlife Refuge

Manahawkin
WMA

Barnegat Light
Loveladies
Harvey Cedars

72

Tuckerton

Surf City
Ship Bottom
Brant Beach
Beach Haven
Crest
Spray Beach

Little

Egg

Harbor

Little Egg
Harbor

Great
Bay

Beach Haven
Holgate

Great Bay Blvd. WMA

THE
NORTHERN
SHORE

4,000 other people on the lawn. There are both classical and pop concerts, musicals, ballets, and ethnic heritage festivals. The Arts Center is located in Telegraph Hill Park, in Holmdel. Take Garden State Parkway to Exit 116.

A few miles south of Long Branch is Deal, the Millionaires' Row of the Jersey Shore. Stately mansions, surrounded by acres of immaculately gardened lawns, hedges, and trees, are found in this all-residential town. It's always fun to turn off Route 36 onto a side road and slowly drive past these great houses to see how the "other half" lives.

Asbury Park

Asbury Park is one of the largest towns on the northern NJ coast, although certainly not the prettiest. This city is best known as the rock-and-roll center of the shore, and the home of The Stone Pony nightclub, where rock star Bruce Springsteen started playing in the early 1970s. In fact, he and his band are still known to show up infrequently to sing a few songs. Though you probably won't be lucky enough to run into the "Boss," you may well encounter people here who knew Bruce back then.

History lovers will appreciate Monmouth Battlefield State Park, a 20-minute drive west. This is where Molly Pitcher became famous during a Revolutionary War battle that turned the tide of the war. There's a good museum to visit as well. The Park is found on Route 33 in Freehold, just off Route 9.

South of Asbury Park, Route 71 is the major highway heading down the shore. The communities found along this 10-mile stretch of highway offer perhaps the greatest diversity of any group of shore towns. Ocean Grove is very Christian, very conservative, and without any bars. In fact, until recently no retail stores could even be open on Sundays. The Great Auditorium in town offers excellent concerts every Saturday evening during the summer, with such "mellow" artists as Ferrante and Teicher, the Osmond Brothers, the Lettermen, and Carol Lawrence. There are also many concerts featuring the works of classical composers such as Mozart, Bach, and Beethoven. Some concerts are also held on Thursday nights as well. For a complete schedule, call 201–775–0035.

Bradley Beach, Avon, and Sea Girt are very quiet, pleasant, residential communities. Each town has a small boardwalk, although only Bradley Beach has amusements.

Belmar and Spring Lake

Belmar has traditionally been one of the party towns of the New Jersey Shore. Every summer, thousands of young adults, usually 21 to 25 years old, pile into rental houses, and hit the bars at night. However, in the last few years, there was a movement to change this. Local officials were cracking down to enforce a law, long on the books, against shared houses. This could change the whole tenor of Belmar.

About five miles south of Belmar is one of the nicest communities on the entire oceanfront—Spring Lake. Everything about this town is immaculate—the houses, the lawns, the public parks. It features Victorian-era houses, and exudes a very quiet, peaceful ambience. A number of fine bed-and-breakfast establishments are here, as well as some good restaurants and shopping.

One of the more interesting side trips on the shore is a few miles west of Spring Lake. Allaire State Park contains a restored Revolutionary War bog-iron community. You can enjoy picnicking, camping, horseback riding, hiking, and exploring a nature center. The Pine Creek Railroad—established in 1963—is the only live-steam, narrow-gauge train ride in New Jersey. The park is off Exit 98 of the Garden State Parkway; from there take Route 547 to Farmingdale.

Shoppers may want to visit Peddlers Village in Manasquan, just south of Spring Lake. This village is filled with craft shops featuring handmade goodies. It's on Route 35 and West Atlantic Avenue in Manasquan and open daily.

Brielle—the next town south—features one of the largest marinas along the coast: the Brielle Marine Basin, at 608 Green Avenue. This is the place to go if you're interested in sailing, water skiing, fishing, or just pleasure boating. Call 201–528–6200.

Point Pleasant and Bay Head

Point Pleasant has many fine restaurants, and its boardwalk is one of the liveliest of this section of the shore, with hundreds of little shops and game booths, and a large amusement center.

Just south of Point Pleasant is upper-middle-class Bay Head. This town is comprised mostly of private second homes of local residents (mostly people who live in New York City and Philadelphia). Some houses are available for rental. In addition, there are a few grand old European-style residential hotels where one has a private room, but shares a bathroom and shower. Bay Head has one of the best beaches on the shore, and the local watering hole— the Bluffs—is extremely pleasant and informal. Bathing suits are the rule, not the exception.

Continuing south on Route 35, the main shore highway south of Point Pleasant, one drives through the small towns of Normandy Beach, Chadwick, Ocean Beach, Lavallette, and Ortley Beach. These are primarily for summer rentals, and offer day visitors few entertainment possibilities. Ortley Beach and Lavallette have small boardwalks.

Seaside

Seaside Heights is one of the more popular and crowded resorts. It has a giant of a boardwalk: two amusement piers, hundreds of booths, games, and other amusements, and some of the best rides on the shore. Major amusement areas include Casino Pier, Palace Arcade, and Henry's Playland, and two super water slides: Wet Banana and Splash Down. All told, there are about 2½ miles of boardwalk, with rides at both ends; try the Log Flume at the south end. In between are scores of booths, snack shops, and T-shirt stores. The best swimming beach is at the south end of the board- walk. Every Wednesday night, if the weather permits, fireworks are displayed.

Island Beach State Park

Island Beach State Park provides a pleasant alternative to the often-crowded boardwalk towns like Seaside. It preserves the natu- ral beauty of the shore: sand dunes, scrub brush, many species of shore birds, and a lovely beach dominate the landscape. Better yet, Island Beach is relatively uncrowded . . . once you get in. Only around 2,200 cars are permitted, so if you don't get there early in the morning on a weekend, you will be turned away. The park is about 10 miles long and contains two major public parking areas, which have changing rooms, showers, snack shops, and souvenir stands. In addition, beach umbrellas, chairs, and so on can be rent- ed for the day. The beaches are huge, so there is plenty of room to spread out. Surf fishing and bird watching are two favorite activ- ities. Those at the southern end of Island Beach can see Barnegat Lighthouse at the far northern tip of Long Beach Island. Island Beach is open from 8 A.M. to 8 P.M. On weekends, get there by 9 A.M. Parking is $4 on weekdays, $5 on weekends, free on Tuesdays.

To visit Long Beach Island, you'll need to backtrack. From Is- land Beach State Park, go north to Seaside Heights, then take Route 37 west to US Route 9. Then take US 9 south to Route 72, the main eastbound route to Long Beach Island. It takes about 45 minutes.

Long Beach Island

Long Beach Island is quintessential New Jersey Shore. It is about 12 miles long, and so skinny that only one main avenue—Long Beach Boulevard—runs all the way from one end to the other. There are about a dozen small communities here, ranging from Barnegat Light at the far north to Holgate at the far south. Thou- sands of summer houses are available for rent in this area, and there are some 100 motels and hotels as well. No boardwalk here, but there are some interesting boutiques, miniature golf and amusement areas for kids, and a host of fine restaurants and bars.

The beach is wide and very clean—no food or drink allowed. Yet its only a few steps from the water to the main drag to find raw clams and beer, pizza, or ice cream. A must-stop is Barnegat Lighthouse at the far northern tip of the Island. The current lighthouse, one of the oldest landmarks on the shore, was built just before the Civil War.

Finally, at the far southern end of this region, is one attraction every shore visitor should experience: the Edwin B. Forsythe Wildlife Refuge. It's on Route 9 in Oceanville. An eight-mile-long auto route weaves through some of the 20,000 acres of wetlands—the home of many species of shore birds. There is also some fine hiking here.

PRACTICAL INFORMATION FOR
THE NORTH SHORE

HOW TO GET THERE AND HOW TO GET AROUND. The best way to get to the North Shore—in all bluntness—is by helicopter. That way, you can avoid the summer traffic altogether. But since most of us can't afford that mode of transportation, the next best thing, by far, is to drive.

For most people, a car offers the best way to get the total shore experience, because it gives you the freedom to enjoy all the attractions each town offers. In most cases, once you've settled into your motel or inn, any attraction you would want to see can be reached within a 10-minute drive of your lodging.

On the other hand, if you want to simply stay put and enjoy the beach, you can get to each shore town via public transportation, although it can be inconvenient, expensive, or both, depending on where you are going.

By car. The Garden State Parkway is the main north-south route leading to the shore. To get to the Parkway from New York City, take the New Jersey Turnpike south to Exit 11, and get on the Garden State Parkway south. From Philadelphia, the Atlantic City Expressway leads directly to Atlantic City and the Parkway. From Trenton, take I–195 to the Parkway.

Most cities are 10 to 15 miles from the Parkway. Expect to pay several 25¢ tolls; bring plenty of quarters!

Try to avoid traveling on a Friday or Sunday afternoon; traffic on the Parkway is murder then. Unfortunately, many of the roads that service the shore towns are 50 years old, and were designed to handle the traffic flow of the 1930s, not the 1980s. On a summer weekend, it would be very difficult *not* to get into a traffic jam of some sort. Accept this fact, and try to live with it.

By bus. Getting to the towns north of Bay Head is fairly easy by bus. Several major carriers go to nearly all points along the coast, from such major cities as Trenton, Philadelphia, Newark, and New York. The main carrier to North Shore points is *New Jersey Transit* (800–772–2222 in 201 area code; 800–589–5946 in 609 area code). The *Asbury Park–New York Transit Company* services a number of shore beaches from New York City, including Asbury Park, Long Branch, and Point Pleasant. Call 201–774–2727 for info.

New Jersey Transit also runs shuttle buses to Island Beach State Park and Seaside Heights on weekends. Cost is $1 round trip. Simply leave your car at Exit 81 of the Garden State Parkway, at the New Jersey Transit Shuttle Parking Lot. Call 201–460–8444 for more information.

By train. *New Jersey Transit Company* operates a rail line that goes to several towns on the North Shore, including Red Bank, Long Branch, Asbury Park, Bradley Beach, Ocean Grove, Belmar, Spring Lake, Manasquan, Point Pleasant, Bay Head, and Seaside Heights. From these towns' train stations you can usually reach the oceanfront motels within a one-mile walk.

NJ Transit also offers a special weekend Shore Package for about $12, which includes round-trip train ticket, free shuttle bus service from the train station to the beach, and a free beach pass for that particular beach. This package includes the hamlets of Long Branch, Asbury Park, Ocean Grove, Point Pleasant, and Seaside Heights. Call 212–363–3360 or 201–507–1500 for specifics. All trains leave from Penn Station in New York City, at 7th Avenue and 33rd Street.

By plane. The closest major airport to the North Shore is Newark. Vacationers planning to spend a week or so at the shore can take all major airlines to this point, and then rent a car from any of the major car-rental companies. From Newark Airport, it can take from 30 minutes (to get to Long Branch) to 1½ hours (Long Beach Island) to reach your final destination . . . assuming you are not trying it on a Friday afternoon.

Philadelphia's airport is farther away, but a viable alternative. For most North Shore points, it will take about an hour longer. For Long Beach Island, it's probably about the same travel time as it would be from Newark.

Taxis are available at the airports, but the cost can be very high.

By taxi. Taxis are rare in the northern shore towns; a few may have one or two. If you need one, contact the local town's chamber of commerce, and request information about taxi services. (A list of chambers of commerce is presented below under Useful Addresses.) Or check the phone book.

One possibility is to take a tour bus to Atlantic City, and go to a major casino; cabs are usually lined up in front of each one. Then negotiate a price for your destination. (It will probably be $50 to $75 for North Shore points.)

The major commuter bus lines that service the North Shore usually stop in Toms River and Lakewood. At those terminals, one can often find standing cabs, which will take you to the North Shore villages for $10 or $15.

By trolley. A few North Shore towns have trolleys that go up and down their main drags in summer. The *Golly Trolley* in Long Beach Island goes from North Beach to Beach Haven Heights. It costs $1, and runs from late June until Labor Day, from 11 A.M. to 12:30 A.M. Call 609–597–4747 for more information. It operates seven days a week.

The *Spring Lake Trolley* circles this pleasant town, hitting the beach area and all main hotels and shopping points. Cost is only 75¢. It runs from 11 A.M. to 7 P.M., about every half hour or so. The trolley runs on weekends only, until late June, then daily until Labor Day. For further information, write to: Spring Lake Trolley Car, 1315 Third Avenue, P.O. Box 7, Spring Lake, NJ 07762. Obviously, you should write at least a couple of weeks before you plan to arrive in Spring Lake. There is no telephone number.

USEFUL ADDRESSES. Potential visitors shouldn't have any trouble getting a ton of useful information from the state's very good, efficient tourism bureaus.

New Jersey Division of Travel and Tourism, CN 826, Trenton, NJ 08625 (609–292–2470).

Monmouth County Department of Economic Development, Division of Tourism, Freehold, NJ 07728 (201–431–7476).

Ocean County Tourism Advisory Council, CN 2191, Administration Bldg., Toms River, NJ 08753 (201–929–2163).

Once you arrive in your town, pick up a copy of the local paper. It will list ads for restaurants, special events, nightclubs, etc. There are two daily newspapers along the North Shore: the *Asbury Park Press* and the *Ocean County Observer. New Jersey Monthly* publishes a special shore issue each June that gives lots of useful information. There are also free entertainment guides easily found in grocery stores, liquor stores, and the like.

Chanbers of Commerce

Asbury Park Chamber of Commerce. P.O. Box 649, Asbury Park, NJ 07712 (201–775–7676).

Barnegat Chamber of Commerce. P.O. Box 362, Barnegat, NJ 08005 (609–698–7170).

Belmar Chamber of Commerce. P.O. Box 297, Belmar, NJ 07719 (201–681–2900).

Greater Point Pleasant Chamber of Commerce. 517 A Arnold Ave., Point Pleasant Beach, NJ 08742 (201–899–2424).

Lakewood Chamber of Commerce. 300 Main St., P.O. Box 656, Lakewood, NJ 08701 (201–363–0012).

Long Branch Chamber of Commerce. 494 Broadway, Long Branch, NJ 07740 (201–222–0400).

Long Beach–Southern Ocean Chamber of Commerce. 265 West 9th St., Ship Bottom, NJ 08008 (609–494–7211).

Manasquan Chamber of Commerce. P.O. Box 365, Manasquan, NJ 08736 (201–223–8303).

Matawan–Aberdeen Chamber of Commerce. 2 Woodland Rd., Holmdel, NJ 07733 (201–739–4883).

Sea Bright Chamber of Commerce. P.O. Box 13, Sea Bright, NJ 07760 (201–842–4390).

Spring Lake Chamber of Commerce. P.O. Box 694, Spring Lake, NJ 07762 (201–449–0577).

Wall Chamber of Commerce. 2100 Hwy. 35, Sea Girt, NJ 08750 (201–223–9255).

ACCOMMODATIONS. Since the New Jersey Shore is so close to the major East Coast population centers (especially New York and Philadelphia), and because it is so popular a place to stay, it is necessary to reserve a room as far ahead as possible for a summer stay. For the better establishments, it's a good idea to get everything set up as early as April or May, for the upcoming summer.

The shore operates on a three-month summer season, and this is when the rates are the highest. Nearly every place, however, has a multiple price structure. As a general rule, accommodations are most expensive in July and August, and somewhat less expensive in June. Then there is another price tier during the fringe months of April, May, September, and October. Winter rates can be as little as half the prime-season rates. Weekend prices are also slightly higher than weekday rates. There is a bright note on lodging fees, however. Many shore towns had "flat" business years in 1987 and 1988, so as a result rates for 1989 have increased very little, if at all.

Prospective vacationers should keep a few things in mind before they leave. First, many places require a minimum stay of at least two nights on summer weekends (sometimes three nights on holiday weekends).

A healthy percentage of the motels and hotels on the shore are at least 50 years old. As a result, these old establishments (although usually clean and well maintained) often do not offer the amenities of modern, luxury hotels. Many do not have air conditioning (which usually isn't needed anyway, because of the shore breezes), television, telephones, or even private bathrooms. At any rate, do not assume that a place offers these amenities. Ask precise questions when making your reservation. Also, double-check that a place takes credit cards; some of the smaller, family-owned motels do not. Expect to pay a deposit of at least one day's stay.

Places on the sea are almost always more expensive than a similar establishment a block from the ocean. And if a motel offers a choice of an ocean view or a non-ocean view, the ocean view room will always be 10 percent to 20 percent more expensive. In fact, rates at a given motel or hotel can vary as much as $50 a night, depending on the type of unit you want.

The prices listed below are the in-season (highest) rates for a standard double room, since most shore visitors come during the peak (summer) season. Rates are significantly lower at other times of the year. The price categories are as follows: *Expensive:* $80 and higher; *Moderate:* $50 to $80; *Budget:* under $50.

We've listed towns from north to south.

SANDY HOOK TO ASBURY PARK

Sandy Hook, Highlands, Red Bank, Monmouth Beach, Long Branch, Deal, and Asbury Park

Expensive

Berkeley–Carteret Hotel. Ocean Ave., Asbury Park, 07712; 201–776–6700. This grand old hotel, dating back to the 1920s, was recently renovated, so guest rooms are now spotless and classy. Recaptures the glory days of the shore. Located next to the boardwalk. Open year-round.

Molly Pitcher Inn. Rte. 35, Red Bank, 07701; 201–747–2500. One of most luxurious hotels on entire North Shore. Located right above Navesink River marina. Swimming pool, luxuriously appointed rooms, huge dining room with river views. Within 10-minute drive of other shore towns. Open year-round.

Moderate

Beach Comber Motel. 384 Ocean Ave., Long Branch, 07740; 201–222–8479. Has 42 rooms, including some efficiency units with kitchens. Every room has a view of the beach, which is right across the street. Open year-round.

Deal Lake Motel. Kingsley and 8th Ave., Asbury Park, 07712; 201–775–7070. About 30 rooms. Free parking. One block from the beach and boardwalk. Open year-round.

Fountains Motel. 160 Ocean Ave., Long Branch, 07740; 201–222–7200. One of the largest motels in the region, with 116 rooms. Outdoor pool. Right across street from ocean. Cable TV. Open year-round. Major credit cards.

Horizon Motor Inn. 217 4th Ave., Asbury Park, 07712; 201–774–1444. One of the nicer, more modern motels in Asbury Park. Features swimming pool, color TV with cable, air conditioning, complimentary breakfast, free beach passes, access to refrigerator. Major credit cards. Open year-round.

OCEAN GROVE TO BRIELLE

Ocean Grove, Bradley Beach, Avon, Belmar, Neptune, Spring Lake, Sea Girt, Manasquan, Brielle

Expensive

Breakers. 1507 Ocean Ave., Spring Lake, 07762; 201–449–7700. First-class luxury hotel. 85 rooms. Modern, well-appointed rooms have color TV; some have own refrigerator and whirlpool. Private swimming pool, private beach. Restaurant serves breakfast, lunch, and dinner. Open year-round.

Warren Hotel. 901 Ocean Ave., Spring Lake, 07762; 201–449–8800. One of the shore's great hotels; many of the guests have been coming for decades. Amenities include freshwater swimming pool, professional putting green, tennis court. Clean, though not lavish, rooms. Some shared baths. Entertainment nightly in cocktail lounge, and at poolside on weekends. Excellent restaurant. Nice bar on the grounds, the Beach House, looks out over the ocean. Open early May to mid-November. Two-night minimum stay on weekends.

Moderate

Hewitt Wellington Hotel. 20 Monmouth Ave., Spring Lake, 07762; 201–449–8220. An old, Victorian-style building located on the lovely lake for which the town is named. Now open year-round. Complimentary breakfast. Beach is one block away.

Howard Johnson's. Asbury Park Cir., Neptune, 07753; 201–776–9000. Newly renovated facility, with all modern amenities. Only three miles from the beach. Swimming pool, color TV with cable, vending machines. Sofa beds in some rooms. Open year-round.

Shawmont Hotel. 17 Ocean Ave., P.O. Box 27, Ocean Grove, 07756; 201–776–6985. An old but immaculately maintained three-story hotel right on the boardwalk. Several guest rooms have private terraces with views of the sea. Nice large porch. Open summer months only.

The Shoreham. Box 225, 115 Monmouth Ave., Spring Lake, 07762; 201–449–7100 or 800–648–4175 (out-of-state). Classy, old-fashioned hotel. More than 100 guest rooms, one block from the beach. Swimming pool, complete with poolside bar. Entertainment and dancing nightly in summer. Room air conditioners and televisions can be rented. Cocktail lounge and elegant restaurant.

TraveLodge. New York Rd., Rte. 35, Neptune, 07753; 201–988–8750. Modern, comfortable facility, about one-half mile from the ocean. Color TV, outdoor pool, and fitness room with Universal equipment. Several restaurants nearby. Overlooks Shark River. Open year-round.

Twin Oaks Motel. 2300 Rte. 35, Manasquan, 08736; 201–223–1247. Recently remodeled, with 18 guest rooms. 1½ miles from the beach. Color TV, swimming pool, picnic area in yard, refrigerator in every room. Open year-round.

Budget

Bath Avenue House. 37 Bath Ave., Ocean Grove, 07756; 201–775–5833. Old, functional, three-story house. 1½ blocks from the beach. Some rooms with private baths.

Cheshire Inn. 27 Webb Ave., Ocean Grove, 07756; 201–775–3053. Newly remodeled under new ownership. 20 guests rooms; some have private baths. A few units are efficiencies, with private bath, refrigerator, and microwave oven. Pleasant patio. One block from the beach. Open year-round.

Sampler Inn. 28 Main Ave., Ocean Grove, 07756; 201–775–1905. 34 clean rooms. Cafeteria. Weekly rates available. A block and a half from the sea. Open May–Sept. No credit cards.

Shamrock Lodge. 414 Central Ave., Spring Lake, 07762; 201–449–9729. Bright, airy rooms. Located just a few blocks from the beach. Close to shopping, tennis courts, restaurants, and amusement parks. 12 rooms. Open May–September.

POINT PLEASANT TO SEASIDE PARK

Point Pleasant, Bay Head, Mantoloking, Normandy Beach, Chadwick, Ocean Beach, Lavallette, Ortley Beach, Seaside Heights, and Seaside Park

Expensive

Sheraton Oceanside. Ocean Ave. and Rte. 35, Point Pleasant, 08742; 201–892–2111. Formerly the Beacon Manor; reopening planned for March, 1989. Outdoor pool; restaurant and cocktail lounge. 85 guest rooms. Located near the beach.

Thunderbird Ocean Resort. Rte. 35, Mantoloking, 08738; 201–793–2000. Weekly condominium rentals only. Very plush, with bay views. Outdoor pool, cocktail lounge. Located near beach.

Moderate

Bay-Berry Motel. 1005 Grand Central Ave., Lavallette, 08735; 201–830–4442. Has 15 rooms. Several restaurants within walking distance. Open year-round.

The Bluffs. 575 East Ave., Bay Head, 08742; 201–892–1114. An old-style hotel with clean, comfortable rooms. Has nice restaurant and most famous bar in town. Near beach. Open year-round.

Cadillac Motor Inn. 201 Hiering Ave., Seaside Heights, 08751; 201–793–5117. 38 rooms. Outdoor pool, coffee shop, public beach. Major credit cards.

Colonial Motel. 210 Arnold Ave., Point Pleasant, 08742; 201–899–2394. Has 23 modern, comfortable rooms. Located near beach. Open year-round.

Sand Dollar Restaurant and Villa. 20001 Rte. 35 North, Ortley Beach, 08751; 201–830–2098. Open late May to late September. 12 efficiency apartments. Restaurant, outdoor pool. Some apartments have two bedrooms.

Seafarer Motel & Efficiencies. Sampson Ave. and the boardwalk. Seaside Heights, 08751; 201–793–1755. 17 rooms; 5 are regular motel rooms; 12 are efficiency apartments with kitchen, bath, bedroom. Open Memorial Day to Labor Day.

Starlight Motel and Apartments. 1963 Rte. 35 North, Ortley Beach, 08751; 201–793–4321. 47 rooms; 27 are efficiency apartments. Open April to late September. Outdoor pool.

Budget

Cove Point Motel. 1609 Bay Ave., Point Pleasant, 08742; 201–892–1208. Offers both regular rooms and efficiency apartments. Not on beach. Three-night minimum in July and August. Open year-round.

White Sands-Ebb Tide Motel. 1100 Ocean Ave., Point Pleasant Beach, 08742; 201–899–3370. On the beach, with 22 rooms. Air-conditioned. Open during season only.

LONG BEACH ISLAND

Barnegat Light, Loveladies, Harvey Cedars, Surf City, Ship Bottom, Brant Beach, Beach Haven, Beach Haven Crest, Spray Beach, and Holgate

Expensive

Engleside Motel. 30 Engleside Ave., Beach Haven, 08008; 609–492–1251. Offers efficiencies with kitchens, as well as regular rooms. Features include a giant swimming pool, modern health spa with sauna and whirlpool, restaurant, and cocktail lounge. Some rooms also have refrigerator and coffeemaker. Open during season only.

The Mariner. 33rd & Blvd., Beach Haven Gardens, 08008; 609–492–1235. 38 modern, luxury units. Swimming pool, color television, free coffee, and refrigerators in every room. Each room has private balcony. Open April–October.

Quarter Deck Inn. 351 W. 9th St., Ship Bottom, 08008; 609–494–9055. Features efficiency apartments and regular rooms. Boasts large dining room. Live entertainment nightly in summer, in cocktail lounge. Beach is one mile away. Open year-round.

Spray Beach Motor Inn. 24th St. and Oceanfront, Spray Beach, 08008; 609–492–1501. On the ocean. Color TV, coffee shop, cocktail lounge. 88 units available, efficiency units and regular rooms, all air-conditioned and with phone. Refrigerators in every room. Swimming pool. Open February–October and weekends during winter months.

Moderate

Ella's Motel. 18th and Central Ave., Barnegat Light, 08006; 609–494–3200. Pleasant, modern rooms near beach, located in the quietest part of Long Beach Island. Rooms have TV and air conditioning. Open year-round.

Lorry's Island's End. 69 Washington Ave., Beach Haven, 08008; 609–492–4875. Located just two blocks from Holgate Wildlife Preserve, at far southern end of Long Beach Island. All rooms have a private bath, TV, and refrigerator. Open from March to November. Restaurant on premises.

Ocean Breeze Motel. 115 E. 8th St., Ship Bottom, 08008; 609–494–4090. Free beach passes, color TV, air conditioning, heated rooms. Each room has wall-to-wall carpeting, two double beds, and full ceramic tile bathroom.

St. Rita Hotel. 127 Engleside Ave., Beach Haven, 08008; 609–492–9192, high-season; 609–492–1704, off season. 23 rooms. Offers both standard guest rooms and suites. (The suites have refrigerators.) Some two-bedroom apartments are available. Near the beach. Open April–end of October.

Sea Spray Motel. 2600 S. Bay Ave., Beach Haven Inlet, 08008; 609–492–4944. 300 feet from beach, heated pool, color TV, Efficiency apartments available. Open year-round.

Budget

Crane's Surf City Hotel. 8th St. and Long Beach Blvd., Surf City, 08008; 609–494–7281. On beach block. Has 23 rooms, in an old-fashioned, three-story house. Hotel features a clam bar. No TV or telephones. Open from early May to early October.

Harborside Motel. 13600 Long Beach Blvd., Beach Haven Gardens, 08008; 609–492–2233. 10 air-conditioned rooms close to both bay and ocean. TV. Open year-round. No credit cards.

BED-AND-BREAKFASTS. For those travelers who prefer a personal touch, bed-and-breakfast establishments provide an entirely different type of living accommodation on the North Shore. These are often managed by a family who lives on the premises along with the guests. Visitors usually stay in immaculately furnished, clean guest rooms, each with its own special flavor and decor. Some rooms have private baths; some don't. In addition, guests share the common rooms: living room, dining room, study, and library.

Most places serve Continental breakfasts with homemade breads and pastries; a few serve full breakfasts. All of the establishments listed here are within walking distance of the beach. (Many inns, incidentally, give their guests free beach and tennis-court tags.)

Although the best selection of bed-and-breakfast inns is found in the Cape May area, a few North Shore towns (especially Spring Lake and Bay Head) have some truly excellent establishments.

When seeking information about these bed-and-breakfast establishments, the first thing one should do is to contact a statewide registering service: *Bed & Breakfast of New Jersey, Inc.,* Suite 132, 103 Godwin Ave., Midland Park, NJ 07432; 201–444–7409. They will send literature.

Keep in mind that these places are usually three-story Victorian houses with a limited number of rooms (usually from six to 18). In summer especially, reservations often need to be made at least a month ahead of time.

It's especially wise, when making reservations, to try to talk to the owners or managers directly. Ask them specific questions about each room, since each guest room is usually designed differently. This is the best way to get a room that best suits your needs and desires.

The rates quoted below are for the high season. Each inn offers discounts in off-season.

Some places stay open throughout the year. Others open in spring, and stay open through late fall. Each inn's opening and closing dates usually vary somewhat from year to year, so be sure to ask about that, too.

Establishments are listed under towns, moving north to south.

Ocean Grove

Keswick Inn. 32 Embury Ave., 07756; 201–775–7506. Under new ownership, this establishment was completely renovated as a bed-and-breakfast in 1987. 19 rooms, one block from the beach. Shared bathrooms only. Shopping and transportation nearby. Breakfast features fresh pastries. Rates: $35–$50.

Pine Tree Inn. 10 Main Ave., 07756; 201–775–3264. A lovely century old Victorian inn. Most of the 13 rooms have ocean views; each has color TV with cable. Rooms are decorated with antiques, and are brightened by fresh flowers. Has rose garden on premises. Daily Continental breakfast; brunch served on Sundays. Located one-half block from ocean. Open year-round. Rates: $50–$65.

Avon

Cashelmara Inn. 22 Lakeside, 07717; 201–776–8727. A charming oceanfront Victorian inn, some 200 feet from the Atlantic. Decorated with antiques, especially huge, walnut Victorian beds. 15 guest rooms; one has its own fireplace. Public rooms include a large living room, sun room, and a very large lobby with a working fireplace. Each room has a private bath. Rates are in the $75–$85 range. Open year-round.

The Sands. 42 Sylvania Ave., 07717; 201–776–8386. A clean, well-maintained inn. Nine quiet guest rooms close to the beach in an 1800s Victorian building. Open Memorial Day to Labor Day. Modest Continental breakfast served. Rates: $40–$50 a night, double room.

South Belmar

Hollycroft. 506 N. Blvd., 07719; 201–681–2254. Features unique architecture more like a ski chalet than a beach house. The living room is dominated by a huge stone fireplace; log beams slice across the ceiling. Both lake and ocean views are offered. The six Victorian-decor guest rooms each have a private bath. A Continental breakfast is served with homemade pastries. Within walking distance of Spring Lake or Belmar beaches. Open year-round. Rates: $65 weekdays; $85 weekends.

Spring Lake

Ashling Cottage. 105 Sussex Ave., 07762; 201–449–3553. Built a century ago—in 1887—this 10-room rambling house is decorated with fine antiques. Serves homemade breakfast every morning. Located one block from sea. Rates for a double room with private bath are about $80–$100, less if bath is shared. Closed January and February.

Carriage House. 208 Jersey Ave., 07762; 201–449–1332. Eight spacious, airy rooms are available; most have private baths. Guests can use the living room with color TV, the big, shaded front porch, and the umbrella tables in beautiful backyard, which has flowers and trees. Complimentary coffee is served in morning. A double room with private bath goes for about $50–$75. Open year-round.

Chateau. 5th and Warren aves., 07762; 201–974–2000. This attractive Victorian building overlooks Spring Lake. Winner of AAA 3-Diamond and Mobil 3-star awards. Each of the 35 rooms has private bath, refrigerator, color cable TV. Some suites available. Free tennis and beach passes. Standard double rooms—about $90 to $100 weekends, less weekdays.

Kenilworth. 1505 Ocean Ave., 07762; 201–449–5327. Only bed-and-breakfast in Spring Lake is right on the beach. 13 of 25 guest rooms have private baths. In addition to Continental breakfast each morning, guests get lemonade and tea in the evening. Open year-round. Rates $55–$75.

La Maison. 404 Jersey Ave., 07762; 201–449–0969. A charming French Victorian guest house offering eight rooms, plus an efficiency cottage. Open year-round. Continental breakfast includes champagne and homemade bread. Located near Spring Lake trolley. Room rates: $70–$95. Private cottage: $135.

Normandy Inn. 21 Tuttle Ave., 07662; 201–449–7172. The 18 guest rooms capture the elegance of the inn's Victorian heritage. The large porch has white wicker tables and chairs. The living room and sitting room have antique clocks, stained glass lamps, gilded mirrors, and cherry, walnut, and oak furniture. Breakfast is served in a large, sunny dining room. Bicycles can be borrowed free of charge. Rooms cost $65–$95. Open year-round.

The Sandpiper. 7 Atlantic Ave., 07762; 201–449–6060. A charming bed and breakfast spot located just a quarter of a block from the ocean. All 12 rooms are equipped with air conditioning, color TV, and private bath. A homey porch and deck for sunning. Most rooms have ocean views. Double occupancy price includes beach passes and continental breakfast. Open year-round. Summer rates: $80–$85, weeknight, $90–$95 weekend. Off-season rates: $55, weeknight, $60, weekend. All major credit cards.

Victoria House. 214 Monmouth Ave., 07762; 201–974–1882. Located near the town's official lake (of the same name) as well as shopping district. House decor features stained-glass and huge floor-to-ceiling windows and a large wrap-around porch. There are 10 guest rooms. Rates are in the $70–$90 range.

Bay Head

Bay Head Sands. 2 Twilight Rd., 08742; 201–899–7016. Nine beautifully appointed rooms, in English decor. Guests congregate in huge, old-fashioned parlor, and relax on wicker furniture on outside porch. Continental breakfast is served Monday through Saturday; on Sunday a full breakfast is served. Tastefully decorated with English antiques. Open from Valentine's Day through mid-September. Rates: $60–$85.

Bentley Inn. 649 Main Ave., 08742; 201–892–9589. Newly renovated, with 20 rooms. All rooms have air conditioning; about one-half have private baths. Rooms are in the $45–$65 range. Open year-round.

Conover's Bay Head Inn. 646 Main St., 08742; 201–892–4664. Has 12 rooms, many filled with antiques. Two rooms have private baths. Owners provide transportation to and from Bay Head train station. Rates vary from $55–$95. Open March–November, some weeks December–February.

Gray Goose Inn. 676 Main St., 08742; 201–899–0767. Ten individually decorated rooms. Free beach passes to guests. Rates: $60–$80. Open year-round.

Beach Haven

The Barque. 117 Centre St., 08008; 609–492–5216. A 19th-century Victorian inn, located one-half block from the Atlantic Ocean. Has nine comfortable rooms, and a spacious porch. Serves a continental breakfast. Rates range from $65–$90.

Green Gables. 212 Centre St., 08008; 609–492–3553. Included in the National Register of Historic Places, this grand, charming old house offers tastefully decorated guest rooms. Continental breakfast served. Open in-season only. Free beach passes. Rate $60–$85.

Sea Girt

Molly Harbor. 112 Baltimore Blvd., 08750; 201–449–9731. Well-named establishment, with holly trees surrounding the inn. 12 guest rooms; complimentary breakfast and newspaper. Rates: $60–$125, depending on accommodations. Open year-round.

RENTALS. In many ways, renting a house on the Jersey Shore can offer you the best of all worlds. For one thing, by the very fact that few houses can be rented for less than a week, you are almost *forced* to relax! Living in a house offers you a lot more freedom to eat what—and when—you want. Other advantages include more space; access to a washer and dryer; the opportunity to barbecue; and a chance to sit out on a quiet lawn at sunset, drink in hand, enjoying the twilight. And if you like cooking at least some meals at home, you can actually save some money, especially if several people rent a house together and share expenses.

The most difficult thing about renting a house is that you must be prepared to make the arrangements a good six months in advance. Yes, the prime house-hunting season is during the brutal winter months of January and February. In fact, by Washington's Birthday (in late February) most of the good houses are already gone.

When planning your dates, keep in mind that peak season runs from the third week of June until Labor Day. Renters can save anywhere from 25 percent to 50 percent if they rent outside of that period. Most check-ins and check-outs are on Saturdays.

It's important to select not only the town you want to be in, but the section. For example, one part of a given town might be inhabited primarily by 21 to 25-year-olds, while another section may be used primarily by families.

You should ask—and answer—several questions before you start looking. How many bedrooms? Bathrooms? Is there a dishwasher? Garbage disposal? Washer and dryer? Amenities that are typical in an average suburban home are not always found in the shore towns. Also, do you want to be near a commercial boardwalk and amusement district? If you have teenagers, the answer is probably yes. If you want a more peaceful environment, the answer might be no.

The chambers of commerce, or local government bureaus, in each shore town will supply a list of rental agents, upon request. It's best to register with several different agencies, and then try to visit them on one long weekend. If you find a house you like, expect to put down a deposit.

Many individual home owners also rent out their homes through classified ads, another source for a summer place.

Shore rentals can vary widely, depending on what town you are in and how close you are to the sea. In parts of Long Beach Island and Seaside Heights, places can be found for as little as $400 a week. In Spring Lake or Mantoloking, large oceanfront homes can cost as much as $4,000 a week.

As a very general rule, rents are somewhat cheaper on the southern end of the shore.

Condominium rentals are becoming popular, although you often get less space for the money. On the plus side, their facilities are generally more modern.

Some people rent their houses over the telephone (through an agent). That's fine if you are a trusting sort, or if you live a long distance away and have little choice. But if it is at all possible, it's far wiser to visit several homes personally, to see if you can get a feel of the marketplace. One last thing—don't be afraid to bargain a little. Some owners *will* take less than they advertise for.

Here's a brief summary of the rental situations in many shore towns. A major contact is listed, which will supply, upon request, a list of certified rental agents. The typical costs of a sample home are also listed, to give you a rough idea of the going market rate.

Avon. There are a few rental opportunities in this tiny town. Apartments can be rented from one weekend up to one month, usually in old, 50-year-old seashore rooming houses. Weekly rents usually run from $600 to $700. Borough Clerk, 301 Main St., Avon, 07717 (201–774–0871).

Belmar. Most rentals are within two blocks of the sea. A typical three-bedroom group house about two blocks from the ocean costs about $7,500 a season. Belmar Chamber of Commerce, Box 297, Belmar, 07719 (201–681–2900).

Lavallette. This quiet, residential village is highly desired by families. A three-bedroom house a couple of blocks from the beach may cost $850 to $950 a week. Borough Hall, P.O. Box 67, Lavallette, 08735 (201–793–7477).

Long Beach Island. This 12-mile-long island offers by far the most units for summer rental: usually around 10,000 a year. This is a family resort area. Most of the houses are modest Cape Cod-design buildings; there are a few duplexes. Since there is no boardwalk, even the most basic home has some sort of beach in the backyard (assuming you are east of the major highway).

The most exclusive houses are the relatively new homes in the hamlets of Harvey Cedars, North Beach, Loveladies, and Webster's Lagoon (a part of Beach Haven).

Waterfront three-bedroom homes in these communities will run as high as $3,000. A block away, weekly rates are "only" $2,000–$2,500. Prices are reasonable elsewhere on Long Beach Island, however. A home right on the water in other communities may cost between $950 and $1,150 per week, while two or three blocks away, $550 to $650 is the norm. Some $400 houses can still be found.

Those people who want other diversions besides the beach should consider Beach Haven. It is perhaps the most bustling town on Long Beach Island, and there are several opportunities for shopping, dining, drinking, and various amusements on the main street.

If you really want to save some money, try Beach Haven West on the other side of Little Egg Harbor Bay. In this pleasant, quiet residential area, houses are in the $450–$550 range (per week). Many are on man-made lagoons. However, keep in mind that you will have to travel over the crowded bridge to get to the beach every day. But for a 15-minute drive, it may be worth it to save $100–$200 in rentals.

Long Beach Island Chamber of Commerce, 265 West 9th St., Ship Bottom, 08008 (609–494–7211).

Manasquan. This is one of the more reasonable rental towns. It caters to families. A clean, nice three-bedroom house a block from the ocean in the quiet northern end can be rented from $650 to $900 a week. In the rowdier southern end of Manasquan, costs are about $6,000 for the season, or $500–$600 a week. Manasquan Chamber of Commerce, 108 Main St., Manasquan, 08736 (201–223–8303).

Ocean Grove. Prices are fairly reasonable in this conservative town. A three-bedroom home near the ocean might cost $500–$600 a week. Mrs. Muriel Smith, Box 277, Ocean Grove, 07756 (201–774–4736).

Pt. Pleasant. A two-bedroom house three blocks from the ocean can rent for as low as $600; a three-bedroom can go for $700. (Some houses are right on the boardwalk; people who don't like excessive noise should keep that in mind). Greater Pt. Pleasant Chamber of Commerce, 517–A Arnold Avenue, Pt. Pleasant Beach, 08742 (201–899–2424).

Seaside Heights. With one of the liveliest boardwalks on the shore, this fun town attracts both singles and families. Groups usually rent houses east of Ocean Avenue; families tend to prefer the quiet northwestern section. Houses are relatively inexpensive; weekly costs range from $450–$750. Accommodations Directory, Borough of Seaside Heights, Box 38R, Seaside Heights, 08751 (201–793–9100).

Seaside Park. This is much quieter and more conservative than its noisier neighbor to the north. It's inhabited mostly by families. A two-bedroom house costs about $675 a week. Borough Clerk, Municipal Building, 6th and Central avenues, Seaside Park, 08752 (201–793–0234).

Sea Girt. Sea Girt is slightly cheaper than its neighbor, Spring Lake. Full-season rentals range from $5,000 to $6,000 for a nice three-bedroom house six or eight blocks from the sea. If the house is only two or three blocks away, the cost is as high as $7,500–$9,500. Borough Clerk, Baltimore Blvd., Sea Girt, 08750 (201–449–9433).

Spring Lake. This quiet, elegant village is very much in demand, and subsequently it is very expensive to rent. Oceanfront rentals run from $15,000 to $30,000 a season, with minimum stays of one month. Five or six blocks inland, an older, three-bedroom home may cost $6,000 a season. Spring Lake Chamber of Commerce, Box 694, Spring Lake, 07762 (201–449–0577).

CAMPING. In the region north of Atlantic City, there are no campgrounds directly on the sea. However, this should *not* discourage camping-oriented families from vacationing in this area. There are a number of excellent private and state campgrounds within a half-hour drive of shore beaches. One could easily camp inland at night, and then spend all day on the shore.

If you plan to vacation during the summer, it's always wise to reserve a site in advance. The telephone numbers of each campground (as well as its address and facilities) are listed below.

Private Campgrounds

Albocondo Campground. 1480 Whitesville Rd., Toms River, NJ 08753 (201–349–4079). 45 acres, 200 sites, flush toilets, sewer hookups, dumping stations, showers, hot water, electric hookups, water hookups, groceries, picnic tables, ice, pets, swimming, boating, fishing, playground, and clubhouse. Year-round.

Atlantic City North Bass River KOA. Stage Rd., P.O. Box 242, Tuckerton, NJ 08087 (609–296–9163). 30 acres, 153 sites, flush toilets, sewer hookups, dumping stations, showers, hot water, electric hookups, water hookups, groceries, refreshments, fire rings, picnic tables, ice, pets, laundry, swimming, boating (nearby), fishing (nearby), playground, and clubhouse. Year-round.

Baker's Acres Campground. Box 104–S, Willits Ave., Tuckerton, NJ 08087 (609–296–2664). 60 acres, 260 sites, flush toilets, sewer hookups, dumping stations, showers, hot water, electric hookups, water hookups, groceries, refreshments, fireplaces, picnic tables, ice, pets, laundry, swimming, boating (nearby), fishing (nearby), playground, and clubhouse. Apr. 15–Dec. 1.

Brookville Campgrounds. 224 Jones Rd., Brookville, Barnegat, NJ 08005 (609–698–3134). 30 acres, 90 sites, flush toilets, sewer hookups, dumping stations, showers, hot water, electric hookups, water hookups, groceries, refreshments, fire rings, picnic tables, ice, pets, swimming, boating (nearby), fishing, and playground. May 1–Oct. 1.

Butterfly Campground. R.D. 2, Box 51–A, Jackson, NJ 08527 (201–928–2107). 15 acres, 135 sites, flush toilets, sewer hookups, dumping stations, showers, hot water, electric hookups, water hookups, groceries, refreshments, fire rings, picnic tables, ice, pets, laundry, swimming, fishing, playground, and clubhouse. Mid-Apr.–mid-Oct.

Cedar Creek Campground. 1052 Rt. 9, Bayville, NJ 08721
(201–269–1413). 30 acres, 150 sites, flush toilets, sewer hookups, dumping
stations, showers, hot water, electric hookups, water hookups, groceries,
refreshments, fire rings, picnic tables, ice, pets, laundry, swimming, boating, fishing (nearby), and playground. Apr. 15–Nov. 1.

Maple Lake Campground. Lakewood/New Egypt Rd., Rte. 528, Box
1209, Jackson, NJ 08527 (201–367–0177). 30 acres, 147 sites, flush toilets,
sewer hookups, dumping stations, showers, hot water, electric and water
hookups, groceries, refreshments, picnic tables, ice, pets, laundry, swimming, boating, fishing, playground, and clubhouse. Apr. 15–Oct. 16.

Pine Cone Campground. P.O. Box 1047, Freehold, NJ 07728
(201–462–2230). 60 acres, 114 sites, flush toilets, sewer hookups, dumping
stations, showers, hot water, electric and water hookups, groceries, refreshments, fireplaces, picnic tables, ice, pets, laundry, swimming, boating
(nearby), fishing (nearby), playground, and clubhouse. Apr. 22–Oct. 2.

Sea Pirate Light. Rt. 9, Box 271, West Creek, NJ 08092
(609–296–7400). 300 acres, 150 sites, flush toilets, sewer hookups, dumping stations, showers, hot water, electric and water hookups, groceries,
refreshments, fire rings, picnic tables, ice, pets, laundry, swimming, boating, fishing, playground, and clubhouse. May 1–Oct. 1.

Surf & Stream. 1801 Ridgeway Rd., Toms River, NJ 08757
(201–349–8919). 20 acres, 252 sites, flush toilets, sewer hookups, dumping
stations, showers, hot water, electric and water hookups, groceries, refreshments, picnic tables, ice, pets, laundry, swimming, boating, fishing,
playground, and clubhouse. Year-round.

Timberland Lake Campground. P.O. Box 48, Jackson, NJ 08527
(609–758–2235). 65 acres, 200 sites, flush toilets, dumping stations, showers, hot water, electric and water hookups, groceries, refreshments, fireplaces, picnic tables, ice, pets, swimming, boating, fishing, playground,
and clubhouse. Year-round.

Tip Tam Camping Park, Inc. R.D. 5, Box 46, Jackson, NJ 08527
(201–363–4036). 20 acres, 200 sites, flush toilets, sewer hookups, dumping
stations, showers, hot water, electric and water hookups, groceries, refreshments, fire rings, picnic tables, ice, pets, laundry, swimming, boating
(nearby), fishing (nearby), playground, and clubhouse. May 1–Sept. 30.

Toby's Hide 'A' Way Campground. 278 Clearstream Rd., Jackson, NJ
08527 (201–363–3662). 6 acres, 30 sites, flush toilets, sewer hookups,
dumping stations, showers, hot water, electric and water hookups, groceries, refreshments, fireplaces, picnic tables, ice, pets, laundry, swimming,
boating (nearby), fishing (nearby), playground, and clubhouse. Apr.
16–Oct. 30.

Turkey Swamp Park. Box 86C, R.D. 4, Nomoco Rd./Georgia Rd.,
Freehold, NJ 07728 (201–462–7286). 500 acres, 64 sites, flush toilets,
dumping stations, showers, hot water, electric and water hookups, refreshments, fire rings, picnic tables, ice, pets, laundry, boating, fishing, playground and clubhouse. Mar. 1–Nov. 30.

Yogi Bear Jellystone Park Resort. R.D. 3, Rte. 528, Jackson, NJ 08527
(201–928–0500). 30 acres, 175 sites, flush toilets, sewer hookups, dumping
stations, showers, hot water, electric and water hookups, groceries, refreshments, fire rings, picnic tables, ice, pets, laundry, swimming, boating,
fishing, playground, and clubhouse. Year-round.

State Parks and Forests

Allaire State Park. Box 220, Farmingdale, NJ 07727 (201–938–2371). 2,985 acres, 55 sites, flush toilets, dumping stations, showers, hot water, groceries (nearby), refreshments, fireplaces, picnic tables, laundry, boating, fishing, and playground. Year-round.

Bass River State Forest. Stage Rd., New Gretna, NJ 08224 (609–296–1114). 17,645 acres, 187 sites, flush toilets, dumping stations, showers, hot water, refreshments, fire rings, picnic tables, laundry, swimming, boating, fishing, and playground. Year-round.

RESTAURANTS. Although many, many types of ethnic restaurants can be found on the New Jersey Shore, the two strong suits of this region are seafood and Italian. Some of the best examples of these two cuisines anywhere on the East Coast can be found right here.

The vast majority of establishments, however, are nice, informal places that serve good—not great—food. The shore restaurants don't go in for show. Instead, they are all very functional, and the hired help—in 99 percent of the cases—actually do seem to be pleasant and courteous. Nearly every shore town has a wide variety of restaurants—from those "quick bite" places along the boardwalks to fancy gourmet establishments overlooking the Atlantic Ocean.

Most restaurants are informal. Only a few require, for example, a coat and tie on men. In most cases, slacks and a sport shirt are all that you will need.

In the summer, many of the better restaurants will have some sort of a line, so be prepared to wait. If a restaurant accepts reservations (many don't) by all means make one, especially on weekends. One nice thing about the shore is that there are so many restaurants in each municipality, that if one is crowded you can simply try another one down the street. Unless you are incredibly picky, you are bound to find something that will please you. Enjoy.

In this section, we have divided the region north of Atlantic City into four separate areas: 1) Sandy Hook south to Asbury Park; 2) Ocean Grove to Brielle; 3) Point Pleasant to Seaside Park; and 4) Long Beach Island.

Within each of these four areas, we have further separated restaurants according to price categories: *Expensive:* $16 and higher; *Moderate:* $10 to $16; and *Inexpensive:* under $10. This represents the price of a typical three-course meal for one person (drink, tax, and tip not included).

Abbreviations: B—breakfast; L—lunch; D—dinner; BR—brunch. AE—American Express; CB—Carte Blanche; DC—Diners Club; MC—MasterCard; V—Visa.

SANDY HOOK TO ASBURY PARK

Sandy Hook, Highlands, Atlantic Highlands, Sea Bright, Rumson, Monmouth Beach, Red Bank, Long Branch, Deal, Asbury Park

Expensive

Bahr's. 2 Bay Ave., Highlands; 201–872–1245. Features seafood and steaks. Live music Friday and Saturday nights, 7 P.M.–midnight. L, 11:30 A.M.–3 P.M. Mon.–Sat.; D, 3–9:30 P.M. Sun.–Thurs.; 3–10:30 P.M. Fri., Sat.; BR, 11 A.M.–2:30 P.M. Sun. AE, DC, MC, V.

Doris & Ed's. 36 Shore Dr., Highlands; 201–872–1565. Excellent seafood appetizers and entrees. Great lobster bisque and Charleston she-crab soups. Open summer only. D, 5–10 P.M. Tues.–Fri.; 5–11 P.M. Sat.; 3–10 P.M. Sun. AE, MC, V.

Harry's Lobster House. Ocean Ave., Sea Bright; 201–842–0205. An institution in this area since 1933. Offers many varieties of fresh seafood and imaginative dishes. Closed Tuesdays. D, 5–10 P.M. daily. AE, DC, MC, V.

The Little Kraut. 115 Oakland St., Red Bank; 201–842–4830. Features German cuisine, especially roast duckling. Attractive atmosphere. Also serves roast duckling, beef roulade, and sauerbraten. L, 11:30 A.M.–4 P.M. Mon.–Fri.; D, 5–10 P.M. Mon.–Thurs.; Fri. and Sat. 5–11 P.M.; Sun., 3–9 P.M. All major credit cards.

Olivia's. Berkeley–Carteret Hotel, Ocean Ave., Asbury Park; 201–776–6700. Located in elegant, turn-of-the-century hotel. Diners eat in a handsome room decorated in beige and pastel pink. Dinner menu features American and Continental cuisines—steaks, chops, and seafood are the specialties. Reservations required. Open daily, from 7 A.M.–midnight. All major credit cards.

Periwinkle's. 1070 Ocean Ave., Sea Bright; 201–741–0041. Cozy, intimate restaurant. Continental fare, with many sauce dishes. Great desserts. L, 11:30 A.M.–2:30 P.M., Mon., Wed.–Fri.; D, 5:30–10 P.M. Sun., Mon., Wed.–Fri.; 5:30–11 P.M. Sat.; BR, 8 A.M.–2 P.M. Sun. Closed Tues. AE, MC, V.

Ristorante Bellavista. 228 New Ocean Ave. at Joline Ave., Long Branch; 201–229–4720. Italian cuisine—specialties are veal, lamb. Seafood imported from Florida. D, 5–11 P.M. Tues.–Thurs.; 5 P.M.–midnight Fri. and Sat.; Sun. 4–10 P.M. AE, DC.

Riverhouse on the Quay. 280 Ocean Ave. (Rte. 36), Sea Bright; 201–842–1994. Offers terrific view of Navesink River. Considered one of the best restaurants on the shore by *New Jersey Monthly* magazine. Menu consists of French, Italian, and American fare. L, 11:30 A.M.–3 P.M. Mon.–Sat.; D, 5–10 P.M. daily; BR, 11:30 A.M.–3 P.M. Sun. All major credit cards.

Moderate

The Left Bank. 8 Linden Pl., Red Bank; 201–530–5930. Serves European dishes. Reservations required. BYOB. L, 11:30 A.M.–2:30 P.M. Tues.–Fri.; 1–4 P.M. Sat. D, 5–10 P.M. Tues.–Fri.; 5–11 P.M. Sat. 3–10 P.M.

Sun. BR, 11 A.M.–4 P.M. Sun. Afternoon tea on weekends. Closed Mon. AE, MC, V.

Memphis Pig Out. 67 First Ave., Atlantic Highlands; 201–291–5533. Informal, fun place, specializing in barbecued ribs, pork, and chicken. Open 4–9 P.M. Mon.–Thurs., 4–10 P.M. Fri., Sat.; 1–9 P.M. Sun. Closed Mon., Tues. No credit cards.

Net Lane's Fisherman. 1605 Ocean Ave., Asbury Park; 201–775–0282. Specializes in local seafood. D, 4–9 P.M. Mon.–Thurs.; 4–10 P.M. Fri., Sat. Open 1–9 P.M. Sun. MC, V.

Oceans 20. 310 Ocean Ave., Long Branch; 201–870–1040. The Garden Room restaurant provides one of the best views of the ocean in this region. Specialties are Italian fare and seafood. All types of fettuccine dishes. L, 11:30 A.M.–4 P.M. Mon.–Sat.; D, 4–11 P.M. Mon.–Sat.; 1–11 P.M. Sun. AE, MC, V, DC.

Olivo's. 1072 Ocean Ave., Sea Bright; 201–842–9857. Serves Italian dishes, veal, seafood. Reservations required. D, 5–10 P.M. Mon.–Thurs.; 5–11 P.M. Fri. and Sat.; 4–9 P.M. Sun. Twilight specials, 5–6:30 P.M. Mon.–Thurs., 5–6 P.M. Fri. All major credit cards.

Peninsula House. 1049 Ocean Ave., Sea Bright; 201–842–2100. A wide variety of seafood and Italian dishes in a refurbished mansion. Reservations suggested. Entertainment provided Wed.–Sun. L, 11:30 A.M.–4 P.M. Sat. D, 5:30–11 P.M. Tues.–Sun. BR, 11:30 A.M.–3 P.M. Sun. AE, MC, V, DC.

The Shore Casino. Atlantic Highlands Yacht Harbor, Atlantic Highlands; 201–291–4300. Southern Italian specialties, including veal parmesan, filet of lemon sole meuniere, and pork chops. Reservations are accepted. Entertainment provided on Fri. and Sat. nights. Noon–10 P.M. Mon.–Fri.; 3–10:30 P.M. Sat.; 2–9:30 P.M. Sun. AE.

Yvonne's. 525 Ocean Blvd., Long Branch; 201–222–3456. Located in a Georgian Colonial-style home, built in 1800s. Specialties include French-style dishes such as duckling à l'orange, frogs' legs, chateaubriand, and coq au vin. Main dining room offers ocean views. 11 A.M.–11 P.M. Mon.–Sat.; 11 A.M.–10 P.M. Sun. Closed from late Nov. to early spring. All major credit cards.

Inexpensive

Casa Comida. 336 Branchport Ave., Long Branch; 201–229–7774. Offering excellent, inexpensive Mexican fare. Specialty is mesquite-grilled seafood. Serves more than 120 different types of beers. 11:30 A.M.–10 P.M. Tues.–Thurs.; 11 A.M.–11 P.M. Fri. and Sat., Sun., noon–10 P.M. AE.

Frank's Deli Restaurant. 1406 Main St., Asbury Park; 201–775–6682. Pleasant, inexpensive coffee shop, with great sandwiches. B, L, D: 6 A.M.–8 P.M. Mon.–Sat.; 6 A.M.–2 P.M. Sun.

Max's. One block west from southern end of beach, Long Branch; 201–571–0248. Maybe the best hot dogs you've ever eaten; the hot relish is legendary. Great onion rings and fries, too. No trip to Long Branch is complete without stopping here.

Sandy Hook Diner. Rte. 36, Leonardo; 201–291–9517. Attracts one of most diverse clienteles in the whole region, from cops to yacht owners. Has great jukebox covering many musical eras. Wide variety in menu. 6 A.M.–10 P.M. weekdays; 24 hours Fri.–Sun. No credit cards.

OCEAN GROVE TO BRIELLE

Ocean Grove, Bradley Beach, Avon, Belmar, Spring Lake, Sea Girt, Manasquan, Brielle

Expensive

Carriage House. 430 Higgins Ave., Brielle; 201–223–1070. One of the few French restaurants on the shore. Entertainment provided 8 P.M.–midnight, Fri., Sat. D, 5:30–10 P.M., Wed.–Sun. AE, MC, V.

Cosmo's. 500 Morris Ave., Spring Lake; 201–449–9000. Relatively new—and elegant—restaurant for this town. Jackets required after 6 P.M. for men. Continental cuisine. Entertainment, dancing on Fri. and Sat. nights. Open 5–10 P.M. weekdays; 5–11 P.M. weekends. All major credit cards.

The Mooring's. River Rd. at Rte. 70, Manasquan; 201–899–9000. Spacious dining room overlooks Manasquan River. Entrees include chicken, seafood, and meats. Boat docking facilities are available. Open 11:30 A.M.–9 P.M. every day. Major credit cards.

Shenanigans. 1904 Atlantic Ave., Wall Township, 201–223–2049. This classy restaurant features a wide variety of selections. In addition, cocktail lounge serves sandwiches until 1 A.M. Full lunch and dinner served from 11:30 A.M. to 10 P.M.; BR, 10:30 A.M.–9 P.M. Sun. All major credit cards.

The Shoreham. 115 Monmouth Ave., Spring Lake; 201–449–7100. Continental cuisine. Entertainment provided 9:30 P.M.–1:30 A.M. Mon.–Sat. 3–6 P.M. Sun. 6–9 P.M. Sun.–Thurs.; 6–10:30 P.M. Fri.–Sat. AE, MC, V.

The Yankee Clipper. 1 Chicago Ave., Sea Girt; 201–449–7200. American and Continental cuisines. Dining room overlooks sea. Several daily specials. Reservations suggested. Entertainment Fri.–Sat. L, 11:30 A.M.–2:30 P.M. Mon.–Fri.; D, 5–10:30 A.M. Mon.–Sat.; BR, 11:30 A.M.–2:30 P.M. Sun. Open 3–10 P.M. Sun. All major credit cards.

Moderate

The Breakers. 1507 Ocean Ave., Spring Lake; 201–449–7700. Italian cuisine. BYOB. Reservations suggested. Located right on sea, in a grand, old-fashioned hotel. Breakfast and lunch served on hotel's veranda. D, 5–10 P.M. Wed.–Thurs.; 5–11 P.M. Fri. and Sat.; 2–9 P.M. Sun. All major credit cards.

Churchill's. Rte. 71, Brielle; 201–528–7833. Continental and seafood dishes. Friday night, several different types of lobster are offered. Diners can eat in one of several different dining rooms; one has a fireplace. L, 11:30 A.M.–4 P.M. Mon.–Sat.; D, 4–10 P.M. Early-bird dinner, 4–6 P.M. Mon.–Sat.; 2:30–6 P.M. Sun.; BR, 11:30 A.M.–2:30 P.M. Sun. AE, MC, V.

Evelyn's. 507 Main St., Belmar; 201–681–0236. Specialty is New England clambake, as well as other seafood. Popular, so be prepared to wait. L, 11:30 A.M.–4 P.M.; D, 4–10 P.M. AE, CB, DC, MC, V.

Jessie's. 607 Union Ave., Brielle; 201–528–7779. Mexican and American cuisines; dining room is filled with antiques. L, 11:30 A.M.–4 P.M.; D, 5–10 P.M. Mon.–Fri.; 5–11 P.M. Sat. and Sun. AE, MC, V.

Rod's Old Irish Tavern. 507 Washington Blvd., Sea Girt; 201–449–2020. Casual restaurant-bar in an elegant turn-of-the-century atmosphere. Serves steaks, burgers, seafood. Dinners served until 1 A.M. Blackboard specials daily. Open every day, 11:30 A.M.–2 A.M. BR, 11:30 A.M.–2:30 P.M. Sun. AE, MC, V.

Sandpiper. 7 Atlantic Ave., Spring Lake; 201–449–6060. Grilled dishes, specializing in lobster, veal, lamb, seafood. Entertainment Fri., Sat. No liquor license. D, 6–11 P.M. daily. All major credit cards.

POINT PLEASANT TO SEASIDE PARK

Point Pleasant, Bay Head, Mantoloking, Normandy Beach, Chadwick, Ocean Beach, Lavallette, Ortley Beach, Seaside

Expensive

Jack Baker's Lobster Shanty. Channel Dr., Point Pleasant Beach; 201–899–6700. Large variety of fresh seafood in a splendid waterfront setting. Dinners range from $6.95 to $13.95, and include a salad bar. An "all-you-can-eat" buffet is offered after 5 P.M. on Fri. Open 5–10 P.M. Mon.–Thurs.; 5–10:30 P.M. Fri.; 4:30–11 P.M. Sat.; 1–9:30 P.M. Sun. All major credit cards.

Bluffs. 575 East Ave., Bay Head; 201–892–1710. Relatively new restaurant, with lovely Victorian garden overlooking the ocean. Continental fare, specializing in gamebirds and pork. D, 5–10 P.M. Tues.–Thurs.; 5–11 P.M. Fri., Sat.; 4–8:30 P.M. Sun. AE, MC, V.

Krone's Lavallette Inn. Rte. 35 North, Lavallette; 201–830–2065. Specialties are seafood dishes such as lobster, shrimp, flounder, scallops . . . plus other daily specials. 11:30 A.M.–10 P.M. Sun.–Thurs.; 11:30 A.M.–11 P.M. Fri. and Sat. AE, MC, V.

Top o' the Mast. 23rd Ave., South Seaside Park; 201–793–2444. Fisherman's combination plate is specialty, as is broiled bluefish. Restaurant located on beach, at entrance to Island Beach State Park. Open noon–10 P.M. Mon.–Thurs.; noon–11 P.M. Fri.; noon–midnight Sat.; noon–11 P.M. Sun. All major credit cards.

Moderate

Baker's Wharfside. 101 Channel Dr., Point Pleasant beach; 201–892–9100. Open year-round. Seafood primarily. Open 11:30 A.M.–10:30 P.M. Mon.–Sat.; 11:30 A.M.–9 P.M. Sun. All major credit cards.

Barmore's Shrimp Box. Inlet Dr., Point Pleasant Beach; 201–899–1637. Mixed bag: seafood, steak, prime rib, fried chicken, etc. Open Apr.–Oct. D, 4:30–10 P.M. Mon.–Sat.; 2–10 P.M. Sun. All major credit cards.

Crab's Claw Inn. 601 Grand Central Ave., Lavallette; 201–793–4447. Full, varied menu, mostly American cuisine. Serves lunch and dinner, from 11 A.M.–1 A.M. All major credit cards.

Europa South. 521 Arnold Ave., at Highway 35, Point Pleasant; 201–295–1500. Spanish and Portuguese cuisines. Reservations required. L, 11:30 A.M.–3 P.M. Mon.–Sat.; D, 3–10 P.M. Mon.–Thurs.; 3–11 P.M. Fri. and Sat.; BR, 11:30 A.M.–2:30 P.M. Sun. All major credit cards.

Filomio's. 15–17 Inlet Dr., Point Pleasant Beach; 201–892–2723. Open Apr. 15–Oct. 30. Italian cuisine; excellent homemade cooking. Set in a small, Mediterranean villa next to the sea. D, 4:30–10 P.M. Sun.–Thurs.; 4:30–10:30 P.M. Fri. and Sat. AE, MC, V.

Fore n' Aft. 20th and Central aves., South Seaside Park; 201–793–2500. Nautical atmosphere. Features lunch, dinner, and blackboard specials. Two-for-one dinner specials. L, noon–3 P.M. Tues.–Sun.; D, 3–11 P.M. Tues.–Sun. All major credit cards.

Inexpensive

Cici's Pizza. 311 Boardwalk and Central Ave., Point Pleasant Beach; 201–892–5005. Serves great pizza and sandwiches; small dining room. Open 11:30 A.M.–10 P.M. Sun.–Thurs.; 11 A.M.–midnight Fri. and Sat. No credit cards.

Copper Hood. Rte. 88 and River Rd., Point Pleasant; 201–295–4960. A pleasant, cheerful place, with a wide variety of choices for breakfast, lunch, and dinner. (Dinners include steaks, ribs, chicken, flounder . . . and salad bar.) Open seven days, 6 A.M.–9 P.M. All major credit cards.

Dorca's. 58 Bridge Ave., Bay Head; 201–899–9365. A first-class restaurant specializing in breakfast and lunch. An institution in Bay Head for nearly 25 years. Features brightly colored umbrella tables. Special homemade touches mark entrees. Closed Feb. and March. Open from spring to fall. L, 11 A.M.–3 P.M. Wed.–Sun.; also D, 6–8 P.M. Fri. From Memorial Day to Labor Day, open 8 A.M.–4 P.M. seven days a week; also 6–8 P.M. Fri. No credit cards.

Joe's Chadwick Diner. Chadwick Beach, Rte. 35 North, Chadwick; 201–830–2288. A fine place to grab a quick bite to eat while enjoying the beach. Open 6 A.M.–8 P.M. Sun.–Thurs.; 6 A.M.–10 P.M. Fri. and Sat. No credit cards.

Ocean Bay Diner. Junction of Rtes. 35 and 88, Point Pleasant; 201–899–2997. Big portions, good food—classic Jersey diner. Open 24 hours. AE.

LONG BEACH ISLAND

Barnegat Light, Loveladies, Harvey Cedars, Surf City, Ship Bottom, Brant Beach, Beach Haven Crest, Spray Beach, Beach Haven

Expensive

Gourmet's Mooring. Ninth St. and Bay Ave., Beach Haven; 609–492–2828. Overlooks Little Egg Harbor Bay. Several seafood specials daily, served with salad bar. L, noon–5 P.M. D, 5–10 P.M. Late-night menu, 10 P.M.–1 A.M. Open June–Sept. only. All major credit cards.

Ketch. 529 Dock Rd., Beach Haven; 609–492–3000. Offers one of best views of ocean on Long Beach Island. Mostly seafood, with some chicken dishes. Reservations suggested. L, noon–4 P.M. D, 5–10 P.M. Bar open until 2 A.M. AE, V.

Owl Tree. 80th St. and Long Beach Blvd., Harvey Cedars; 609–494–8191. One of most popular spots in northern LBI. Diners eat Continental and seafood entrees in a Victorian-decor dining room. Place is known for its bright, friendly, attractive waiters and waitresses. L, 11:30 A.M.–4 P.M. D, 5–10 P.M. No credit cards or reservations accepted.

Port-O-Call. Engleside Ave. at the bay, Beach Haven; 609–492–0715. Open year-round. Features seafood and prime rib. Lobster tanks. D, 5–9:30 P.M. every day; 2–9 P.M. Sun. All major credit cards.

Moderate

Bayberry Inn. 1302 Long Beach Blvd., Ship Bottom; 609–494–8848. Traditional seafood. L, 11:30 A.M.–3 P.M.; D, 4–9:30 P.M. Mon.–Thurs.; 4:30–10:30 P.M. Fri. and Sat.; 4–9:30 P.M. Sun. BR, 10 A.M.–1:30 P.M. Sun. All major credit cards.

Carroll's Caravelle Inn. Rtes. 9 and 72, 609–597–7522. Located on other side of bridge, just west of Long Beach Island. Delicious seafood and Continental cuisine, served seven days a week. Open 11:30 A.M.–9:30 P.M. Early-bird specials: 2–6 P.M. Mon.–Sat. AE, MC, V, CB, DC.

Charlie's Seafood Garden. 8611 Long Beach Blvd., Beach Haven Crest; 609–492–8340. Plenty of plants and a small waterfall create a relaxing, cheerful atmosphere. Restaurant specializes in homemade seafood specialties. BYOB. D, 5–10 P.M. daily. From Sept.–May, open only Fri.–Sun. AE, MC, V.

Giancarlo Ristorante. 357 W. 8th St., Ship Bottom; 609–494–4343. Italian specialties, focusing on Northern Italian cuisine. Homemade pastries. D, 5–11 P.M. Tues.–Sat.; 5–10 P.M. Sun. No credit cards. BYOB.

Harvey Cedars. Long Beach Blvd., Harvey Cedars; 609–494–7112. Great clams and oysters and a variety of seafood—very reasonably priced. Very casual. Be prepared to wait. BYOB. Open summers only, 11 A.M.–10 P.M. for outdoor market; D, 4:30–10 P.M.

Morrison's Seafood Restaurant. 2nd St. and bayfront, Beach Haven; 609–492–5111. Offers terrific view of Little Egg Harbor Bay. Mainly seafood. BYOB. Closed Nov.–Jan. Open 8 A.M.–9 P.M. during summer; 11:30 A.M.–9 P.M. May and Sept. Open weekends only Feb.–Apr. and Oct. AE, MC, V. Reservations not accepted.

Ott's Sea Ketch. 7800 Long Beach Blvd., Beach Haven Crest; 609–494–4224. American and seafood entrees. Nonalcoholic bar. B, 7–11:30 A.M.; L, 11 A.M.–5 P.M.; D, 5–10 P.M. No credit cards.

Polish Peasant. 122 N. Bay Ave., Beach Haven; 609–492–0134. Specializes in Eastern European foods, such as stuffed cabbage and kielbasa. Desserts are all homemade. Open 8 A.M.–8 P.M. daily, in summer; open same hours weekends only, Oct.–May. No credit cards or liquor license.

Quarter Deck Inn. 351 W. 9th St., Ship Bottom; 609–494–3334. Seafood. D, 4–10 P.M. Mon.–Sat.; open 11 A.M.–10 P.M. Live entertainment Fri., Sat. nights. 9:30 P.M. Sun. AE, MC, V.

Inexpensive

China Pearl. 1305 Long Beach Blvd., Ship Bottom; 609–494–4332. Good Chinese fare; lunch specials every day. BYOB. Open 11:30 A.M.–10:30 P.M. No credit cards.

Cranberry Bog. 31 North Main St., Manahawkin; 201–597–1999. New restaurant with wide menu, from burritos to burgers to ribs. No reservations. Major credit cards.

Pumpernickel Deli. 33rd St. and Bay Ave., Beach Haven Gardens; 609–492–2766. Offers huge selection for both breakfast and lunch. BYOB. Open 8 A.M.–3 P.M. June; 8 A.M.–8 P.M. July and August. No credit cards.

Seaport. 7801 Long Beach Blvd., Harvey Cedars; 609–494–4389. Features excellent menu for breakfast and lunch. Open 6 A.M.–3 P.M. during summer. BYOB. No credit cards.

PARKS, GARDENS, AND FORESTS. Though the best nature refuges are in the southern part of the state, a few good parks can be enjoyed north of Atlantic City as well. These tend to get extremely crowded in summer, since they're used heavily by local residents of Pennsylvania and southern New York State as well as New Jersey. Always call for more information.

Allaire State Park. Off route I–95 in Farmingdale; 201–938–2371. Named after James Allaire, who in 1822 bought the existing bog-ore furnace and established an iron foundry–and the town itself. Today, this village has been restored. The general store sells souvenirs, and during the summer one can see craftsmen do weaving, candle-making, and carving. There are also nature trails, a state-owned golf course, and horseback riding trails. The Pine Creek Railroad is the only narrow-gauge train in New Jersey.

Barnegat State Park. Long Beach Island; 609–494–2016. This is the smallest state park in New Jersey, and is located at the far northern tip of Long Beach Island. Its main feature is "Old Barney," the Barnegat Lighthouse, which dates back to the 1850s. The beach offers swimming, fishing, and picnicking.

Cattus Island County Park. Fischer Blvd., off Route 37, Toms River; 201–270–6960. Features salt marsh creatures, such as snapping turtles. The 500-acre park is open from 10 A.M. to 5 P.M. Don't miss free tour of Cooper Ocean Environmental Center, given hourly on Saturdays and Sundays. You can take a self-guided tour on or off marked trails. The park naturalist conducts boat and van tours. There are also summer programs for children; call for details.

Double Trouble State Park. Off Garden State Parkway, Exit 80, on Double Trouble Road West, in Berkeley; 201–349–1903. In this restored village, you can see an old sawmill and cranberry bogs. It's about 10 miles southwest of Seaside Heights.

Edwin B. Forsythe Wildlife Refuge. Great Creek Rd., Oceanville; 609–652–1665. More than 20,000 acres of wetlands make this a birdwatcher's mecca. There are some 40 species in summer, including shore birds, peregrine falcons, ducks, geese, and ospreys. There is a guided auto tour, and hiking. The refuge is open from sunrise to sunset, and is free. Early afternoon and morning and late afternoon are considered the best times to visit.

Gateway National Recreation Area. Off Rte. 36, Sandy Hook; 201–872–0092. Features sand dunes, historic Fort Hancock, and a wonderful holly tree grove. Sandy Hook Lighthouse. Excellent public beaches with snack shops, etc. On clear days, New York City's World Trade Center towers can be seen about 18 miles away.

Holgate Wildlife Refuge. Southernmost end of Long Beach Island; 609–698–1387. Excellent for birdwatching, and has preserved natural fauna of the Jersey Shore. Also a good place for surf fishing. Long Beach Island visitors will especially like this small but beautiful refuge; it offers a nice alternative to the hustle and bustle of Long Beach Boulevard.

Island Beach State Park. South Seaside Park, Berkeley; 201–793–0506. An excellent undeveloped beach, which includes a botanical preserve, wildlife sanctuary, and two bathing beaches. Great spot for swimming, surfing, picnicking, and surf fishing. It is open 8 A.M.–8 P.M. Parking costs $4 weekdays; $5 on weekends. Free on Tuesdays. Nature center is open from 9 A.M.–5 P.M. and guided tours are offered at 11 A.M. It's wise to get there by 9 A.M. on weekends, since only a limited number of cars are permitted.

Shark River Park. School House Rd., Neptune, 07753; 201–922–3868. Inlet of Atlantic Ocean, next to Belmar. Facilities include fishing pond, hiking/fitness trail, ballfields, picnic table.

Wharton State Forest. Batsto, R.D. 4, Hammonton, 08037; 609–561–3262. Located about 20 miles west of Long Beach Island, this forest offers excellent horseback riding and hiking. It's located in the Pine Barrens, a large wild area with pine forests and cedar swamps. The four rivers that cut through the forest (the Batsto, Oswego, Wading, and Mullica) provide some outstanding canoeing.

BEACHES. Perhaps the main attraction of the shore—the reason for its existence as a resort—is its wonderful beaches. In this section, you will find a detailed listing of the facilities offered on the beach of each major North Shore town. Also included are the towns' phone numbers, where you can get more information about beach facilities, and the latest (as we went to press) prices for beach tags. (Note: These can change overnight, but they are likely to be accurate within $1.) All beaches are open to the public, though in some very residential communities, (like Deal, for instance) it may be difficult to find public access.

Asbury Park: 201–775–0900. Boardwalk, amusements, rafting, and bathhouses. *Beach tags:* $35 season, $18 senior citizens; $3 weekdays, $5 weekends and holidays.

Avon: 201–774–0871. Boardwalk, rafting, and beachfire permits. *Beach tags:* $40 season; $30 June, July; $25 Aug. $4 weekdays, $6 weekends and holidays.

Barnegat Light Township: 609–494–7211. Surfing, rafting, and bathhouses. *Beach tags:* $11 season, $8 weekly, $3 daily.

Bay Head: 201–899–2424. Surfing, scuba diving, and rafting. *Beach tags:* Available by mail from Box 42, Bay Head, NJ 08742.

Beach Haven: 609–494–0111. Amusements, surfing (after hours), scuba diving, beachbuggy permits, beachfire permits, and bathhouses. *Beach tags:* $5 season to June 15, $8 after.

Belmar: 201–681–1176. Boardwalk, surfing, scuba diving, rafting, beachbuggy permits, and bathhouses. *Beach tags:* $35 season, $20 half-season; $4 weekdays, $8 weekends.

Bradley Beach: 201–776–2999. Boardwalk, amusements, surfing, picnicking, and bathhouses. *Beach tags:* $30 season, $20 monthly, $4 weekdays, $6 weekends.

Deal: 201–531–1454. Surfing, rafting, and bathhouses. *Beach tags:* $110 season with bathhouses (waiting list applications only), $55 season with lockers, $35 season; $4 weekdays, $5 weekends and holidays.

Harvey Cedars: 609–494–2843. Surfing, scuba-diving, rafting, beachbuggy permits (off-season), and bathhouses. *Beach tags:* $10 season; $5 weekly.

Island Beach State Park: 201–793–0506. Surfing, rafting, scuba-diving, beachbuggy permits, beachfire permits, and picnicking. *Beach tags:* $4 per car weekdays, $5 weekends. Free Tuesdays. Arrive as early as possible weekends and Tuesdays.

Lavallette: 201–793–7477. Boardwalk, surfing, and rafting. *Beach tags:* $23 season; $7 weekly, $5 senior citizens, $5 weekends and holidays.

Long Branch: 201–222–7000. Boardwalk, amusements, surfing, scuba-diving, picnicking, and bathhouses. *Beach tags:* $20 season, $15 students 12–17; $2 daily, $1.50 students; $3 weekends, $2 students.

Manasquan: 201–223–0544. Boardwalk, amusements, surfing, rafting, and bathhouses. *Beach tags:* $36 season, $22 ages 14–16, $12 senior citizens; $4.50 daily, $6 weekends and holidays.

Ocean Grove: 201–775–0035. Boardwalk, surfing, scuba-diving, rafting, beachfire permits, picnicking, and bathhouses. *Beach tags:* $47.50 season; $31.25 monthly; $15.50 weekly; $4.50 daily, $5.50 weekends and holidays.

Ortley Beach: 201–341–1000. Boardwalk and rafting. *Beach tags:* $15 season; $8 half-season; $8 weekly.

Point Pleasant: 201–892–1118. Boardwalk amusements, surfing, scuba-diving, and picnicking. *Beach tags:* $35 season; $1.50 daily, $2.50 weekends.

Sandy Hook: 201–872–0115. Surfing, scuba-diving, beachfire permits (off-season), picnicking, and bathhouses. *Beach tags:* $2 per car weekdays, $3 weekends and holidays. Arrive before 1 P.M.

Sea Bright: 201–842–0099. Boardwalk, rafting, picnicking, and bathhouses. *Beach tags:* $40 season, $25 half-season; $3 weekdays, $3.50 weekends.

Sea Girt: 201–449–9433. Boardwalk, surfing, scuba-diving (off-season), rafting, and bathhouses. *Beach Tags:* $40 season; $5 weekdays, $7 weekends and holidays.

Seaside Heights: 201–793–8700. Boardwalk, amusements, surfing, scuba-diving, rafting, and bathhouses. *Beach tags:* $25 season; $2 weekdays, $3 weekends.

Ship Bottom: 609–494–7211. Amusements, surfing, rafting, and bathhouses. *Beach tags:* $6 season; $3 weekly.

Spring Lake: 201–449–8920. Boardwalk, surfing, and rafting. *Beach tags:* $45 season; $7 weekdays, $8 weekends and holidays.

Surf City: 609–494–7211. Surfing, rafting, beachbuggy permits (off-season), and bathhouses. *Beach tags:* $8 season; $3 weekly.

PARTICIPANT SPORTS. People who enjoy sports will be extremely satisfied with the opportunities presented at the Northern Shore. This is one of the best regions on the entire East Coast for water-oriented sports such as fishing, boating, swimming, waterskiing, sailing, scuba-diving, jet-skiing, and boardsailing. Swimming can be done everywhere; the ocean waves are usually consistent and gentle; the water is warm; and most beaches are rock-free. Scores of marinas up and down the North Shore rent boats for fishing, boating, waterskiing, sailing, and boardsailing. Because of the hundreds of wrecks at the bottom of the Atlantic, the Jersey Shore offers some of the best scuba-diving anywhere in the United States.

Bicycle-riding can be done down the quiet side streets of every shore town (they are basically nice and flat). Those towns that have boardwalks usually allow bike-riding for a few hours during the early morning. Most shore towns have public tennis courts a few blocks from the major resorts. Except for weekend mornings, these courts are usually not too crowded. Most of the public golf courses are inland a few miles from the ocean. They *do* get crowded, so reservations are advised.

The addresses and telephone numbers of establishments that specialize in certain types of sports are listed below.

Bicycle Rentals. *A–1 Bicycles.* 642 Arnold Ave., Point Pleasant Beach, 08742; 201–295–2299.

Brielle Cyclery. 205 Union Ave. (Rte. 71), Brielle, 08730; 201–528–9121.

C & R Cycles. Rte. 35, Lavallette, 08735; 201–830–1616.

DJ's Cycles. 15th and Main, Belmar, 07719; 201–681–8228.

DJ's Cycles. 9th and Barnegat Ave., Ship Bottom, 08008; 609–494–2223.

Ed's Rent-A-Bike. 811 North Bay Ave., Beach Haven, 08008; 609–492–3481.

Mark's Bicycle Shop. 15 Atlantic Ave., Spring Lake, 07762; 201–449–8747.

PJ's Rental & Sales Co. 16 Blaine Ave., Seaside Heights, 08751; 201–830–3474.

Point Pleasant Bicycles. 2701 Bridge Ave., Point Pleasant, 08742; 201–899–9755.

Rossi's Rent-A-Rama, Inc. 1607 Ortley Rd., Ortley Beach, 08751; 201–793–8573.

Tyres Bicycles. 1900 Boulevard, Seaside Park, 08752; 201–830–2050.

Boating (rentals, cruises, and instructions). (See also sailing, canoeing, and fishing.)

Aggie's Sailing School. White's Marina, Ship Bottom, 08008; 609–494–0248.

Al's Boats. 52 Shrewsbury Ave., Highlands, 07732; 201–291–1115.

Anchor Reef Marina. 3404 Rte. 37 E., Toms River, 08753; 201–929–1585.

Barnegat Bay Sailing School and Rentals. 1 Corrigan Ave., Pine Beach, 08741; 201–244–2106.

Barnegat Boat Basin. 491 E. Bay Ave., Barnegat, 08005; 609–698–8581.

Bay Harbor Marina. 27th and Bay, Beach Haven Gardens, 08008; 609–492–9735.

Bayside Marina. Rte. 35 and Bay Blvd., Seaside Heights, 08751; 201–793–8554.

Bob's Rowboats. 6th and Bay Blvd., Ortley Beach, 08751; 201–793–9476.

Campbell's Boat Basin, Inc. Newark and Bay Blvd., Lavallette, 08735; 201–793–1900.

Charlie's Landing. 930 Main St., Bayville; 201–269–9899.

Ed's Boat Rental. 9th and Bayview Aves., Barnegat Light, 08006; 609–494–2447.

Fisherman's Den. Rte. 35, Belmar, 07710; 201–681–6677.

Furie Sailing Center. 25th St. and Long Beach Blvd., Spray Beach, 08008; 609–492–8550.

Gateway Marina. 5 Port Monmouth Rd., Port Monmouth, 07758; 201–787–2213.

Harvey Cedars Marina & Sailing School. 6318 Long Beach Blvd., Harvey Cedars, 08008; 609–494–2884.

Houghton's Rowboats. 83rd St., Harvey Cedars, 08008; 609–494–2052.

Inlet Marine. 16th St. and Bayview Ave., Barnegat Light; 609–494–0425.

Long Beach Island Sailing School. 1812 Bay Terr., Ship Bottom, 08008; 609–494–9568.

Ocean Beach Marina. Box 171, Rte. 35 South, Lavallette, 08735; 201–793–7460.

Polly's Rowboats. 112 N. West Ave., Beach Haven, 08008; 609–492–2194.

River Belle. Bogan's Basin, 800 Ashley Ave., Brielle; 201–524–6620.

Schneider's Marina. 14th St. on the bay, Beach Haven, 08008; 609–492–2961.

Teal Sailing Academy. 668 Main Ave., Bay Head, 08742; 201–295–8225.

Van's Boat Rentals. P.O. Box 382, Bayview Ave., Barnegat Light, 08006; 609–494–2447.

Canoeing. *Art's Canoe Rentals.* 1052 US 9, Bayville, 08721; 201–269–1413.

Jersey Paddler. 900 Rte. 70, Brick Twp. 08723; 201–458–5777.

Mohawk Canoe Livery & Recreation. Squankum–Yellowbrook Rd., Farmingdale, 07727; 201–938–7755.

Pineland Canoes. Whitesville Rd., Jackson, 08527; 201–364–0389.

Surf & Stream Canoe Rentals. Rte. 571, Toms River, 08753; 201–349–8919.

Winding River Park & Nature Center. Rte. 37, Toms River, 08753.

Golf Courses (public). *Asbury Casino Corp.* (miniature). 2nd Ave. & Boardwalk, Asbury Park, 07712; 201–776–6323.

Atlantis Country Club. Country Club Rd., Little Egg Harbor, 08087; 609–296–2444.

Bel-Aire Golf Club. Allaire Rd. and Rte. 34, Allenwood, 08720; 201–449–6024.

Belmar Playland–Rides, Inc. (miniature). 1400 Ocean Ave., Belmar, 07719; 201–681–5115.

Bey Lea Municipal Golf Course. Bay Ave., Toms River, 08753; 201–349–0566.

Cedar Creek Golf Course. Tilton Blvd., Berkeley Twp., 08721; 201–269–4460.

Fairway Mews Golf Shop. Clubhouse Dr., Spring Lake Heights, 07762; 201–449–8883.

Hominy Hill Golf Courses (county). Mercer Rd., Colts Neck, 07722; 201–462–9222.

Howell Park Golf Course (county). Preventorium Rd., Howell, 07731; 201–938–4771.

Jumping Brook Golf & Country Club. Jumping Brook Rd., Neptune, 07753; 201–922–8200.

Lakewood Country Club. West County Line Rd., Lakewood, 08701; 201–363–8124.

Ocean Acres Country Club. 925 Buccaneer Lane, Manahawkin, 08050; 609–597–9393.

Old Orchard Country Club. 54 Monmouth Rd., Eatontown, 07724; 201–542–7666.

Quail Ridge Driving Range (miniature). State Hwy. 34 and Hurley Pond Rd., Wall, 07719; 201–681–0918.

NORTH OF ATLANTIC CITY 87

Shark River Golf Course (county). Old Corlies Ave., Neptune, 07752; 201–922–4141.
West Long Branch Golf Range. Rte. 36, West Long Branch, 07764; 201–544–8787.

Horseback Riding. *Batta Farms.* 362 Birdsall Rd., Farmingdale, 07727; 201–938–9741.
Batta Farms. 1556 Church Rd., Toms River, 08753; 201–240–9738.
Bill's Lazy B Riding Stables & Tack Shop. 103 S. New York Rd., Oceanville; 609–652–1973.
Circle A Riding Stable. 336 Squankum Rd., Howell, 07731; 201–938–2004.
Duchess Pines Ranch. Bowman Rd., Jackson, 08527; 201–928–3131.
Footlight Farm. Freehold area, 07728; 201–780–7701.
Garalee Acres. 830 Cross St., Lakewood, 08701; 201–364–6060.
Hidden Valley Ranch. 4070 Bay Shore Rd., Cold Springs; 609–884–8205.
Lakewood Riding Center. Cross St., Lakewood; 201–367–6222.
Muddy Creek Farm. 568–A, Ramtown–Greenville Rd., Howell, 07731; 201–840–8977.
New Horses Around. Bermar Rd., Farmingdale; 201–938–4480.
Slope Hollow Farm. 132 Rte. 537, Colts Neck, 07722; 201–542–1770.
Tall Oaks Farm. Oak Glen Rd., Howell, 07731; 201–938–5445.
Windward Farm. Baileys Corner Rd., Wall, 07719; 201–449–6441.

Jet-Skiing (rentals and instructions). *Jet-Ski Rentals.* Maryland Ave. and the bay, Somers Point; 609–927–3738.
Jet-Ski of Sea Isle. 88th St., Sea Isle City; 609–263–7572.
Pier One Jet Ski Shop, Rte. 37, Toms River; 201–270–0914.

Sailing. (See also Boardsailing, below.) *Barnegat Bay Sailing School and Rentals.* 1 Corrigan Ave., Pine Beach, 08741; 201–244–2106.
C & C Sail & Trawler Charters. Bay Ave. P.O. Box 691, Point Pleasant, 08742; 201–295–3450.
C & C Sailing Charters. River Ave., Point Pleasant; 201–295–3450.
Chapman's Boat Sales and Service, Inc. State Hwy. 70, Brick Twp., 08723; 201–840–9100.
Furie Sailing Center. 25th St. and Long Beach Blvd., Spray Beach, 08008; 609–494–8550.
New Horizons Sailing School. 1 First St., Rumson; 201–530–3237.
Pelican Harbor. State Hwy. 37 East, Pelican Island, 08751; 201–793–1700.
Pier 88. 88th St., Sea Isle City; 609–263–8811.
Sailin' Center. 3121 Rte. 37 East, Toms River, 08753; 201–270–1919.
Sailing Rentals. 17 Central Ave., Island Heights, 08732; 201–929–0505.
Teal Sailing School. 688 Main Ave., Bay Head; 201–295–8225.
Todt's Sailing Center. 25th St. and Long Beach Blvd., Spray Beach; 609–492–8550.
Trixie's Landing. 305 Brennan Cncse., Bayville; 201–269–5838.
Water Sports Inc. 3100 Blvd., Brant Beach, 08008; 609–494–2727.

Scuba Diving. *Diver's Cove.* State Hwy. 35, Lawrence Harbor; 201–583–2717.

Diver's Two Inc. 1 Main St., Avon, 07717; 201–776–7755.

Dosil's Sports Center. 261 State Hwy. 36, E. Keansburg, 07734; 201–787–0508.

East Coast Diving Service, Inc. 340–F Spring Valley Rd., Morganville, 07751; 201–591–9374.

Four Divers Inc. 56 Broadway, Point Pleasant; 201–899–7753.

Harbor Divers, Inc. 73 Tiller Dr., Waretown; 609–693–8999.

Professional Divers, Inc. 70 State Hwy. 35, Neptune City, 07753; 201–775–8292.

Triton Divers. 4404 Long Beach Blvd., Brant Beach, 08008; 609–494–4400.

Underwater Discovery, Inc. 2716 Rte. 37 East, Toms River, 08753; 201–270–9100.

World of Innerspace, Inc. 2805 Long Beach Blvd., Beach Haven Gardens, 08008; 609–492–0982.

Surfing and Boardsailing. The following locations in each Northern Shore town are the best beaches for surfing and boardsailing. Both activities are unsupervised (without lifeguards), although in the summer there will surely be other people in the vicinity enjoying these same sports who can supply help and friendly tips, if necessary.

Barnegat Light. 22–24th Sts., Barnegat Light, 08006.

Beach Haven. Nelson Ave., Beach Haven, 08008.

Harvey Cedars. Salem Ave., Harvey Cedars, 08008.

Lavallette. Ortley Ave., Brooklyn Ave., and Princeton Ave., Lavallette, 08735.

Long Beach Township. Janet La., Long Beach Township, 08008.

Point Pleasant Beach. Beacon Beach, Point Pleasant Beach, 08742.

Seaside Heights. Any Beach, Seaside Heights, 08751.

Seaside Park. Brighton Ave., Seaside Park, 08752.

Ship Bottom. Any Beach, Ship Bottom, 08008.

Surf City. South 1st St., Surf City, 08008.

In addition, the following shops sell all equipment and accessories affiliated with these sports, and the sales people in these stores are usually very knowledgeable about local conditions. Don't hesitate to ask them for their advice.

Bay Head Windsurfing. 76 Bridge Ave, Bay Head,; 201–899–9394.

Grog's Surf Palace. 910 Central Ave., Seaside Park; 201–793–0097.

H&S Concession. Gateway National Recreation Area, Sandy Hook; 201–872–0025.

Island Style Sun & Surf, 1302 Ocean Ave., Sea Bright, 07760; 201–681–4502.

Y-Knot Surf Shop, 8 Long Beach Blvd., Surf City; 609–494–4204.

Zodiac Water Sports. 703 Belmar Plaza, Belmar, 07719; 201–681–4502.

Swimming. See also Beaches, above. *Brookside School.* State Hwy. 35, Sea Girt, 08750; 201–449–4747.

Casino Pier & Pool. Sherman Ave. and Boardwalk, Seaside Heights, 08751; 201–793–6488.

Chelsea Swimming Pool and Beach. 65 Ocean Ave., Long Branch, 07740; 201–222–0005.

Dosil's Swim Program. 45 S. Ave., Atlantic Highlands, 07716; 201-291-4013.

Ocean Acres Recreation Society Pool. 925 Buccaneer La., Manahawkin, 08050; 609-597-9393.

Silton Swim School. 1701 Atlantic Ave., Manasquan, 08736; 201-223-4181.

Tennis. *Allaire Racquet Club.* Rte. 38, Wall Twp., 07719; 201-681-3366.

Barnegat Township Tennis Courts. Off Lower Shore Rd., Barnegat, 08005.

Deal Casino Tennis Courts. Ocean Ave., Deal, 07723; 201-531-0234.

Harvey Cedars Borough Court. 6204 W. Long Beach Blvd., Harvey Cedars, 08008; 609-494-3521.

Madison Indoor Tennis Club. Rte. 34, Matawan, 07747; 201-583-1010.

Matawan Indoor Tennis Club. Line Road, Aberdeen,; 201-566-5200.

Seaside Heights. Bay Blvd., Seaside Heights, 08751.

Spring Lake Bath & Tennis Club. Ocean and Jersey Ave., Spring Lake, 07762; 201-449-6400.

Tennis Center of Ocean County. 485 Locust St., Lakewood, 08701; 201-367-3600.

Thompson Park (county). Newman Springs Rd., Lincroft, 07738; 201-842-4000.

Tuckerton Lake County Park. Rte. 9, Tuckerton, 08087.

Veterans' Park. Tilton Blvd., Berkeley Twp., 08721.

Water Skiing. *Bayside Boats.* Rte. 35 and Bay Blvd., Seaside Heights, 08751; 201-793-8535.

Bayside Marina. 421 Bayside Terr., Seaside Heights, 08751; 201-793-8535.

Bayview Water Ski School. 104 West 28th St., Ship Bottom, 08008; 609-494-5405.

Lawasaki Wheelhouse. 501 Atlantic Ave., Point Pleasant,; 201-899-4050.

Maurita's. 8th and 9th sts., Ship Bottom, 08008; 609-494-7211.

Maurita's. 2800 Rte. 37, Toms River, 08753; 201-270-6404.

Pelican Harbor. Rte. 37 East, Pelican Island, 08751; 201-793-1700.

Shore Ski School. 1154 17th Ave., Belmar,; 201-681-3838.

Wet & Wild. Pier One, Rte. 37, Toms River, 08753; 201-929-2723.

Wild Wayno's Water Sports. Rte. 37 West at Lobster Time Restaurant, Pelican Island, 08751; 201-793-0996.

Fishing. Some of the best saltwater fishing in the country can be found right off the New Jersey Shore. There are a couple of reasons for this. First, the very deep Hudson Canyon, an underwater trench about 50 miles offshore, is a submarine "highway" for tuna, marlin, and other big-game fish. The thousands of shipwrecks in the nearby Atlantic also attract lots of species. Finally, many species migrate from northern waters to southern waters and vice versa, so there are always new species showing up.

Species often caught here include bluefish, striped bass, mackerel, fluke, weakfish, bonito, and sometimes even sharks, tuna, and marlin. Surf fish-ers often catch bluefish, striped bass, and fluke from the surf off Manasquan, Belmar, Spring Lake, and Sea Girt.

Several piers in towns are open to the public. The ones at Long Branch, Brigantine, Seaside Heights, and Belmar are often productive.

Fishing licenses are needed only for freshwater fishing; contact the Division of Fish, Game, and Wildlife; CN 400, Trenton, NJ 08625 (609–292–2965).

Both charter boats and party boats, which accommodate up to 100 people, are available for rent at several marinas up and down the coast. Party boats cost from $20 to $30; charter boats cost from $150 to $400.

All shore-county tourism offices have brochures that list fishing-boat captains. Another excellent source is *New Jersey Fisherman,* 339 Herbertsville Road, Bricktown, NJ 08724 (201–840–8600). It lists weekly news about saltwater and freshwater fishing, and costs $17.50 a year.

Aruba Reba II. Clarks Landing Marina, Point Pleasant, 08742; 201–929–0805.

Barnegat Boat Basin. 491 E. Bay Ave., Barnegat, 08008; 609–698–8581.

Bayview Marina. 13th and Bayfront, Barnegat Light, 08006; 609–494–7450.

Barnegat Light Yacht Basin, 18th St. and Bayview Ave., Barnegat Light, 08006; 609–494–8956.

Bay Harbor Marina, 27th and Bay Ave., Beach Haven Gardens, 08008; 609–492–9735.

Bayside Marina, 421 Bayside Terrace, Seaside Heights, 08751; 201–793–8535.

Big Mohawk II, Marine Basin, Belmar, 07719; day phone, 201–364–5600; night phone, 201–681–7812.

Black Fin II, Captain's Cove, Highlands, 07732; day phone, 201–291–1166; night phone, 201–681–7812.

Black Whale. Beach Haven Fishing Centre, Centre St. and the Bay, Beach Haven, 08008; 609–494–0333.

Campbell's Boat Basin, Inc., Neward and Bay Blvd., Lavallette, 08735; 201–793–1900.

Clark's Landing Marina. 847 Arnold Ave., Point Pleasant, 08742; 201–892–5559 or 899–5589.

Happy Hour. Marine Basin, Belmar, 07719; day phone, 201–775–1454; night phone, 201–892–1015.

Harvey Cedars Marina. 6318 Long Beach Blvd., Harvey Cedars, 08008; 609–494–0111.

Invader. Hoffman's Anchorage, Brielle, 08730; 201–920–9678.

Inlet Basin Deep Sea Fishing. 57 Inlet Dr., Point Pleasant Beach, 08742; 201–295–1020.

Margo's Marina. 1432 East Bay Ave., Manahawkin, 08050; 609–597–8909.

Miss Belmar. Belmar Marina, Rte. 35 S., Belmar; 201–681–2266.

Nimrod. Brielle Yacht Club, P.O. Box 344, Brielle, 08730; 201–528–7600.

Osprey. Marine Basin, Belmar, 07719; day phone, 201–566–0986; night phone, 201–566–7760.

Outlander. Captain's Cove Marina, 2 Washington St., Highlands, 08742; 201–739–6936.

Perpetual Care. Howes Marina, 4th St., Beach Haven, 08008;
201–226–2404.

Prime Time. Hoffman's Anchorage, Brielle, 08730; day phone,
201–528–6160; night phone, 201–899–1327.

Sabre. Hoffman's Anchorage, Brielle, 08730; day phone, 201–793–4444;
night phone, 201–458–2072.

Sea Witch. Marine Basin, Belmar, 07719; day phone, 201–681–8531;
night phone, 201–458–2072.

Sly Fox. Hoffman's Anchorage, Brielle, 08730; day phone,
201–548–1120; night phone, 201–548–0786.

Temptation. Hoffman's Anchorage, Brielle, 08730; day phone,
201–343–9111; night phone, 201–845–4558.

Yachtsman's Anchorage Marina. 6th and Bay Blvd., Ortley Beach,
08751; 201–793–9476.

SPECTATOR SPORTS. There are no major spectator sports in the
northern shore region, though some first-class auto and horse racing can
be enjoyed. *Monmouth Park* draws some of the best **thoroughbred race-
horses** in the East during its season. Monmouth Park is located on Oceanport Avenue in Oceanport (201–222–5100). Racing is done from late May
through August. Monday through Saturday. Post time is 1:30 P.M. Admission to grandstand is $2.25.

Another racing spot is *Raceway Park,* Route 527, Englishtown
(201–446–6370). This is the home of the National Hot Rod Association's
Summer Nationals. There's **drag racing, motorcross, bicycle motorcross.**
It's open from March to November. Tickets range from $6–$12.

Auto racing fans will enjoy *Wall Stadium,* Route 34, Wall
(201–681–6400), about five miles west of Spring Lake. Races are held
every Saturday night, beginning at 7 P.M., for various classes of stock cars.
Demolition derbies also are occasionally held. Grandstand seats are $8,
reserved seats are $9, children 6 to 12 are $2.50.

The best spectator sports on the Northern Shore, though, take place
at the local level. Many shore towns sponsor some sort of annual sports
event each summer, so check the local weekly or daily paper in your area,
and look for notices of such events.

There is an annual **bocce tournament** in Asbury Park in June. Call
201–774–7232 for details.

Pro **basketball** fans will enjoy the *Miller Lite Pro–Am Jersey Shore Summer League.* The games occur at the Headliner in Neptune
(201–775–6200). Adults' tickets are $15.00; high school and college stu-
dents' are $1; children's under 12 are 50 cents. Call 201–775–6200 for a
schedule.

The *Walsh Offshore Grand Prix,* a series of **powerboat races,** takes place
in late July. Best viewing areas are around Manasquan and Point Pleasant,
although the races can be seen along the shore from Asbury Park all the
way to Seaside Park. Call 201–929–1667 for information.

BERRY PICKING. In summer, a few places offer sumptuous, juicy ber-
ries, which can be obtained at half price. Wear long pants and sleeves.

Blueberries (late June–mid-Aug.) Sweetwater Farm, Lower Shore Rd.,
Barnegat, 609–698–7862; B&B Farm, Egg Harbor, 609–965–4351.

Raspberries (July–Oct.) The Berry Farm, Colt's Neck (10 miles west of Long Beach), 201–583–0707; Fralich Farm, May's Landing, 609–625–0492.

Strawberries (late May–mid-June) Butterhoff Farm, Egg Harbor, 609–965–4696; Fraligh Farm, May's Landing, 609–625–0492.

SPECIAL-INTEREST TOURS AND HISTORIC SITES. If you asked a sample group of people to name 500 things you could do near the New Jersey Shore, the chances are good that the one thing they would *not* answer is "a winery tour." Yet there are wineries within a short drive of many shore towns that are worth visiting on a rainy day (see also Atlantic City). Tours—and samples—are offered.

People interested in history will enjoy touring Batsto Historic Site and Wheaton Village—two restored villages that recapture the flavor of this region in its infancy.

Revolutionary War buffs will have to see Monmouth Battlefield, site of one of the most significant battles in that conflict, with a crucial impact on our nation's history.

The places named below will offer you very pleasant and interesting half-day excursions. See also Museums.

Batsto Historic Site. Batsto Rd. No. 4, Hammonton; 609–561–3262. Another restored village—the site of the Batsto Furnace and Iron Works—dates back to 1766. Factory furnished firearms for Revolutionary War. You can tour Iron Master's house, visit craftmakers' cottages. $2 parking fee in summer. $1 admission for mansion tour, which takes one hour. Advance reservation preferred for tour.

Towne of Historic Smithville. Rte. 9, 12 miles north of Atlantic City,; 609–652–7777. This beautiful little village is a replica of an 1800s Colonial village. It has cobblestone paths, a little pond, and about 30 specialty shops. Open daily. Free.

Monmouth Battlefield State Park. Rte. 33, Freehold, just off Route 9; 201–462–9616. The place where Molly Pitcher became famous during a Revolutionary War battle. This is also the setting for the historic Craig House, visitors center (which contains many displays), and playgrounds.

Renault Winery. 72 N. Bremen Ave., Egg Harbor; 609–965–2111. Established in 1864, this is one of the East Coast's oldest wineries; a gourmet restaurant is also found here. There are guided tours. Hours: 10 A.M.–5 P.M. Mon.–Sat.; noon–5 P.M. Sun.

Twin Lights Historic Site. Lighthouse Rd., Highlands; 201–872–1814. Constructed in 1862, this beautiful lighthouse sits atop the highest bluff on the North Shore. Offers spectacular views. Visitors can climb to the top of the North Tower. Open daily, 9 A.M.–5 P.M. Free.

Wheaton Village. Glasstown Rd., Millville; 609–825–6800. This is a replica of a late 1800s glassmaking town. You can see glassmaking on the premises and shop in a nice glass store. Open seven days a week, 10 A.M.–5 P.M. Admission: $3.50 adults, $2.50 students.

MUSEUMS AND GALLERIES. There are only a few noteworthy museums and galleries in the region north of Atlantic City. However, if you want to get away from the beach for a few hours some afternoon, these places are worth a visit. See also Historic Sites, above.

Barnegat Light Museum. 5th and Central aves., Barnegat Light,;
609–494–3407. Original one-room schoolhouse of Long Beach Island now
houses original lens from the lighthouse. Also includes collection of historical items and memorabilia from the island's past. Open daily in summer,
2–5 P.M. No charge but donations accepted.

Long Beach Island Historical Association Museum. Engleside and Beach
aves., Beach Haven,; 609–492–0700. A series of exhibits portrays Long
Beach Island life of long ago. Photos, books, and charts show the history
of the commerce, leisure, and recreation of the area. Open 2–4 P.M. weekends; 7–9 P.M. weekdays, during summer. Charge: $1 adults, 25 cents for
children. Formal programs Mon. nights at 7:45 P.M., during July and August.

National Broadcasters Hall of Fame. 22 Throckmorton St., Freehold,;
201–431–4656. Contains antique radios; nostalgic tapes of famous radio
personalities; and exhibits, films, and slide shows dealing with the history
of radio.

Noyes Museum. Lily Lake Rd., Oceanville,; 609–652–8848. One of the
better museums in the area. Has good rotating exhibits, plus collection
of American art from Fred Noyes. There are working decoys and decoy-
carving demonstrations. Open 11 A.M.–4 P.M. Wed.–Sat.; noon–4 P.M. Sun.
Admission: $1.50, adults, $1 senior citizens, 50 cents children.

SHOPPING. Virtually every shore town has small retail stores that
carry the basic goods needed while on vacation. There are a few malls in
the larger towns.

The most interesting shopping, however, is presented by a number of
very good antique centers and flea markets. They offer hundreds of unusual items . . . and occasionally some terrific bargains.

The Red Bank Antique Center, West Front St., **Red Bank**
(201–842–3393) is one of the better antique markets on North Shore. It
features large, wide aisles, and has pieces from more than 100 dealers.

The *Seaview Square Mall,* routes 36 & 66 at **Asbury Park Circle**
(201–922–8100) is one of the largest and nicest shopping centers on the
North Shore, with three department stores and nearly 100 specialty shops.
Open daily 10 A.M.–9:30 P.M. Mon.–Sat.; noon–5 P.M. Sun.

Another good antiques spot is the *Antique Emporium,* Bay and Trenton
Ave., **Point Pleasant Beach** (609–892–2222). It is similar to other ones:
spacious, and all goods are well labeled for easy identification.

A fun book store, which specializes in secondhand books, is *Escargot
Books,* 503 Rte. 71, **Brielle** (201–528–5955). It's fairly large, and the sales
people are courteous and knowledgeable. There are plenty of books on
the history of New Jersey and Monmouth County, and many interesting
biographies.

Bridge and Main Aves. in **Bay Head** feature several small stores that
specialize in handmade, unique products, especially embroidered pillows.

In wealthy **Deal,** walk down Norwood Avenue; there are a number of
specialty stores. *Pitti Bimi,* 266A Norwood Ave. (201–531–3676) sells a
number of items from France and Italty. *The Country Fair,* 266 Norwood
Ave. (201–531–8009) sells high-fashion women's clothing under its own
label.

Collingwood Park Flea Market is open Fri. and Sat. from 10 A.M.–9:30
P.M., and Sun. from 10 A.M.–6:30 P.M. With more than 600 dealers, it's one of

the largest flea markets in the state. Located at the junctions of Rtes. 33 and 34, **Collingwood.** Call 201–938–7941.

Peddlers Village in **Manasquan** contains a number of interesting crafts shops. It's on Rte. 35 and W. Atlantic Ave., and is open on Fri., Sat., and Sun. Call 201–223–2300.

If you are in **Seaside Heights** during the off-season, visit the *Businessmen's Association Flea Market.* It runs from Sept. through Dec. 8 A.M.–4 P.M. Sun., and outdoors from Feb. through Apr. Casino Pier Parking Lot, Grand Ave. and the Boulevard, Seaside Heights. There are about 30 dealers.

BOARDWALKS AND AMUSEMENTS. The boardwalk is the very symbol of the New Jersey Shore. These wooden, wide, elevated sidewalks are the center of all social activity on the shore. They are used by young and old alike, from early morning to late night. Lovers, young mothers with strollers, bike riders and joggers, and hordes of teenagers all share the same walkway.

Several shore towns do not allow any commercial enterprises at all on their boardwalks. For naturalists who just want to enjoy the beach, these towns should be considered first.

Those with amusements are pretty much dominated by teenagers. With the exception of Seaside Heights, the attractions found in these boardwalk amusement areas remain pretty much the same: carnival rides, booths with games of chance, video arcades, miniature golf, and scores of sourvenir shops and fast-food places.

No matter what type of boardwalk town you're in, you should treat yourself—at least once during your visit—to an early morning walk beside the beach. The boardwalks are practically deserted then. As you walk along the surf, you can see the sun rising above the Atlantic and think—if only for a moment—what a special place the shore must have been before it was settled.

The towns with noncommercial boardwalks are: Ocean Grove, Bradley Beach, Avon, Spring Lake, Sea Girt, Ortley Beach, and Lavallette. In these municipalities, one must be content to simply enjoy the sand, sea, and sun. There are no restaurants, bars, or amusement parks.

Boardwalk towns with amusements areas of some sort are Asbury Park, Beach Haven, Belmar, Long Branch, Point Pleasant, Manasquan, and Seaside Heights. A short summary of the major amusement areas of these towns follows.

Asbury Park. Its amusement area features the Casino Carousel, built in 1932, and one of the classiest and most elegant on the shore. Call 201–988–8585.

Beach Haven. Although there is no boardwalk anywhere on Long Beach Island, the Fantasy Island Casino Arcade—the next best thing to being in Atlantic City—is worth mentioning. There are blackjack and poker machines, miniature golf, rides and many other video games as well. Located at 320 West 7th, phone 609–492–4000.

Belmar. One of the wildest towns on the shore; most of the action centers along its 1½-mile boardwalk. There are five beachfront bars, and many carnival rides and other amusements. Teenagers will love Wizard's World Arcade (201–280–8271). Children will enjoy Belmar Playland–Rides (201–681–5115).

Long Branch. Kid's World is a perfect amusement area for small children. Call 201–222–0005. There's a great haunted house here, too, geared for children during the days; scarier after 8:30 P.M.

Manasquan. The one-mile-long boardwalk is bordered by houses, fast-food establishments, an arcade, and a water slide. The southern part of the boardwalk has several bars, and is frequented by young adults. One of the best amusement areas is Manasquan Pavilion (201–223–9551).

Point Pleasant Beach. Besides the well-known children's train, the boardwalk here has rides, a water slide, booths with games, a miniature golf course, and some pinball in the arcades. There are several snack shops as well.

One fun train trip for kids is the Point Pleasant Beach Train (609–729–0586), which stops at Jenkinson's Pavilion and Manasquan Inlet. Kids will love it, as it goes right along the beach.

Seaside Heights. This is arguably the busiest, and perhaps longest (2½ miles) boardwalk on the entire shore north of Atlantic City. It has everything. One unique ride is the Airwave (201–793–6488)—a chairlift that runs for 1,600 feet, from the pier to the end of the boardwalk. It offers a great view of the beach. Perhaps the most famous ride is the Log Flume (201–830–5481), which dominates the southern end where there is also a swimming beach. Another well-known amusement is the Alpine Bob roller coaster. The Waterworks, 800 Ocean Terrace (201–793–6495) has about a dozen water slides. One, the "corkscrew," is 300 feet long.

All along the boardwalk is an endless procession of food stands, selling everything from saltwater taffy to soft pretzels to steak sandwiches. There are many, many game booths as well, where one can win stuffed animals, cameras, even bicycles. In the evening, young adults over 21 cram into the bars, while the boardwalk teems with adolescents seeking some action.

Every Wednesday night, weather permitting, Seaside offers fireworks from the boardwalk. This, Seaside's best show of all, is free.

ARTS AND ENTERTAINMENT. Cultural opportunities are somewhat limited in the region north of Atlantic City, but there are a few good theater companies, and music festivals are held throughout the summer.

Once you arrive at your destination, the wisest thing to do is to pick up the local weekly or daily newspaper that lists that week's events. Visit the town's chamber of commerce: Since the shore towns depend so much upon tourists, their chambers of commerce usually provide very complete brochures and pamphlets about the cultural opportunities available during the high-season summer months.

The following organizations offer top-notch entertainment.

Clearwater Festival. Fort Hancock, Sandy Hook (201–842–9420). Every August, this annual music festival features a wide range of singers. Call for exact schedule.

Cold Spring Village. 735 Seashore Rd., Cold Spring (609–884–1810). A wide variety of music—country, classical, and choral—is performed. Square dancing is also offered.

Garden State Art Center. Garden State Pkwy., Exit 116, Holmdel (201–442–9200). Besides rock groups, classical music is performed throughout the summer, by such groups as the New York Philharmonic and the New Jersey Symphony Orchestra. For details, call 201–442–9200. Ticket prices vary, according to the performer.

Long Beach Island Foundation of the Arts and Sciences. 120 Long Beach Blvd., Loveladies (609–494–1241). Sponsors occasional classical, folk, jazz, and other concerts. Cost is about $5. In addition, the Foundation also sponsors occasional film festivals. Last August, for example, it showed a number of children's movies, such as *Old Yeller* and *The Ugly Dachshund.* Call for details about this summer's films.

Noyes Museum. Lily Lake Rd., Oceanville (609–652–8848). Classical music and string quartets perform throughout the summer. For schedules, call the museum.

Ocean Grove Great Auditorium. Auditorium Square, Ocean Grove (201–775–0035). One of the true meccas for classical music lovers on the North Shore. Weekly concerts are offered throughout the summer, usually on Thurs. or Sat. nights. For example, there was a Mozart Festival last summer (1986).

Spring Lake Theater Company. Spring Lake Memorial Community House Theatre, 3rd and Madison Ave., Spring Lake (201–449–4530 or 201–449–1415). One of the finest theater companies on the shore. Four or five well-known plays run throughout the summer. Ticket costs range from $6 to $9; most performances start at 8:30 P.M.

Surflight Summer Theater, corner of Engleside and Beach avenues, Beach Haven (609–492–9477). Presents leading Broadway plays and musicals throughout the summer. $15.

NIGHTLIFE. The New Jersey Shore's nightlife is truly one of its major attractions. Few resort areas anywhere offer such a terrific variety of good night spots: from rock-and-roll bars to quiet, mellow piano bars, to lovely outdoor terraces overlooking the sea.

The North Shore has a rich rock-and-roll history. Here, rock superstar Bruce Springsteen got his start at the Stone Pony rock club in Asbury Park in the early 1970s. Springsteen started a tradition that still continues, for today there are many truly excellent bands performing at the shore's 100 or so night spots that offer live music. One can listen to folk, jazz, and blues . . . but good old-fashioned rock-and-roll remains the mainstay of the shore clubs. As a general rule, these clubs have clienteles comprised of people in their 20s. Expect a line in front of them on weekends.

There are also scores of quiet, out-of-the-way piano bars in nearly every shore town, either in the adjoining cocktail lounges or restaurants, or as part of the hotels themselves. These can provide a pleasant evening for people who want a more mellow experience.

Finally, many lounges simply serve drinks, and perhaps offer a jukebox.

On the Jersey Shore, each town has its own closing hours, but during the busy summer season, nearly every establishment is open till at least 1 A.M. or 2 A.M. Bands start playing relatively late (after 8:30 P.M.), so people can go home after a day at the beach, relax, eat dinner . . . and then hit the town.

Here's a representative list of many of the finest bars and clubs found north of Atlantic City, and what they offer.

Albert Music Hall. Rte. 9, Waretown Plaza, Waretown; 609–693–4188. This is *the* place for you if you like the country sound. Every Saturday night there are hootenannies that feature local musicians playing folk, country, and bluegrass. No liquor is served; bring your own. Most customers are over 30.

The Bluffs. 575 East Ave., Bay Head; 201–892–1114. The only bar in Bay Head, this is a local institution. It's extremely informal; many people wear bathing suits in early afternoon. Features a dart board and a great jukebox. Can be hard to find; there's no sign. If you see a bunch of people sort of converging to the same spot, that will be, no doubt, the Bluffs. Hours vary; early afternoon to late evening.

Brighton Bar. 121 Brighton Ave., Long Branch; 201–870–1030. Without a doubt one of the most popular bars on the North Shore, with a great assortment of live bands that play rock. Always cramped and crowded, but drinks are cheap. Caters to a 21-to 25-year-old crowd. Music Thurs. through Sun., beginning at 10:30 P.M.

Brownies Lounge. Poplar Ave., Bargaintown; 609–927–5556. A favorite of country music buffs in the southern part of this region. Everyone gets into the act, which is dancing. On Tuesday, tacos are three for $1; shots of tequila are 50¢. Never a cover charge. Open every day except Mon.

Buckalewe's. Centre St. and Bay Ave., Beach Haven; 609–492–1065. Live performers play piano-bar-type mellow music every night of the week.

Cafe Bar. 115 Ocean Ave., Long Branch; 201–229–9725. Pleasant place to have a drink, stare out to sea, and watch the action on the Long Branch boardwalk. This establishment has a disco that plays current music geared to a young audience (early to mid-20s). In addition, it just completed a new addition that will include another dance area in which more mellow 1960s and 1970s music will be featured. The clientele here is expected to be older—people in their 30s.

Columns by the Sea. 601 Ocean Ave., Avon; 201–988–3213. Great spot for a late-afternoon drink, on a marvelous veranda with spectacular view of the sea.

Crane's. 8th and Long Beach Blvd., Surf City; 609–494–7281. Music starts every night at 9 P.M. This is a rowdy sing-along bar that gets packed with people of all ages. The clam bar next door is perfect for an after-beach beer.

Deck House. 517 East Lake Ave., Asbury Park; 201–988–0076. Presents live rock and roll; some former members of Bruce Springsteen's band play here. Rhythm and blues, soul, and blues bands occasionally play here.

Gourmet's Mooring. Bay Village, Ninth St. and Bay Ave., Beach Haven; 609–492–2828. Lively piano bar. Local performers sing here every night of the week, and patrons often join in on the fun. Entertainment from 9:30 P.M.–1:30 A.M.

Green Parrot. Rte. 33, Neptune (201–775–1991). One of the leading rock clubs on the entire shore, featuring many up-and-coming groups. Live music Wed. through Sat. nights; live reggae Thurs. nights.

Headliner. Rte. 35, Neptune; 201–775–6200. Some of the best Top 40 bands in the state play here. One favorite is a Bruce Springsteen tribute band: Backstreets. The dance floor is always full, and there is an excellent sound system. Eight bars. On Fri. and Sat. nights, expect a line.

Jason's. 1604 F Street, South Belmar (201–681–9782). The only full-time jazz club left on the North Shore. Live music is offered from 9:30 P.M.–2 A.M. every night during peak season.

Jimmy Byrne's Sea Girt Inn, Rte. 71, Sea Girt; 201–449–8300. One of the great late-night spots on the northern coast for a quiet, pleasant nightcap. Has a very friendly, casual ambience exuded by both bartenders and customers.

Joe Pop's. 20th and Blvd., Ship Bottom; 609–494–0558. Large bar right on main drag on Long Beach Island features a variety of live bands that play music ranging from oldies to Top 40 hits. Also sponsors comedy nights with stand-up comics. Even has teen nights, for adolescents. Crowded and lots of dancing.

The Ketch. 2nd St. and Dock Rd., Beach Haven; 609–492–3000. One of the most popular clubs on Long Beach Island. Plays both original and popular tunes. The bar features wall-to-wall carpeting, three-dimensional murals, sophisticated lighting, and a superior sound system. Clientele is well-dressed yuppies.

Krone's Lavallette Inn. 1307 Grand Central Ave., Lavallette; 201–830–3113. During the summer, live entertainment is provided seven nights a week in the lounge. There is also live music every Fri. and Sat. night throughout the year.

Miller's Inn. Rte. 9, Tuckerton; 609–296–3102. Live bands play mostly rock and roll or country-western music.

Mrs. Jay's Beer Garden. 909 Ocean Ave., Asbury Park; 201–775–1695. Located in charming, classic 60-year-old vintage New Jersey Shore building. Features a very pleasant outdoor patio perfect for a late-afternoon beer. Later, at night, bands play country music every night. Also has dance floor, two pool tables. Crowd is mostly in their late 20s–early 30s.

Montego Bay. 104 4th Ave., Belmar; 201–681–5922. This huge bar is one of the more active singles spots in this region. A DJ plays music seven nights a week, from 12 noon to 12 midnight. Happy hours are offered Fri., Sat., and Sun. afternoons. Caters to 21–29 age group.

Murphy's Law. Ocean and Chelsea avenues, Long Branch; 201–229–5175. Rock-and-roll bar with both live bands and DJs. Features longest bar on the shore. Mixed clientele: rock-and-rollers from their 20s to their 40s. Open daily, noon–2 A.M.

Osprey. 201 1st Ave., Manasquan; 201–223–0707. An institution in Manasquan. Housed in a 50-year-old hotel. Populated mostly by young singles in their 20s, although a few people in their 30s and 40s stop by also. There are two big dance floors. In one, a DJ plays music; in the other, a live rock band performs. Also serves hamburgers, hot dogs, etc. Open, May to Sept., noon–2 A.M.

The Owl Tree. 80th St. and Long Beach Blvd., Harvey Cedars; 609–494–8191. Live performers specialize in folk-rock. Soloists appear during the week, duets on weekends. Hours vary depending on season; call ahead.

Parker House. 8–12 Beacon Blvd., Sea Girt; 201–449–0442. A longtime shore hangout for college kids and young adults, it's an old, three-story, wooden hotel. The ground level houses the dance floor, where bands perform on Fri. and Sat. nights. The upper level is a cocktail lounge. Open from late May until early Sept.

Pete's Bar and Grill. Rte. 35 and Delaware Ave., Point Pleasant; 201–892–3382. Has both good food and good live music. Very informal. One of the most popular clubs on the northern shore. Visitors dance to the music played by a DJ every night during the summer. Open 11 A.M.–11 P.M. Mon.–Sat.; 10:30 A.M.–11 P.M. Sun.

Rick's American Cafe. 4th and Broadway, Barnegat Light; 609–494–8482. Few clubs on Long Beach Island offer the musical diversity of Rick's, which features an atmosphere out of the movie *Casablanca,* with ceiling fans, tropical plants, and wicker furniture. Along with rock and roll and blues, Rick's often offers reggae music on Thurs. nights. Upscale crowd.

Rod's Olde Irish Tavern. 507 Washington Blvd., Sea Girt; 201–449–2020. Elegant cocktail lounge in an early 1900s decor. Mellow taped music, from oldies to current hits. Fine spot for late-night drink.

Sand Bar. 1 Chicago Blvd., Sea Girt; 201–449–7200. Located in bottom floor of Yankee Clipper restaurant. A singles spot during the summer, crowd is mid- to late 20s.

Sea Shell Club. Centre St. and the ocean, Beach Haven; 609–492–4611. Live entertainment most nights of the week.

Shenanigans. 1904 Atlantic Ave., Wall; 201–223–2049. Large cocktail lounge next to restaurant, dancing every Fri. and Sat. night. One of newest and classiest places on North Shore.

Smiles Cantina. Rte. 9, West Creek; 609–597–4134. A live group plays different types of music, ranging from country and western to oldies.

The Stadium. Plaza Blvd., Sea Girt; 201–449–1444. Perhaps the best-known sports bar on the northern shore. Owned by former New York Giant running back Alex Webster. Visiting pro athletes sometimes stop in.

Stone Pony. 913 Ocean Ave., Asbury Park; 201–988–7177. Most famous rock club on the whole shore, without a doubt. Bruce Springsteen opened his successful *Born in the USA* tour at this club a few years ago. The crowd is comprised of serious rock fans—some come from all parts of the country. Lines are common in summer, so arrive early. Tickets for many shows can be bought at Ticketron.

Tide Dancebar. Bay Village, Ninth St. and Bay Ave., Beach Haven; 609–492–2828. Lively, very danceable bar, with both live entertainment and DJs providing the music. Sponsors special evenings such as "Hawaiian Nights."

Tsunami. 160 Ocean Ave., Long Branch; 201–870–9292. One of the hottest new bars on the North Shore, catering to Yuppies. Somewhat dressy. Valet parking available. This establishment has four bars and a large dance floor. A DJ plays a wide variety of music. Happy hour 4 P.M.–9 P.M. Fri.

Warren Lounge. Mercer Ave., Spring Lake; 201–449–8800. Entertainment in Spring Lake centers around this old hotel's famous lounge. It presents big bands on Thurs. nights, dual pianists Tues., a Dixieland band Sat. afternoons, and singers Sat. and Sun. nights. Lounge is open from May to Sept.

Werx. Sumner Ave. and the Blvd., Seaside Heights; 201–830–3555. The bands here play original music, and are generally quite sophisticated; some groups have gone on from here to record their own albums. Unfortunately, there is no dance floor, just a stage. Customers sit in bleachers along the walls.

THE SOUTHERN SHORE

South of Atlantic City

by
JEROME E. KLEIN

Jerome Klein is a writer who knows the New Jersey Shore well. He is the author of the Fodor's book Views to Dine By Around the World.

Located between the waters of the Atlantic Ocean and the Delaware Bay, the southern shore area of New Jersey has been known for its resorts almost as long as there has been a United States. The beaches and generally tranquil waters of the sea and inland waterway, as well as the wooded countryside, have attracted people from the big cities, like Philadelphia, New York, and Washington, D.C., for centuries. Even presidents have spent their holidays here—Lincoln, Grant, Arthur, Buchanan, Hayes, and Benjamin Harrison among them. The area has long been the perfect place to find beauty and peace and quiet, an escape from the pressures of the hectic daily life of the metropolis.

Nearly 100,000 people live year-round in this area, so, unlike many other resorts in the northeastern United States, the southern NJ shore doesn't close its doors after Labor Day.

It is easy to reach the southern shore region. The Garden State Parkway travels the full length of NJ, north to south. Closer to the ocean is the delightful Ocean Drive, which, although slower, is actually the best means of enjoying the unique beauty of this historic area. You can take what could be considered a "land cruise" along this 40-mile oceanside route, which connects the charming island communities. Start on the Ocean Drive in Atlantic City, and enter the southern shore region at Ocean City, traveling south through Strathmere, Sea Isle City, Townsends Inlet, Avalon, Stone Harbor, North Wildwood, Wildwood, Wildwood Crest, and arriving at the end in Cape May City and Cape May Point.

Coming from the west by car, you can come by way of the Atlantic City Expressway or New Jersey Route 47. If you are coming from the south, you can take the Cape May–Lewes (Delaware) Ferry. This is the only connection between the southern terminal of the Garden State Parkway and US 13 (Ocean Highway) on the Delmarva Peninsula. The 16-mile trip across the Delaware Bay is a delightful mini-cruise, and takes about an hour and ten minutes on a sleek new bayliner. A lot of people use the ferry to continue on southward after relaxing in one of the southern shore region resorts for a few days.

The region is approximately 150 miles from New York City, 120 miles from Washington, D.C., and 80 miles from Philadelphia, in fact, less than a day's drive from nearly all the major cities in the eastern United States and Canada.

SOME HISTORY

The region's first settlers were the Lenni-Lenape Indians, who were a part of the Algonquin Indian Nation. They hunted and fished along the cape until the late fifteenth and early sixteenth centuries. Then the flow of visitors started—European explorers and settlers arrived, disrupting the tranquility of the Indians.

A Dutchman from Nieuw Amsterdam (now Manhattan) arrived in 1623. Captain Cornelius Mey liked the area so much that he named it after himself, and that is how Cape May—the county, the city, and the point—were named. Other settlers, including the Pilgrims, were attracted by the offshore whaling and the shelter provided by the Delaware Bay. Soon the area was alive with activity—shipbuilding, whaling, fishing, timber harvesting, and some modest farming. While some of these occupations are still to be found, the major business these days is relaxation and recreation.

The tourist business started with the creation of convenient transportation. Steam-powered ferries came down the Delaware River, and, inland, the railroad found its way south. Soon rail spurs were added from the mainland to the barrier islands off the southern coast, and these islands became the chain of resorts that feature particularly Ocean City, the Wildwoods, and Cape May.

THE BEACHES TODAY

The barrier islands all have fine, white, clean beaches, some more than 1,000 feet wide. The sunny summer climate makes these beaches very popular, although rarely as crowded as the beaches farther north. Also important is the gentle slope of the ocean bottom away from the beach. This slope and the mild currents mean that the water temperature reaches a very pleasant 70-degrees-plus during the summer. In most places the undertow is negligible. Safety is assured by the lifeguards that the resort communities all provide at designated bathing beaches.

Highly residential and mostly family-oriented in feeling, all of the southern shore region resorts welcome vacationers. There are over a thousand hotels, motels, motor inns, bed and breakfasts, and small apartments available for seasonal rental.

Each of the beach resorts has its own personality. Some do have the popular boardwalks lined with fast-food shops, restaurants, souvenir shops, boutiques, and amusement centers. Others are more peaceful, with no boardwalk at all, and no noise-making attractions. On this shoreline, you can find what you want. If it's nightlife, it can be found in the Wildwoods. Other resorts are far more conservative, such as Ocean City, about eight miles south of Atlantic City.

Ocean City

Ocean City is dedicated to being the ideal family resort, concerned about the quality of family safety and entertainment, since its inception in 1881.

Founded by the Lake brothers, all of them ministers, the community was established as "a proper Christian summer resort." The brothers ordained that no liquor would ever be sold here; and to this day this ruling has not been altered.

A city with a year-round population of nearly 16,000, its population reaches well over 100,000 during the peak summer season. This community-conscious resort has well-maintained community services and exceptionally clean, wide, and secure beaches. And, during the summer—particularly at its delightful Music Pier— there is a complete calendar of special events, many happening after the summer season ends.

The Music Pier, first built at the turn of the century, is one of the biggest attractions on the two-and-a-half-mile boardwalk and features all types of summer concerts. The rest of the boardwalk is lined with shops and amusements.

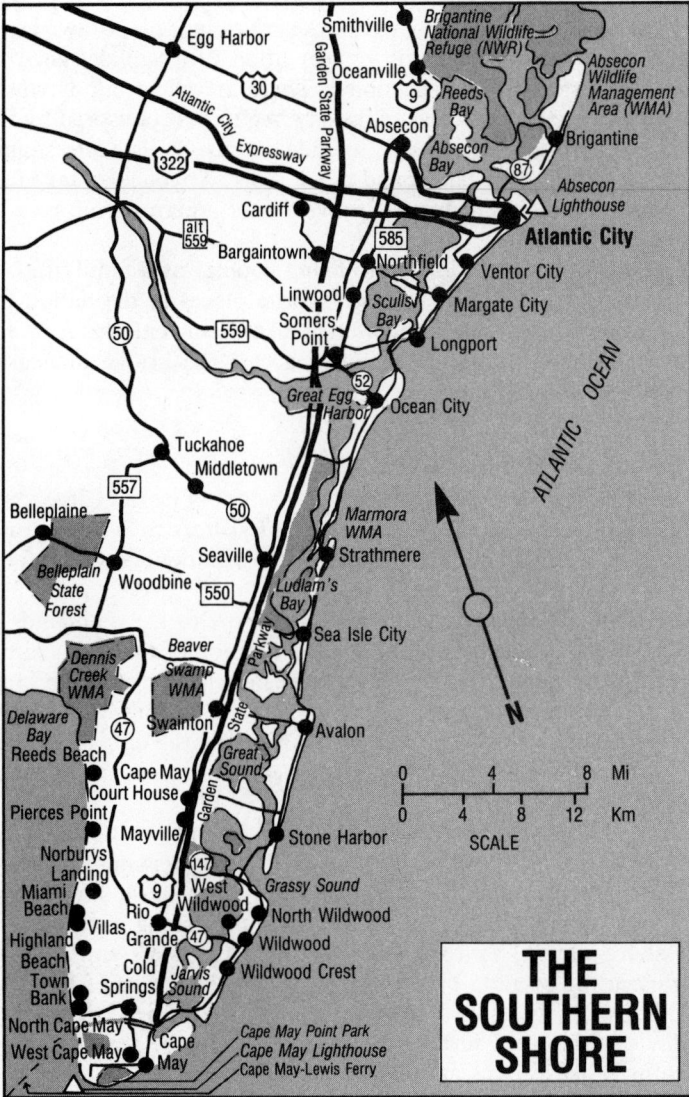

THE SOUTHERN SHORE

Fishing is a very popular pastime in Ocean City. You see people fishing everywhere—from jetties, bridges, piers, from the shore, and from boats both in the sea and in the calm waters of the inland waterway separating the island from the mainland.

Families come to Ocean City for the entire summer, drawn especially by the excellent summer recreation program designed to keep youngsters happily occupied. There are playgrounds where counselors are on hand the entire day. Activities sponsored by the city's recreation department include tennis, volleyball, square dancing, gymnastics, chess, and much more. Anyone can take tennis lessons, play shuffleboard, or even enter a hermit-crab race or a freckle contest.

Over the years, in addition to being popular as a family resort, Ocean City has been one of the favorite places in the nation for religious retreats, seminars, conferences, and conventions. And, for those interested, liquor is available across the bridge in nearby Somer's Point.

Sea Isle City

Another dedicated family resort, just south of Ocean City, is Sea Isle City. A century ago, a train brought visitors to Sea Isle Junction, near the village of Seaville, then the vacationers took a four-horse stage coach, boarded a barge, and finally arrived at Sea Isle City. By 1882, the railroad linked the resort to the mainland.

Hotels were built to try to meet the demand of the new visitors from Philadelphia and the other bigger mainland cities. One hotel was the Continental, which, for a while, was the biggest hotel on the entire Atlantic Coast, with five stories and the only steam-run elevator in the area. By 1900, there were more than thirty hotels and about 300 cottages.

Today, the five-mile long beach is still the major attraction because it is so clean and safe for sunbathing and swimming.

Sea Isle City is one of the largest lobster ports on the East Coast, and you'll see the vessels of a number of the fishing companies in the shore waters. Visitors enjoy watching the boats and the nets drying in the evening breezes, much as on the coasts of Portugal and Spain. Party boats take visitors out to sea off Sea Isle City for a day of fishing, or just to enjoy the sun and the sea. There are evening bluefish trips as well.

The summer offers activities such as oceanside surfing contests, lifeguard races, an annual baby parade, a skimmer weekend, fireworks, and free Wednesday evening concerts. Other fun includes an Antique Car Parade and an oceanside Flea Market.

Sea Isle City is home to the Philadelphia Flyers hockey team during the summer, and they play an annual softball game.

Avalon

Farther south, is Avalon. The townspeople, through tough zoning laws, have protected their resort, allowing it to develop slowly and comfortably to assure its beauty and calmness. Avalon got its name from the mythical resting place of Celtic lore—and the local people want for themselves and their visitors a truly delightful and restful resort.

Avalon is on the northern end of what is known as the Seven Mile Beach, with Stone Harbor at the other end. The street plan for Avalon was drawn in 1880 and it is still in use today.

There are a few hotels and motels, but mostly rental apartments, duplexes, condominiums and cottages.

Beaches and jetties are host every day to a lot of visitors who enjoy fishing; others prefer to fish in the calmer inland waterways. The beautiful clean, white-sand beach has lifeguards. Tennis and golf are popular with visitors.

Perhaps what Avalon is most famous for is its natural treasures. Very few of the fine New Jersey shore sand-dunes are left, but those that remain are in Avalon, thanks to a most fruitful and aggressive dune protection effort. The World Wildlife Fund owns 1,000 acres of natural meadowland also in the area. When visiting either spot, visitors are cautioned to stay on designated paths so that at least here nature's efforts will not be destroyed.

Stone Harbor

Occupying the lower half of the Seven Mile Beach is Stone Harbor. It is a lagoon development, consisting mainly of family homes.

The first building in Stone Harbor was an inn built in 1892 near 80th Street. Today, about 1,200 people live here.

Stone Harbor is popular today as the haven for all kinds of boats, including luxurious pleasure boats, skiffs, chartered fishing vessels, and ocean-going excursion boats. All are found at Stone Harbor's marina facilities. A public boat ramp provides an easy access for those with trailered boats.

Fishing and crabbing are the popular inland water activities. If you prefer ocean fish, space can be reserved on an excursion boat, or you can cast from the shore or one of the piers. Fish found in these waters include marlin, tuna, flounder, channel bass, and bluefish.

The beautiful beaches are popular for sunners and swimmers. The first lifeguard was assigned to this beach in 1912. Today there are 48 lifeguards and a beach doctor. There is a small beach fee to help defray the costs of preservation activity and safety maintenance.

A wonderful bird sanctuary, nationally famous for its heronry, is part of the resort. There is a fine recreation program for all ages, including a complete tennis program on 16 excellent courts. Another sort of recreation can be found at Springers, which has been serving homemade ice cream for over 50 years.

The Wildwoods

Northernmost of the communities known as The Wildwoods is the city of North Wildwood, which had its start in the 1890s as a tiny fishing village called Anglesea, where Swedish settlers first netted fish. Soon, along with Gloucester, Massachusetts, Anglesea became one of the great fishing ports on the Atlantic coast.

Eight miles off the North Wildwood shore is a feeding ground for a variety of species of fish—today a popular gathering place for those who enjoy fishing. Here, too, people fish everywhere. North Wildwood, in fact, sponsors a surf-fishing championship every year. Contestants bring in large catches of sea trout, blue fish, and striped bass.

The boardwalk is a typical seashore fun spot for the family, whether your interests be a healthy stroll, the shops, the games, or the rides. Bicycling seems to be one of the favorite pastimes here, particularly on the wide North Wildwood streets.

In the center of the Wildwoods is Wildwood proper, at the midpoint of the Five Mile Beach. It is a city with great appeal for teenagers and everyone who enjoys the mix of old-fashioned and modern amusements that fill the boardwalk and seven piers—more than any other resort on the New Jersey Shore. This amusement area (which is said to have more rides and amusements than Disney World) extends almost three miles along the Atlantic Ocean with a dazzling array of arcades, souvenir shops, restaurants, and rides. When night overtakes the city, Wildwood is aglow with thousands of multi-colored lights along this boardwalk strip. Local nightclubs feature top entertainers and plenty of room to dance.

Wildwood's free beach is considered one of the finest and cleanest in the world. It is expansive, as wide as 1,000 feet in some areas. In summer, the ocean water reaches more than a 76 balmy degrees; there is a full staff of trained lifeguards on duty.

Every day, deep-sea fishing excursion boats leave the harbor and you can join the fishing enthusiasts who will be catching sea bass, bluefish, and black drum. You can, if you prefer, rent your own boat for a day of quiet fishing or crabbing in the waters of the inland bay. Popular, too, are waterskiing and jet skiing, along with windsurfing and sailing.

The main street of Wildwood is Pacific Avenue. It has a wide range of retail stores, specialty and variety shops, and restaurants offering, of course, seafood freshly caught, as well as prime ribs, pizza and cold beer, cocktails, and all kinds of tantalizing sweet snacks and desserts.

This area has plenty of neon motels in all price ranges. There are also rental apartments and cottages for various periods of time, including the whole summer season.

At the southern end of the Five Mile Beach of The Wildwoods is Wildwood Crest, a quieter spot than Wildwood. Its special claim to fame is that it has two beautiful coastlines: one is the coast of the Atlantic Ocean, and the other is along Sunset Lake and the inland waterway on the west. This western coast is adorned with landscaped parks offering truly serene and tranquil settings—a particular delight each day as the sun sets. Anyone who enjoys sailing loves the waters of this calm lake. But it's not always quiet; often you'll see sailboat regattas, jet skiers, water skiers, and lots of spectators on the shore of Sunset Lake.

Fishing is very popular in this Wildwood, too: daily excursions are available on both the ocean and bay, the latter sailing from the Crest docks at Sunset Lake.

The community provides entertainment for visitors and residents. A favorite is the series of regularly scheduled free municipal concerts at the Gazebo Park at Rambler Road, taking place throughout the week, beginning in May and continuing through September. At the Gazebo Park is the Wildwood Crest Tourism Council's Information Center, the Nebitt Center, where you can find out about other local activities.

There are no nightclubs in Wildwood Crest. Visitors wanting to enjoy the nightlife haven't far to go—just next door, in Wildwood, farther to North Wildwood, or drive or take a limo or boat to the casinos in Atlantic City. The Wildwood Crest residents prefer a family atmosphere for their resort and they find that the visitors they welcome and who return again and again feel the same way.

Cape May

Cape May City, at the end of the Cape May peninsula and the Ocean Drive as well as the Garden State Parkway, has been a renowned resort since the 1800s. During the last decade, thanks to the renaissance efforts of its citizens, the city, the county, and the state, it has become one of the favorite resorts on the New Jersey Shore.

A branch of the Lenni-Lenape Indians, the Kechemeches, enjoyed summers here. But one of the earliest European visitors to Cape May was not on a holiday. It was said that the pirate Captain Kidd, came here to fill his casks at the area's Lily Pond.

Perhaps it was a farmer, Robert Parsons, who gave Cape May its start as a resort. On June 26, 1766, he ran an advertisement in the *Pennsylvania Gazette* telling its readers that he now had plenty of room in his house for guests because the children had grown

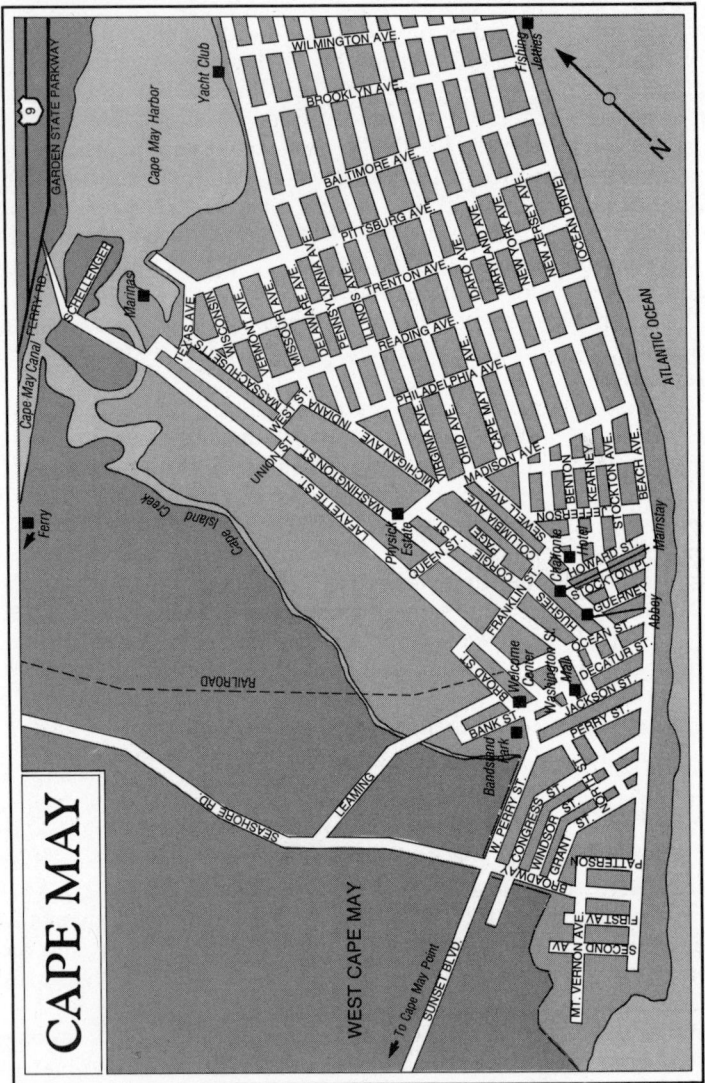

CAPE MAY

WEST CAPE MAY

GARDEN STATE PARKWAY

9

Cape May Harbor

Cape May Canal FERRY RD.

Yacht Club

Cape Island Creek

Ferry

RAILROAD

To Cape May Point

SUNSET BLVD.

SEASHORE RD.

LEAMING

WILMINGTON AVE.

BROOKLYN AVE.

BALTIMORE AVE.

PITTSBURG AVE.

TRENTON AVE.

READING AVE.

PHILADELPHIA AVE.

Fishing Jetties

ATLANTIC OCEAN

OCEAN DRIVE

NEW JERSEY AVE.

NEW YORK AVE.

MARYLAND AVE.

IDAHO AVE.

CAPE MAY AVE.

MADISON AVE.

BEACH AVE.

TEXAS AVE.

SCHELLENGER

Marinas

CHALLENGER

WASHINGTON ST.

LAFAYETTE ST.

TENNESSEE AVE.

WISCONSIN

MASSACHUSETTS AVE.

VERNON AVE.

MISSOURI AVE.

DELAWARE AVE.

PENNSYLVANIA AVE.

ILLINOIS AVE.

INDIANA AVE.

MICHIGAN AVE.

VIRGINIA AVE.

OHIO AVE.

COLUMBIA AVE.

HUGHES

BENTON

KEARNEY

STOCKTON AVE.

JEFFERSON

Mainstay

Abbey

GURNEY

STOCKTON PL.

HOWARD ST.

Physick Estate

QUEEN ST.

CORGIE

FAGER

UNION

FRANKLIN ST.

DECATUR ST.

JACKSON ST.

PERRY ST.

OCEAN ST.

Welcome Center

Washington St. Mall

BANK ST.

Bandstand Park

W. PERRY ST.

CONGRESS ST.

WINDSOR ST.

GRANT ST.

BROADWAY

FIRST AV.

SECOND AVE.

MT. VERNON AV.

PATTERSON

Carpenters

N

and left. He pointed out that Cape May was a very healthful place, particularly because of the bathing possible in the local waters on the shore not far from his house.

It was really after the War of 1812 that Cape May became a popular resort. Visitors came by horseback, sailboat, or stagecoach, taking two or three days to make the journey from such places as Camden and Philadelphia. With the coming of the railroad and the steamboat during the 1840s and 1850s, the resort business grew substantially.

In the mid-nineteenth century Cape May became known as the "Presidents' Playground" because Lincoln, Grant, Arthur, Buchanan, Hays, and Benjamin Harrison had vacationed there. In its heyday, it rivaled Newport as a summer escape for the socialites. People like John Wanamaker and Horace Greeley had built homes here.

Today the entire town has been proclaimed a National Historic Landmark because of its beautifully designed Victorian buildings, many of which were restored recently. Cape May actually owes its abundance of Victorian architecture to a tragedy. Fire had destroyed parts of the community several times before, because wood was the main building material of the villas and mansions in the area, but in 1878, a full 30 acres of the town was devastated. The world's finest craftsmen and architects were brought to the city that year (and in the years immediately following) to rebuild the homes of the wealthy residents. The world's finest furniture and fabrics were brought in to help create what would become one of America's outstanding collections of magnificent Victorian homes.

During the past decade, an ambitious townwide project has restored more than 600 Victorian buildings to their original splendor.

Cape May doesn't have the flash and noise of Atlantic City and the upper Wildwoods, but rather prides itself on the old-fashioned Victorian look and tempo it has successfully maintained. A small town, of about 5,000 residents, it is a proud community, that offers the unique pleasure of enjoying the best of two centuries. There is no other place in New Jersey quite like it.

The residents have the attitude that they would rather renovate than build. You can see the result of their heartfelt efforts on a variety of walking and trolley tours. Stroll under the shade trees of Washington Street Mall and admire the magnificent private residences. This Victorian pedestrian mall is set with sidewalk cafes and flickering gas lamps amid the gingerbread structures of a century ago. Somehow you lose sight of where you are, as you notice a Southern-type ambience, quite a different pace than the lifestyle commonly associated with New Jersey beach resorts.

Cape May has hotels, motels, and, most delightful of all, restored bed-and-breakfast inns. These smaller residences may not have all the modern amenities of the hotels and motels, but they make up for that with honest Victorian decor, charm, and atmosphere. You feel this when you have breakfast or tea on the veranda, or sit sipping sherry in the parlor.

There's much more to Cape May than its Victorian setting. There is, for example, a large harbor that holds crafts of all sizes, excellent for sailboating and other small-boat activities. Fishing is popular here, too, particularly because the point at which the Atlantic Ocean and Delaware Bay meet is a wonderful spot for the sport.

The Cape May Point Lighthouse is a particularly interesting landmark. Built in 1859, it is the oldest lighthouse still commissioned by the U.S. Coast Guard as a navigational aid. It is set in Cape May Point State Park, which has a fine bird observatory, nature trails, and a natural history museum. The beach here is beautiful (and free) and has none of the commercial activity of the Cape May beach.

You can even find your own diamonds here. "Cape May Diamonds," which many visitors take home with them, are actually pure quartz, rounded by the ocean waves and found mainly on the shores of Delaware Bay, in a variety of sizes, from that of a small pea to the size of a walnut. Many are colorless and look like real diamonds; others have tints of amber-brown or yellow. The pebbles are bright and clear when wet, but, alas, become dull once they dry off. The largest "diamond" ever found at Cape May weighed almost half a pound and was about the size of a chicken's egg. There is a great display of these fake diamonds at the Cape May County Historical Museum in nearby Cape May Court House, New Jersey.

While in Cape May, ask to be shown the wreck of the British sloop of war *Martin,* which blockaded Delaware Bay during the War of 1812 and was attacked in 1813, grounded on the shoals, and burned. It had been buried in the sand for over a century, when it was salvaged to be displayed to visitors in 1954.

Another nautical side trip takes visitors to the remains of a colossal failure: the concrete ship *Atlantus,* one of several experimental ships built during World War I in an effort to overcome the shortage of steel. While the *Atlantus* was waiting to become a part of a ferry wharf, it broke anchor and was blown aground. It is now a historic site of the State of New Jersey and is at the foot of Sunset Boulevard in Cape May Point.

A great mini-cruise is to take one of the ocean-going ferries that travel the waters of the Lower Delaware Bay between Cape May and Lewes, Delaware. The Cape May–Lewes Ferry is a one-hour-and-ten-minute ride on the beautiful waters of the bay. The shorelines are scenic and ocean vessels pass by as they enter the bay to go to such Delaware River ports as Philadelphia, Wilmington, and Chester. These ferries run year-round, and have frequent departure times.

The resorts of the southern New Jersey Shore are dedicated to a love of the sun, sand, water, and things in and along it. Everyone can find at least one resort that offers fun and relaxation to his or her liking. Indeed, this area of the Jersey Shore offers delights to history buffs, boaters, fishing enthusiasts, campers, nature lovers, sun and water worshippers, and antique collectors. It is a region for all people, for all seasons.

PRACTICAL INFORMATION FOR
THE SOUTHERN SHORE

HOW TO GET THERE AND HOW TO GET AROUND. The area is
about 150 miles from New York City, 120 miles from Washington, D.C.,
and about 80 miles from Philadelphia. It is less than a day's drive from
virtually every major city in the eastern United States and Canada.

By car. Most visitors to the Southern Shore Region of New Jersey prefer
to go by car. Not only is it easy for the one third or so of the nation's
population who live less than a tankful of gas from the area, but it is useful
to have the car available to explore the area and get to many delightful
places beyond walking distance.

Those traveling from New England get to the New Jersey Turnpike
from US 95, enter the Garden State Parkway near Perth Amboy, then
head south for about 150 miles to reach the southern resort area. The exits
to each of the resorts are clearly marked, all going over small bridges to
the barrier island on which they are located. If you prefer to go slowly,
through the New Jersey towns, take Route 9 which runs almost parallel
to the Garden State Parkway; for a small portion it is the same road. Exit
25 is to Ocean City. Those traveling from New York City and Northern
New Jersey can also use the Turnpike to the Parkway or Route 9.

Coming from the west, US 80, 78, 76, and 276, all eastbound, are used.
On Route 76, continue through to the Atlantic City Expressway, then go
south along the 40-mile-long Ocean Drive. This begins at the southern
end of the island Atlantic City is on (Absecon Island), crosses into Cape
May County at Ocean City, and continues as a very pleasant highway
through each of the resort barrier islands until it reaches Cape May at
the southern tip of New Jersey.

The Ocean Drive travels through typical shore areas—salt marshes,
sounds, islands, and their inlets—and across five bridges that connect the
coastal barrier islands. Each crossing has a toll of 40¢. You'll enjoy the
ocean breezes and the cries of the sea gulls and other shore birds. And
you'll enjoy driving through all the different resorts, some of which have
magnificent waterfront homes. Delightful, too, are the marina communities on the inland waters. In some areas, the islands are so narrow you
see the Atlantic Ocean on one side and the calm inland water on the other
side of the road as you drive. You'll have plenty of opportunity to sightsee
because the speed limit in many areas on the Ocean Drive is 25 miles an
hour.

Coming from Northern Delaware, drivers use US 95 and then go southeast on state routes 49 into 47 reaching Cape May and its northern cluster
of neighbors, The Wildwoods.

By ferry. Coming from Southern Delaware and most other areas in the
South is probably the most fun, because you can take a one-hour-and-ten-
minute mini-cruise across Delaware Bay starting at Lewes, Delaware, and
landing at Cape May, New Jersey. During the summer, the sleek, modern
ferryboats leave Lewes starting at 8:40 A.M., with the last leaving at mid-

night; there are 15 departures. In the winter, and fall, and spring you may leave Lewes beginning at 9:30 A.M. There are four departures in winter, the last being at 8:40 P.M. In spring and fall, there are as many as nine departures, with the last leaving at 10:30 P.M.

If you wish to reverse the trip, and go south from Cape May, in summer you may leave as early as 7 A.M., or 7:30 A.M. the rest of the year. There are approximately the same number of departures to Delaware, with the last at 10:20 P.M. in summer, 7 P.M. in winter, and 8:30 P.M. in spring and fall. For exact departure times and fees call the Cape May–Lewes Ferry. The Cape May Terminal number is 609–886–2718, and the Lewes Terminal number is 302–645–6313.

By airplane. Flight schedules are changed every season. In order to fly to either Bader Field in Atlantic City (just across the Albany Avenue bridge on the mainland) or to the Ocean City Airport, it is necessary to call for flight information and to make reservations: *Allegheny Airlines,* for flights from Philadelphia, Washington, D.C., and New York City. Call 800–428–4253. For charter flight information call: *Air Taxi,* Bader Field, Atlantic City, 609–344–5555. Ocean City Airport, 609–399–0907. *Southern Jersey Airways,* 609–886–1161.

By bus. *New Jersey Transit Bus Service.* Call the transit information center in your area for times and other details of the connections to Ocean City, Cape May, and The Wildwoods. In North Jersey call 800–772–2222. In Pennsylvania call 215–569–3752. In South Jersey call 800–589–5946. In New York call 201–460–8444. There are regular departures from New York City and Philadelphia. Stops are all resorts from Ocean City south to Cape May. Rates and times are changed frequently so it is important to check at time of trip.

Local bus lines: *Ocean City Transportation Center,* 10th and Haven Avenues, Ocean City, 609–398–9030; *Sea Isle Variety & Bus,* 4601 Landis Ave., Sea Isle City, 609–263–6832.

By limousine. Limousines are popular for trips to Atlantic City. See also Casinos. In Ocean City: *Lion Limousine Service,* 812 Ocean Ave., 609–399–6701; *Casino Limouisine Service,* 1320 Boardwalk, 609–398–8522; *Maher Limousine Service,* 609–398–7132. In Wildwood Crest: *Luxury Limousine,* 6700 New Jersey Ave., 609–729–4800. Because of the popularity of limousine trips to the casinos in Atlantic City, it is wise to make reservations as far in advance as possible.

By taxi. Ocean City: *Ocean City Yellow Cab,* 609–927–8471, serves both Ocean City and Atlantic City. Cape May: *Stiles Taxi Service,* 609–884–5999, serves local, Atlantic City, Philadelphia, and New York airports from anywhere in Cape May County.

USEFUL ADDRESSES. *Cape May County Chamber of Commerce,* P.O. Box 74, Cape May Court House, NJ 08210, 609–465–7181.

Chamber of Commerce of Greater Cape May, P.O. Box 109, Cape May, NJ 08204, 609–884–5508.

Cape May Welcome and Information Center, 405 Lafayette St. (across from bandstand), 609–884–8411, ext. 28, or 884–9562. Open daily 1–3 P.M. for information on tours, accommodations, restaurants, and more.

Chamber of Commerce, P.O. Box 422, 212 96th St., Stone Harbor, NJ 08247.

North Wildwood Tourism Commission, Box 814, North Wildwood, NJ 08260, in NJ call 609–522–4520; outside of NJ call 800–223–0317.

North Wildwood Motel–Hotel Association (Senior Citizen Committee), P.O. Box 814, North Wildwood, NJ 08260, in NJ call 609–522–4520, outside of NJ call 800–223–0317.

Greater Wildwood Chamber of Commerce, Box 823, Wildwood, NJ 08260, 609–729–4000.

Wildwood Crest Tourism Commission, Rambler Rd. and the Beach, Wildwood Crest, NJ 08260, 800–524–2776, in NJ 800–648–0236.

Borough of Wildwood Crest, Department of Tourism, 6101 Pacific Ave., P.O. Box 529, Wildwood Crest, NJ 08260, 609–522–7788.

Public Relations Dept., City Hall, Ocean City, NJ 08226, 800–225–0252, local, 609–399–6344.

City of Wildwood, Dept. of Tourism, Boardwalk & Schellenger Ave., Wildwood, NJ 08260, 800–WW–BY–SEA.

Emergency Telephone Numbers

Beaches: *Cape May Beach Patrol,* 609–884–9520. *Wildwood Beach Patrol,* 609–522–8258. *Wildwood Crest Beach Patrol,* 609–522–3825. *North Wildwood Beach Patrol,* 609–522–7500.

Police: Avalon, 609–967–3411. Cape May, 609–884–9500. Ocean City, 609–399–9111. Sea Isle City, 609–263–4311. Stone Harbor, 609–368–2111. Wildwood, 609–522–0222. Wildwood Crest, 609–522–2456. North Wildwood, 609–522–2411.

Fire: Avalon, 609–967–3411. Cape May, 609–884–9510. Ocean City, 609–399–9116. Sea Isle City, 609–263-4311. Stone Harbor, 609–368–2111. Wildwood, 609–522–0222. Wildwood Crest, 609–522–2456. North Wildwood, 609–522–2411.

Hospitals: *Burdette Tomlin Memorial Hospital,* Cape May Court House, Lincoln Ave., 609–465–2000. *Shore Memorial Hospital,* Somers Point, New York Ave., 609–653–3531.

General Information: *Weather,* 609–976–1212. *Time,* 609–976–1616.

ACCOMMODATIONS. Accommodations at the southern shore range from century-old inns to 1950's motels, to hotels built just recently. Off-season rates are significantly less expensive. Most hotels and motels take credit cards, but many bed and breakfasts and inns do not. You should double-check this. *Deluxe:* $100 or more; *Expensive:* $80–$100; *Moderate:* $60–$80; *Inexpensive:* under $60. Prices are for double occupancy during high season.

Avalon

A small, quiet resort community with a few accommodations, generally rather pleasant and comfortable.

The Concord Motor Inn. *Deluxe.* 7800 Dune Dr., Avalon, NJ 08202; 609–368–7800. Open Apr.–Dec. *Moderate* off-season. 90 rooms, all with kitchens. TV, A/C, pool, wading pool, sun deck, lawn games. Golf, tennis, boat marina, bicycles, miniature golf nearby. Has lifeguard. *The Heron's Nest Cafe-Restaurant & Lounge* is on the premises and open daily. Located a short block from the beach, close to sports and town center. Two large swimming pools.

Golden Inn Hotel and Conference Center. *Deluxe.* Oceanfront at 78th St., Avalon, NJ 08202; 609–368–5155. 152 rooms; 75 kitchens; 15 suites. Open year-round, with a *Moderate* price range off-season. Amenities include TV, A/C, pool, wading pool, room service, sun deck, art gallery, and gift shop. Golf and tennis off premises. Coffee shop and restaurant. Bar from noon–2 A.M.

Desert Sand Resort Complex. *Expensive.* 7888 Dune Dr., Avalon, NJ 08202; 609–368–5133. 89 rooms, 22 kitchens, 15 suites. Open Apr.–Oct. *Moderate* off-season. TV, A/C, two heated pools. One block from the beach. No credit cards. *The Mirage,* new dining room serving continental cuisine year-round (weekends only in winter).

Cape May

The favorite accommodations here are the bed-and-breakfast inns. There are many in Cape May—and they are delightful. Some outdo each other in the breakfasts they serve, and a few are so good they even have their own cookbooks for sale. Some of these ornately restored Victorian villas or mansions (a villa is a place that had four servants; a mansion had more) have as few as two guest rooms; some a dozen or more. While they are fun to stay in, not everyone likes a taste of the Victorian times. You have to go up stairs to your room, so the handicapped may have problems here; some rooms share bathrooms, there is no air conditioning, and there are often no room phones or TV. It's good to remember that there is a more communal feel to these inns than you'll find at the usual motel—you are, after all, sharing a house with others and you may be having breakfast together.

Some visitors may enjoy exploring the old Victorian inns on tours, but decide to stay where there is TV, A/C, and things the Victorians didn't know about. The waterfront Victorian guest houses are cooled usually by the ocean breezes, but the most exciting furnishings and breakfasts are in the heart of the city.

Victorian Bed-and-Breakfast Inns

Columns by the Sea. *Expensive.* 1513 Beach Dr., Cape May, NJ 08204; 609–884–2228. Eleven guest rooms; open Apr.–Nov. Restored oceanfront Victorian, decorated with antiques. Tea and sherry served on ocean-view veranda or in parlor. TV available, as are bicycles.

The Queen Victoria. *Expensive.* 102 Ocean St., Cape May, NJ 08204; 609–884–8702. Twelve guest rooms, open year-round. One block from beach, two blocks from shopping and historic district. Breakfast and afternoon tea for guests. Grill and picnic tables; golf available off premises.

White Dove Cottage. *Expensive.* 619 Hughes St., Cape May, NJ 08204; 609–884–0613. A guest house by the sea built circa 1866 with collections of antique dolls and wood sculptures. Spacious bedrooms with private baths; one air-conditioned suite. Open all year. No pets or children under 10.

Captain Mey's Inn. *Moderate–Expensive.* 202 Ocean St., Cape May, NJ 08204; 609–884–7793. Eight guest rooms; open year-round. About one and a half blocks to the beach and to the Washington Street Mall. Inn is named for Cornelius J. Mey, the founder of Cape May. No pets. Victorian courtyard, room service, tea served. Beach passes, sand chairs, beach towels. No credit cards.

The Mainstay Inn. *Moderate–Expensive.* 635 Columbia Ave., Cape May, NJ 08204; 609–884–8690. Thirteen guest rooms; three suites; open Mar.–Dec. Two blocks from the ocean, in the heart of the historic district, the Mainstay is one of the favorites of the Wednesday evening "gaslight" tours; the main floor is part of tours of the fine Victorian inns. Verandas, lawn games, tea served. No credit cards.

The Abbey. *Moderate.* Columbia Ave. and Gurney St., Cape May, NJ 08204; 609–884–4506. Seven guest rooms; open Apr.–Dec. In heart of historic district, one block from beach and shopping. The Abbey is an authentically restored 1869 Gothic Revival villa, furnished throughout with appropriate Victorian antiques. The downstairs is one of the stops on Wednesday night gaslight tours. Delightful tea served; lovely lawn.

Abigail Adams' Bed and Breakfast by the Sea. *Moderate.* 12 Jackson St., Cape May, NJ 08204; 609–884–1371. Six guest rooms, three with ocean views; one ocean-view suite with sitting room. Open Apr.–Nov. 15. One hundred feet from the beach in primary historic district, close to shopping and restaurants. Tea and beverages served. On request, breakfast served in room in spring and fall. No credit cards.

Barnard-Good House. *Moderate.* 238 Perry St., Cape May, NJ 08204; 609–884–5381. Six guest rooms; one suite, open Apr. 1–Nov. 15. Two blocks from main swimming beach; easy walking to historic area and restaurants. Features a gourmet breakfast lauded in many publications. Ceiling fans in bedrooms; the setting is a step back in time.

Bell Shields House. *Moderate.* 501 Hughes St., Cape May, NJ 08204; 609–884–8512. Six rooms, one with kitchen; one apartment; open Feb.–Oct. Victorian house; full breakfast served on wraparound porch, two blocks from beach, one block from Washington Mall. No credit cards.

The Gingerbread House. *Moderate.* 28 Gurney St., Cape May, NJ 08204; 609–884–0211. Six guest rooms; open year-round. Listed in National Register of Historic Places. Artfully decorated: photographs and shell collection of innkeepers. Front lawn has colorful flower garden in bloom late spring until late fall. Half-block from ocean, walking distance to restaurants and other historic homes.

Hanson House. *Moderate.* 111 Ocean St., Cape May, NJ 08204; 609–884–8791. Five guest rooms and two suites; open year-round. Breakfast is served on the porch in summer and in the dining room in winter. One block to beaches, restaurants, Washington Mall. Family heirlooms among Victorian furnishings. Large TV in living room; tea and wine served. No credit cards.

The Manse. *Moderate.* 510 Hughes St., Cape May, NJ 08204; 609–884–0116. Five guest rooms; open Mar.–Dec. One block from the village mall and the beachfront. Tea served. No credit cards.

The Mason Cottage. *Moderate.* 625 Columbia Ave., Cape May, NJ 08204; 609–884–3358. Five guest rooms; open May–last week in Oct. One of the oldest family-run inns (since 1947) in heart of historic district, one block from ocean and shopping mall. Afternoon tea; sun deck.

Twin Gables. *Moderate.* 731 Columbia Ave., Cape May, NJ 08204; 609–884–7332. Four guest rooms; open Apr. 1–Dec. 1. Well restored to original Victorian splendor. Walking distance to beach and Washington Mall. No credit cards.

The Victorian Rose. *Moderate.* 715 Columbia Ave., Cape May, NJ 08204; 609–884–2497. Ten guest rooms, three with kitchens; three suites;

open Apr. 1 to Dec. 24. Ocean is three blocks away and restaurants nearby. Music from the '40s is played in the parlor, and breakfast is served around a big old Victorian table at 9 A.M.—usually to candlelight and Mozart. Everything is roses—the bedsheets, towels, and wallpaper. Guests call the place romantic and acclaim its attention to details. Three rooms have TV; two rooms are air-conditioned. There are picnic tables. No credit cards.

Windward House. *Moderate.* 24 Jackson St., Cape May, NJ 08204; 609–884–3368. Eight guest rooms; two suites; open year-round. Half a block to the ocean. Rooms large, spacious, and airy. On Jackson Street, oldest inn in Cape May. Wraparound front porch filled with wicker; a second floor porch is for private use of two guest rooms; third floor sundeck. Some rooms with A/C.

The Brass Bed Inn. *Inexpensive–Moderate.* 719 Columbia Ave., Cape May, NJ 08204; 609–884–8075 Eight guest rooms; open year-round. An original 1870s summer cottage, two blocks from beach. Each of eight guest rooms has a restored, period brass bed; two in some rooms. A sun porch, tea served.

The Duke of Windsor Inn. *Inexpensive–Moderate.* 817 Washington St., Cape May, NJ 08204; 609–884–1355. Nine guest rooms; open Feb.–Dec. Near end of Garden State Parkway, four blocks to beach, two blocks to shopping, restaurants, tennis, this is an 1896 Queen Anne home. Breakfast is in a large formal dining room with ornate plaster walls and five ceiling chandeliers. Parking, beach tags; serves a lovely afternoon tea.

The Victorian Lace Inn. *Inexpensive–Moderate.* 901 Stockton Ave., Cape May, NJ 08204; 609–884–1772. Four guest suites, all with kitchens; open year-round. Weekly rates off-season. This is a 16-room 1869 house, the fourth off the beach. The front suites have ocean views. Lovely porch. Two suites have TVs. There is a grill, picnic tables, and a nice lawn. No credit cards.

The Sevilla. *Inexpensive.* 5 Perry St., Cape May, NJ 08204; 609–884–4530. Seventeen guest rooms; open May 15–Oct. 1. Two hundred feet from beach; one block from Washington Mall; view of beach from wraparound front porch. No credit cards.

The White House Inn. *Inexpensive.* 821 Beach Dr., Cape May, NJ 08204; 609–884–5329. Eight guest rooms; open Apr. 1–Oct. 20. Located right on the beach, within walking distance of restaurants, shopping, and entertainment. Three rooms have TVs; all rooms have fans. Picnic tables; tea is served.

Woodleigh House. *Inexpensive.* 808 Washington St., Cape May, NJ 08204; 609–884–7123. Four guest rooms; open year-round. No credit cards.

Victorian Inns and Guest Houses

Like the bed and breakfasts, these establishments have a communal feel. Shared bathrooms and parlors are often featured. These do not offer breakfast.

The Dormer House. *Moderate.* 800 Columbia Ave., Cape May, NJ 08204; 609–884–7446. Eight suites with kitchens; open year-round. Located three blocks from beach and shopping mall. Very pretty large suites all with private baths. Built in 1890s for a Philadelphia marble dealer, John Jacoby, and retains much of the original marble and furniture. During 1940s was a favorite guest house for people from foreign embassies. Weekly only in July and August. No maid service. Cable TVs, bicycles, picnic tables, solarium.

John Wesley Inn. 30 Guerney St., Cape May, NJ 08204; 609–884–1012. One of the newest and finest restorations of an 1869 building. Rooms and apartments. Open all year. Centrally located, not far from the beach.

Carroll Villa. *Inexpensive.* 19 Jackson St., Cape May, NJ 08204; 609–884–9619. 26 guest rooms; open from Mar.–Nov. Well situated—half a block from ocean, half a block from center of town. Site of the very popular restaurant *The Mad Batter.*

Columbia House. *Inexpensive.* 26 Ocean St., Cape May, NJ 08204; 609–884–2789. One guest room; three suites; open year-round. One block from beach in center of historic district. Owner-occupied and furnished with 19th-century antiques. TV.

Holly House. *Inexpensive.* 20 Jackson St., Cape May, NJ 08204; 609–884–7365. Six guest rooms; open year-round. Overlooks the beach, at heart of historic district. Has a circular staircase, porch with ocean view, art collection, porch swing, piano.

May Caper Guest House. *Inexpensive.* 815 Beach Dr., Cape May, NJ 08204; 609–884–1106. Nine guest rooms with kitchens; six apartments; open June 1–Oct. 1. Oceanfront, with some balconies. One of few establishments which welcomes children. Has off-street parking. No credit cards.

The Sand Castle. *Inexpensive.* 829 Stockton Ave., Cape May, NJ 08204; 609–884–5451. Seven guest rooms; three efficiency apartments with cooking facilities and private baths. Open mid-Apr.–mid-Oct. Tea and coffee in the morning; bicycles, beach chairs; fans, refrigerators in rooms. Carpenter-Gothic house built in 1873, one block from ocean; short walk to shops, restaurants. House has large wraparound veranda. Allows children over 5 years of age in guest rooms.

Hotels

Congress Hall. *Inexpensive/Moderate.* Beach Ave., between Perry and Congress sts., Cape May, NJ 08204; May–Oct. call 609–884–8421; Nov.–April call 609–858–0670. Landmark hotel, started 1812. The oceanfront President rooms are restored and furnished with Victorian antiques. The regular rooms are unrestored, inexpensive with decor of the '50s.

The Grand Hotels of Cape May. *Deluxe.* Oceanfront at Philadelphia Ave., Cape May, NJ 08204; 609–884–5611, 800–257–8550, 800–482–5991 (in NJ). 173 guest rooms, 111 with kitchens; 52 suites; open year-round. Closed Christmas. Largest accommodation in Cape May. Facilities all-inclusive, even to a ballroom. Well situated on the oceanfront. Popular as a year-round convention hotel. TVs, A/C, heated pool, wading pool, sun deck, lawn, sauna, jacuzzi, shops, shuffleboard, lifeguard on duty. Restaurants and bar.

Marquis de Lafayette Inn on the Beach. *Deluxe.* 501 Beach Dr., Cape May, NJ 08204; 609–884–3431, 800–257–0432, 800–582–5933 (in NJ). 74 rooms, 43 with kitchens; open year-round. This is a Best Western hotel and is well located at center of Cape May, right on the drive along the promenade and the beach. Every room is oceanfront. Restaurants, lounge, entertainment. TVs, A/C, pool, shops, sauna.

The Chalfonte Hotel. *Expensive.* 301 Howard St., Cape May, NJ 08204; 609–884–8409. 75 guest rooms, 2 with kitchens; open from May–Oct.

Rates include breakfast and dinners. Built in 1876, oldest hotel in Cape May, and although not perfectly renovated the Chalfonte does provide a pleasant atmosphere of the past with a friendly staff and entertainment, including nightly cocktail parties, classical concerts, comedy groups, jazz piano, and other weekly music events. The restaurant is known for its Southern-style family meals; the cozy King Edward bar is open until 1 A.M.

The Inn of Cape May. *Moderate–Expensive.* Beachfront at Ocean St., Cape May, NJ 08204; 609–884–3483. 125 guest rooms, 3 with kitchens; 25 suites; open Apr. 15–Nov. 1. The Colonial Hotel is right on the oceanfront in the center of the beachfront area, and near everything. Oceanfront breakfast and dinner at Aleatha's; The Inn Place is the popular bar and lounge. Horsedrawn trolley tours of Cape May begin in front of the building. Decor is really "contemporary Victorian"; a newer structure has been added to the original Victorian—you have a choice of the modern motor lodge or the historic hotel. TVs, A/C, pool, room service, sun deck. No credit cards.

Motels/Motor Inns

The Atlas Motor Inn. *Deluxe–Expensive.* 1035 Beach Dr., Cape May, NJ 08204; 609–884–7000, 800–257–8513, 800–642–3766 (in NJ). 42 guest rooms, 38 with kitchens; 50 suites; open year-round. This is a delightful motor hotel, providing spacious accommodations, all with excellent ocean views. Features a spectacular Sunday champagne brunch. Offers a variety of spring, fall, and winter package programs for both individuals and groups. TVs, A/C, pool (with food service), wading pool, sun deck, sauna, grill, picnic tables, restaurants, bar, entertainment.

Heritage Motor Inn. *Expensive.* Beach Drive & Stockton Pl., Cape May, NJ 08204; 609–884–7342. 21 guest rooms, 7 with kitchens; open Easter–Nov. 1. Situated on beach, well located for things to see and do. Places to eat across the street and next door. TVs, A/C, pool, sun deck, lawn.

Jetty Motel & Restaurant. *Expensive.* Second Ave. & Beach Dr., Cape May, NJ 08204; 609–884–4640. 30 guest rooms, 18 with kitchens; 1 suite; open mid-Apr.–Oct. 28. Located at good beach area. A family-style motel with TVs, A/C, heated pool, wading pool, shuffleboard, sun deck, restaurant.

Montreal Inn. *Expensive.* Beach at Madison Ave., Cape May, NJ 08204; 609–884–7011. 70 guest rooms, 42 with kitchens; open 7 suites; open Mar.–Dec. The Montreal Inn is right on the ocean and is run by the Hirsch family as a family resort. The motor inn, the restaurant, the bar, and a liquor store are all family-operated. TVs, A/C, pool, room service, sun deck, sauna, grill, picnic tables.

Sea Crest Inn. *Expensive.* Oceanfront at Broadway, Cape May, NJ 08204; 609–884–4561. 40 guest rooms, 30 with kitchens; open Apr.–Nov. Well located, on beachfront, three blocks from Washington Mall; lovely landscaping. TVs, A/C, heated pool, sun deck, lawn, grill, picnic tables, shuffleboard, lifeguard.

Periwinkle Inn. *Expensive.* 1039 Beach Dr., Cape May, NJ 08204; 609–884–9200. 34 guest rooms; 14 suites with kitchens. Open Apr.–Oct. TVs, A/C, pool, wading pool, grill, shuffleboard. Across from ocean. No credit cards.

Camelot Motel. *Moderate–Expensive.* Howard and Stockton sts., Cape May, NJ 08204; 609–884–1500. 36 guest rooms, 28 with kitchens; open year-round. Less than a block from the ocean. Parking facilities, elevator, all units are oceanfront. TVs, A/C, heated pool, wading pool.

Blue Amber Motel. *Moderate.* 605 Madison Ave., Cape May, NJ 08204; 609–884–8266. 40 guest rooms, 10 with kitchens; open May–mid-Oct. Decor is modern, cedarwood. Next to Emlen Physick Estate; near the William Moore Tennis Club. Short walk to the beach and Washington Street shops. Comfortable, quiet, convenient. TVs, A/C, pool, grill, picnic tables, enclosed children's play area.

Madison Motel. *Moderate.* 601 Madison Ave., Cape May, NJ 08204; 609–884–4838. 12 guest rooms, 6 with kitchens; 4 suites; open year-round. On edge of the historic district; short walk to beach and most attractions. TVs, A/C, pool.

Sea Breeze Motel. *Moderate.* Pittsburg and New York aves., Cape May, NJ 08204; 609–884–3352. 13 guest rooms; open Apr. 1–Oct. 31 Two blocks from ocean, four blocks from bathing beaches. All rooms have double beds, color cable TVs, A/C, and small refrigerators. Pool. No credit cards.

Surf Motel and Apartments. *Moderate.* 211 Beach Dr., Cape May, NJ 08204; 609–884–4132. 23 guest rooms, 8 with kitchens; open year-round. Overlooks the beach; within walking distance of Washington Mall.

Jersey Cape Motel. *Inexpensive.* 769 Rte. 9, Cape May, NJ 08204; 609–884–7382. 28 guest rooms, 18 with kitchens; 2 suites; open early spring–Nov. Reasonable rates because it is on Route 109, two miles from the beach. Very quiet, friendly setting. TVs, A/C, heated pool, wading pool, lawn, grill, picnic tables.

Ocean City

Because of the strong family orientation of Ocean City (and the fact that liquor cannot be sold), the town has few hotel- or motel-style accommodations. There are many small guests houses, which have families returning year after year. Most summer visitors rent private apartments for the season.

The Flanders Hotel. *Deluxe.* 11th St. and the Boardwalk, Ocean City, NJ 08226; 609–399–1000, 800–345–0211. 213 guest rooms; 1 penthouse suite with kitchen. Open year-round The Flanders is unique and is called the last of the old traditional hotels in both decor and service. The lobby with its magnificent antiques is a delight. It still attracts guests who have been coming here since the '20s. The Flanders has meeting rooms for modest conferences, seminars, and conventions. The duplex penthouse suite is truly magnificent, used for corporate executive conferences, etc. as well as VIP guests. Right on the boardwalk. Many ocean views. TVs, A/C, heated pool, room service, sun deck, porches, sauna, miniature golf, bicycles, grill, barber shop, beauty parlor, shopping arcade, tea, concerts, movies, lectures, shuffleboard, exhibitions.

Port-O-Call Hotel. *Expensive.* 1510 Boardwalk, Ocean City, NJ 08226; 609–399–8812. 98 guest rooms. Open year-round. TVs, A/C, pool, room service, sun deck, sauna, boutique. Tennis and golf nearby. Fresh flowers in guest rooms and nightly turn-down service. Located right on the boardwalk, overlooking the ocean. Modest lobby, with up-to-date modern motor-inn appearance. *The Portsider Restaurant.*

Strathmere

A small resort community with very few accommodations. Visitors mostly rent apartments (some in condominiums) and homes for the season.

Deauville Inn. Willard Rd. on the bay, Strathmere, NJ 08248; 609–263–2080. Rates on request; open year-round. One block from the beach. There are free beaches in Strathmere, so no beach tags are required. There's a restaurant and lounge, a dockside bar, barbecue, and a luau on Thurs. nights.

The Wildwoods

Wildwood is the city of motels—there are more than 500 of these neon-sign buildings with their 1950s aesthetic, as well as apartments and guest houses. Many visitors are families who come for the summer and rent homes or apartments. The Greater Wildwood Motel/Hotel Association publishes a free accommodations directory listing briefly more than 200 places in Wildwood, North Wildwood, and Wildwood Crest. While it doesn't list rates and provides only some credit-card information, it does give addresses, phone numbers, and some of the amenities. You may write for a copy to: *Greater Wildwood Motel/Hotel Association,* P.O. Box 184, Wildwood, NJ 08260, or call 609–522–4546.

Wildwood

Ala Moana Motel. *Expensive.* 5300 Atlantic Ave., Wildwood, NJ 08260; 609–729–7666. 43 rooms with kitchens; 35 suites. open May–Oct. TVs, A/C, large heated pool, wading pool, room service, sun deck, grill, picnic tables. One block from the beach and boardwalk.

Beach Holiday Motor Inn. *Moderate–Deluxe.* Pine and Atlantic aves., Wildwood, NJ 08260; 609–522–1922. Holiday suites with two rooms & kitchenette, two full baths and two TVs. Heated pools, refrigerators, A/C, sun deck.

Quebec By The Sea. *Moderate–Expensive.* Spicer and Atlantic aves., Wildwood, NJ 08260; 609–522–4664. Efficiency suites, deluxe motel rooms. Color TV, heated pools, A/C, refrigerator in all units.

Knoll's Resort Motel. *Moderate.* Roberts and Atlantic aves., Wildwood, NJ 08260; 609–522–8211. 40 guest rooms, each with 2 double beds, cable color TV, refrigerator, bath with tub and shower. Heated swimming pool.

Mar Lane Motel. *Moderate.* 4310 Atlantic Ave. at Montgomery, Wildwood, NJ 08260; 609–522–7463. 27 guest rooms; open Mar.–Oct. TVs, A/C, heated pool, wading pool, sun deck, refrigerators, grill, miniature golf, barber shop, beauty parlor, boutique, nearby shopping, tennis across street. One block to beach and boardwalk; restaurant and stores across street.

Sea Gull Motel. *Moderate.* 5305 Atlantic Ave., Wildwood, NJ 08260; 609–522–3333. 66 guest rooms, 30 with kitchens; eight suites. Open May–Oct. TVs, A/C, pool, wading pool, sun deck, grill, picnic tables. Half block to beach and the beginning of the boardwalk.

North Wildwood

Donaraile Motel and Apartments. *Expensive–Deluxe.* 438 East 21st St. and the beach, North Wildwood, NJ 08260; 609–522–5275. 20 guest rooms, 17 with kitchens; 8 suites. Open May 1–Oct. 1. TVs, A/C, heated pool, wading pool, room service, sun deck, grill, picnic tables, miniature golf, shuffleboard. Right at the beach.

Long Beach Lodge. *Inexpensive–Expensive.* 9th Ave. at the beach, North Wildwood, NJ 08260; 609–522–1520. 24 guest rooms with kitchens; open May–Oct. Beach and eating facilities across the street. Ocean views; some two-bedroom apartments. TVs, A/C, pool, sun deck, grill, picnic tables, shuffleboard. Golf nearby.

King's Inn. *Moderate–Expensive.* On the Boardwalk at 23rd Ave., North Wildwood, NJ 08260; 609–522–7508. Beachfront rooms—one-, two-, and three-room efficiencies—with fully-equipped kitchens. Cable TV, A/C.

Candlelight Inn. *Moderate.* 2310 Central Ave., North Wildwood, NJ 08260; 609–522–6200. Bed-and-breakfast inn with 9 rooms; open year-round. Three blocks from the beach and boardwalk. Tea is served. House dates back to 1905. Authentic antiques.

Suitcase Motel. *Moderate.* 15th and New Jersey aves., North Wildwood, NJ 08260; 609–522–7208. 18 guest rooms; open May 15–Oct. 15. In center of Wildwood, close to beach, boardwalk, and restaurants. TVs, A/C, pool, grill, picnic tables, shuffleboard.

Thunderbird Inn. *Moderate.* 24th and Surf aves., North Wildwood, NJ 08260; 609–522–6901. 62 guest rooms; open mid-Mar.-mid-Nov. TVs, A/C, room service, bicycles. Golf nearby. Great sun area around lovely pool set in tropical-style gardens. Poolside snacks available at cocktail bar. Restaurant overlooks pool and gardens.

Wildwood Crest

Lotus Motor Inn. *Expensive-Deluxe.* 6900 Ocean Ave., Wildwood Crest, NJ 08260; 609–522–6300. 10 guest rooms, 45 two-room efficiency suites, and 4 one-room efficiency suites. Open May 1 until Oct. 5. TVs, A/C, heated pool, wading pool, sun deck. View of the beach and sand dunes. Hospitable staff.

Carriage Stop Motel. *Expensive.* St. Paul on Atlantic Ave., Wildwood Crest, NJ 08260; 609–522–6400. 48 guest rooms, 32 with kitchens; 12 suites. Open Apr.1–Oct. 1. TVs, A/C, heated pool, wading pool, sun deck, lawn games, tennis, grill, picnic tables, shuffleboard. Golf available off premises. Right on the beach. Clean, well-kept. Certified baby-sitters.

Barcelona Motor Inn. *Moderate-Expensive.* 9001 Atlantic Ave., Wildwood Crest, NJ 08260; 609–522–3678. One- and two-room efficiencies one block from the beach. Cable TV, A/C, refrigerators. Pool and kiddie pool.

Nautilus Motel. *Moderate-Expensive.* 6401 Atlantic Ave., at Columbine Rd., Wildwood Crest, NJ 08260; 609–522–2177. 19 guest rooms; 3 efficiency units. Open May–Oct. Half block from beach, close to coffee shops and restaurants; very friendly, very well kept and clean. TVs, A/C, heated pool, wading pool, sun deck, public tennis across the street, grill, picnic tables, ping-pong table. No credit cards.

The Singapore Motel. *Moderate–Expensive.* On the ocean at 515 E. Orchid Rd., Wildwood Crest, NJ 08260; 609–522–6961. This Oriental-style motel offers "honeymoon temples in the sky." There is a heated pool and a kiddie pool on the premises, and all rooms have refrigerators, A/C, and TV. The *Bamboo Nosheri* serves, breakfast, lunch, and snacks.

Apollo and St. Paul Motels. *Moderate.* St. Paul Ave. and the beach, Wildwood Crest, NJ 08260; 609–522–9300. 44 guest rooms, 29 with kitchens; 2 suites. Open May–Oct. TVs, A/C, heated pool, wading pool, room service, sun deck, grill, picnic tables. No credit cards. On the beach.

Aqua Motel and All Star Motel. *Moderate.* Morning Glory Rd., Wildwood Crest, NJ 08260; All Star, 609–522–6845; Aqua, 609–522–6507. Open Apr. 1–Oct. 15. Ask about 3- and 4-night packages which include round-trip visits to Atlantic City casinos. Some efficiencies and deluxe suites; rooms have A/C, cable TV, stereos. Coffee shop and heated pool on premises.

Madrid Resort Motel. *Moderate.* 427 E. Miami Ave. on the beach, Wildwood Crest, NJ 08260; 609–729–1600. 54 guest rooms, 24 with kitchens; 12 suites. Open Apr.–Oct. All rooms are ocean front. Guests return year after year. TVs, A/C, heated pool, wading pool, room service, sun deck, shuffleboard, picnic tables. Golf available off premises.

Satellite Resort Motel. *Moderate.* 5909 Atlantic Ave., Wildwood Crest, NJ 08260; 609–522–5650. 25 guest rooms, 4 with kitchens. Open Apr. until Oct. TVs, A/C, pool, wading pool, room service, sun deck, near tennis and the Crest Pier. *Schuman's Restaurant* is adjacent. All units with microwave ovens. Children complimentary guests. Right near the beach.

Siesta Motel. *Moderate.* 5410 Ocean Ave., Wildwood Crest, NJ 08260; 609–522–2527. 54 guest rooms, 41 with kitchens; 24 suites. Open Apr. until Oct. TVs, A/C, heated pool, wading pool, sun deck, grill, picnic tables. Situated at the end of the boardwalk, within walking distance of shops and restaurant, and about 200 feet from the beach. All rooms face the ocean. Private golf club privileges at the Wildwood Golf and Country Club.

Topaz Motel. *Moderate.* 7010 Seaview Ave., Wildwood Crest, NJ 08260; 609–522–2723. Cozy motel featuring one-, two-, and three-room fully equipped efficiencies. Pool and kiddie pool. Ask about their family summer specials, and special weekend packages in May, June, and Sept.

RENTALS. House and apartment rentals—by the day, week, month, or season—are popular at the shore. Your search for a summer house or apartment should start early—soon after Christmas. Listed are rental agencies that can give you some information.

Avalon

Avalon Real Estate Agency, 30th and Dune Dr., Avalon, NJ 08202; 609–967–3001.

Holiday Realty, Inc. of Avalon, 2150 Dune Dr., Avalon, NJ 08202, 609–967–7571.

Ferguson–Dechert Real Estate, Inc., 2789 Dune Dr., Avalon, NJ 08202; 609–967–4200.

Leahy Realty, Inc., Realtor, 2688 Dune Dr., Avalon, NJ 08202; 609–967–5070.

Newbold Real Estate Company, Inc., 68th and Ocean Dr., Box #1, Avalon, NJ 08202; 609–967–8300.

Stone Harbor Realty Company, Inc., 30th and Dune Dr., Avalon, NJ 08202; 609–967–7701.

Cape May

Roth's, Suite 140, 510 Bank St., Cape May, NJ 08204; 609–884–2806, toll free 800–227–3639 (out-of-state).
Coastline Realty, 1400 Texas Ave., Cape May, NJ 08204; 609–884–5005.
Sol Needles Real Estate, 512 Washington Mall, Cape May, NJ 08204; 609–884–8428.

Ocean City

The Richards Agency, 1717 Asbury Ave., Ocean City, NJ 08226; 609–399–1612 or 1–800–843–0172.
Hager Real Estate, Inc. 111 Atlantic Ave., Ocean City, NJ 08226, 609–399–1856.
Monihan Realty, 32nd & Central Ave., Ocean City, NJ 08226, 609–399–0998.
French Real Estate, 1 Atlantic Ave., Ocean City, NJ 08226, 609–399–5454.

Sea Isle City

Arthur W. Laricks Agency, 4110 Landis Ave., Sea Isle City, NJ 08243; 609–263–8300.
Charles A. McCann and Sons, Inc., 21 44th St., Sea Isle City, NJ 08243; 609–263–7422.
First Eastern Realty, Inc., John F. Kennedy Blvd. and Landis Ave., Sea Isle City, NJ 08243; 609–263–1171.
Freda Real Estate, 6216 Landis Ave., Sea Isle City, NJ 08243; 609–263–2271.
The Lamanna Agency, 4400 Landis Ave., Sea Isle City, NJ 08243; 609–263–2233.
N.J. Realty Company, 5020 Landis Ave., Sea Isle City, NJ 08243; 609–263–2267.
Pleasure Realty Company, Inc., 23 38th St., Sea Isle City, NJ 08243; 609–263–6909.
Sea Isle Realty, 106 West Jersey Ave., Sea Isle City, NJ 08243; 800–223–1916.
Sofroney Realty Inc., 4201 Landis Ave., Sea Isle City, NJ 08243; 609–263–2206.
Tracey Real Estate Agency, 4100 Promenade, Sea Isle City, NJ 08243; 609–263–1411.

Stone Harbor

Avalon Real Estate Agency, 376 96th St., Stone Harbor, NJ 08247; 609–368–1101.
Diller & Fisher, 9614 Third Ave., Stone Harbor, NJ 08247; 609–368–3311.
Stone Harbor Realty Co., Inc., 9600 Third Ave., Stone Harbor, NJ 08247; 609–368–1440.

The Wildwoods

Wildwoods Realty, 2101 New Jersey Ave., North Wildwood, NJ 08260; 609–729–1701.

Calloway Realty, 7601 Pacific Ave., Wildwood Crest, NJ 08260; 609–522–7777.

Hoffman Realtors Agency Inc., 6301 Pacific Ave., Wildwood Crest, NJ 08260; 609–522–8177.

Nesto Ranalli Realty Co. Inc., 7th and New Jersey Ave., North Wildwood, NJ 08260; 609–729–1100.

CAMPING. In Cape May County there are 31 excellent campgrounds on the mainland, most just a short distance from the shore resorts and their beaches and amusements, and not far from fishing, sailing, boating—even not far from the casinos of Atlantic City.

All of those listed here are members of the Cape May County Campgrounds Association and are pledged to serving the needs of campers whether they come with tent, trailer, or motorhome, for a weekend, a week, or the entire season. You'll find them with fresh-water lakes, swimming pools, modern bath facilities, campground stores, laundromats, video arcades, full hookups, and other amenities.

Acorn Campground, Box 151, Green Creek, NJ 08219; 609–886–7119.

Avalon Campground, 492 Shore Rd. (US 9), Clermont, NJ 08210; 609–624–0075, (winter) 609–522–3747.

Beachcomber Campground, 462 Seashore Rd., Cape May, NJ 08204; 609–886–6035.

Big Timber Lake Camping Resort, Box 366, Cape May Court House, NJ 08210; 609–465–4456.

Cape Island Campground, 709 Rte. 9, Cape May, NJ 08204; 609–884–5777.

Cedar Lake Campground, Box 7, Dennisville, NJ 08214; 609–785–0712.

Cold Spring Campground, 541 New England Rd., Cape May, NJ 08204; 609–884–8717.

Dennisville Lake Campground, Box 36, Dennisville, NJ 08214; 609–861–2461.

Driftwood Campground, 478 Shore Rd. (US 9), Cape May Court House, NJ 08210; 609–624–1899.

Fort Apache Campground, Rte. 47 at Fulling Mill Rd., Rio Grande, NJ 08242; 609–886–1076.

Frontier Campground, 90 Newbridge Rd., Ocean View, NJ 08230; 609–390–3649.

Green Holly Campground, Box 193, Goshen, NJ 08218; 609–465–9602.

Hacienda Campground, Box 35, Rte. 47 N., Cape May Court House, NJ 08210; 609–465–7688.

Hidden Acres Campground, Box 354C, R.D.1 (Rte. 83), Cape May Court House, NJ 08210; 609–624–9015.

Holly Shores Best Holiday Trav-L-Park, 491 Rte. 9, Cape May, NJ 08204; 609–886–1234.

King Nummy Trail Campground, 205 Rte. 47 S., Cape May Court House, NJ 08210; 609–465–4242.

Lake Laurie Campground, 669 Rte. 9, Cape May, NJ 08204; 609–884–3567.

North Wildwood Campground, 527 L Shellbay Ave., Cape May Courthouse, NJ 08210; 609–465–4440.

Oak Ridge Campground, 518 South Shore Rd., P.O. Box 598, Marmora, NJ 08223; 609–390–0916.

Ocean View Campground, Box 607 C, Ocean View, NJ 08230; 609–624–1675.

Pine Haven Campground, Box 606, Ocean View, NJ 08230; 609–624–3437.

Sea Grove Campground, Box 603, Ocean View, NJ 08230; 609–624–3529.

Seashore Campsites, 720 Seashore Rd., Cape May, NJ 08204; 609–884–4010.

Seaville Shores Trailer Resort, 98 Corson Tavern Rd., Ocean View, NJ 08230; 609–624–0564.

Shady Oaks Campground, 62 State Hwy. 50, Ocean View, NJ 08230; 609–390–0431.

Shellbay Campground, 527 N. Shellbay Ave., Cape May Court House, NJ 08210; 609–465–4770.

Tamerlane Campground, Box 510, Ocean View, NJ 08230; 609–624–0767.

Whippoorwill Campground, 810 South Shore Rd., Marmora, NJ 08223; 609–390–3458.

RESTAURANTS. Restaurants in the southern shore area naturally feature seafood. They get quite crowded during the season, so reserve in advance, or if that's impossible, be prepared to wait. Not all restaurants listed here are open year-round, nor do all have liquor licenses—it's wise to call ahead to be sure of the situation. Price categories for a dinner: *Expensive,* $20–$30; *Moderate,* $10–$20; *Inexpensive,* below $10. (This does not include liquor, tax, or tip.) AE—American Express; CB—Carte Blanche; DC—Diners Club; V—Visa; MC—MasterCard. Area code for all restaurants is 609.

Avalon

Golden Inn Restaurant. *Moderate.* Ocean front at 78th St.; 368–5155. American/European cuisine. Specialties include bouillabaisse, blackened redfish, roast duck, and steak au poivre. All meals served, including Sunday brunch. A windowed wall overlooks the dunes on the beach. Dancing in season. AE, MC, V.

Whitebriar Inn. *Moderate.* 260 20th St.; 967–5225. American cuisine in elegant setting. Specialties include seafood combination, veal Oskar, prime rib. Restaurant is open year-round, but hours vary, so call in advance. Reservations are suggested. Lunch, Dinner, Sunday brunch, late snacks to midnight. AE, MC, V.

Cape May

Mad Batter Restaurant. *Expensive.* 19 Jackson St.; 884–5970. Specializes in unusual foods from around the world—all with a *nouvelle cuisine* touch. Dine on the porch or in the pleasant dining room. Very popular, so make reservations, especially mid-season. Fun eating in a national landmark Victorian building, in the heart of the historic area. Menus change daily, weekly, and monthly. BYOB. All meals served, including Sunday brunch. Late snacks until 11 P.M. MC, V.

The Swallows. *Expensive.* 400 South Broadway at Congress St.; 884–0400. Continental cuisine in casual, candlelight elegance of a Victorian mansion. Specialties include homemade pasta, fresh veal and seafood, inventive appetizers, soups, and salads. Incredible desserts. Everything is fresh and prepared to order. The restaurant is furnished with the owner-chef's paintings and other artwork. BYOB. Open May–Oct., Dinner only. AE, MC, V.

The Bayberry Inn. *Moderate–Expensive.* Corner of Perry St. and Congress Pl.; 884–8406. Turn-of-the-century dining room with antiques and a large fireplace; outdoor seating, on a picturesque veranda. International cuisine with an Asian flair. Specialties include fresh local seafood unusually prepared; a favorite: Thai chicken wings, shrimp, apples, and snowpeas. Open from Easter until New Year's Eve. Special holiday menus at Thanksgiving and Christmas. Check off-season hours, and make reservations. BYOB. Dinner only. AE, DC, MC, V.

410 Bank Street. *Moderate–Expensive.* 410 Bank St.; 884–2127. New Orleans French food and mesquite-grilled seafood and steaks in a restored 1840 Victorian residence surrounded by a lush garden. Interior is light, airy, casual. Most tables on porches and patios. Some tables have views of the Cape May Victorian bandstand and gazebo. Very popular so make reservations; highly acclaimed in reviews. BYOB. Open in season, Dinner only. AE, CB, DC, MC, V.

Frescos 412. *Moderate.* 412 Bank St.; 884–0366. Italian dining featuring seafood and pasta in a restored pink-and-gray Victorian house. Interior is contemporary Italian with *faux marbre* wainscoting, Art Deco highlights. Porch dining, too. Food is Italian without being stereotyped as northern or southern. Menu features many salads and light appetizers. Specialties include shrimp sautéed with feta, tomatoes, and fresh basil over fettucini; rigatoni with wild mushrooms and fennel sausage in a fresh tomato sauce; veal chop sautéed with sage and white wine; swordfish with tomato-basil sauce. Restaurant well received when opened in July 1986 by owners of 410 Bank Street, next door. Reservations. Open in season, Dinner only. CB, DC, MC, V.

Huntington House Buffet. *Moderate.* One block off Beach Dr. on Grant St.; 884–5868. Circa 1878 hotel dining room in a charming Victorian house (second oldest in Cape May), serving American cuisine buffet-style. Full dinner buffet includes Huntington corn pudding, apple and raspberry crisp; cold tables with 35 salad, pickles, sweet and sour items; beef, ham, seafood. Open in season, Dinner only, 4:30–9 P.M. BYOB. AE, CB, DC, MC, V.

The Lobster House. *Moderate.* Fisherman's Wharf, at Parkway entrance to town; 884–8296. Large seafood restaurant at the marina. Be prepared to wait—but that, too, can be pleasant as you enjoy cocktails aboard the Schooner *American,* anchored here. Open year-round. Lunch and dinner. AE, MC, V.

Restaurant Maureen. *Moderate.* Beach and Decatur; 884–3774. French food in a 192–year-old building, right on the oceanfront boulevard. Specialties include medallions of veal served over a bed of lobster, shrimp, and crab; veal au poivre; swordfish jardiniere. Dinner only. AE, DC, MC, V.

Watson's Merion Inn. *Moderate.* 106 Decatur St.; 884–8363. American regional food in a Victorian setting. Swinging leaded-glass-and-mahogany entrance doors, 1903 original cherrywood bar, period Victorian and American art, pink table settings, fresh flowers, leaded windows. Specialties include baked Merion potato cup, broiled stuffed lobster tail, Merion surf & turf, fresh fish, steak dijon, fresh vegetables (mostly local in season), homemade desserts, fresh fruit glaze pies. This restaurant has been in business since 1885. The early-bird special (4:30–6 P.M.) is popular, so come early. Dinner only. MC, V.

A & J Blue Claw Restaurant. *Inexpensive–Moderate.* 991 Ocean Hwy.; 884–5878. Waterfront dining in nautical setting; intimate cocktail lounge. A large assortment of broiled, sautéed, and fried seafood. Homemade desserts. Dinner only. MC, V.

Crystal Room. *Inexpensive–Moderate.* Atlas Motor Inn, 1035 Beach Dr.; 884–7000. Continental cuisine, emphasis on seafood and veal. Elegant restaurant and lounge with crystal chandeliers. Ocean view. All meals served, including Sunday champagne brunch. Late snacks to 1 A.M. AE, CB, DC, MC, V.

Peaches Cafe. *Inexpensive–Moderate.* 322 Carpenters La. at Washington St. Mall and Sawyer Walk; 884–0202. International cuisine, including Thai specialties. The decor is cheerful and warm: peach-colored walls with turquoise fabric and gray trim, hanging plants, paintings from around the world. Outside terrace under canopy with hanging petunias. Fresh flowers. Right in the heart of the Victorian historic district with views of vintage architecture and horse-drawn carts. Dinner, Sat. and Sun. brunch. MC, V.

Summers. *Inexpensive–Moderate.* Beach and Decatur St.; 884–3504. American seafood in a restored 110–year-old building with tin ceilings, vitreous tiles, stained glass. Specialties include grilled fish, pasta, lobster, shrimp, and crab dishes. Right on the beach. Frozen cocktails. Entertainment at 9:30 P.M. Lunch, Dinner. AE, MC, V.

The Lord Nelson. *Inexpensive–Moderate.* The Grand Hotels of Cape May, Oceanfront at Philadelphia Ave.; 884–5611. International cuisine in a nautical setting; seafood and steaks, with an ocean view. All meals served. AE, MC, V.

La Toque. *Inexpensive–Moderate.* In the Old Post Office at 210 Ocean St.; 884–1511. French food served in an intimate bistro of pinks and blues with French lithographs. Small—only 38 seats. The place was designed with affection by the owner. Open year-round. BYOB. There are no menus at the table—all of the day's specialties are listed on blackboards. Freshly baked croissants, cappuccino, and espresso are always available. The omelettes, filled with all kinds of things, are especially delightful, all day long. B, L, D. No credit cards.

Washington Inn. *Inexpensive–Moderate.* 801 Washington St.; 884–5697. American cuisine with a French touch. Victorian atmosphere with fireplaces, a garden room, porch and patio dining, and a lovely wicker porch and bar. Fresh seafood specials, veal dishes with flair, uniquely prepared chicken dishes, fresh vegetables. Fabulous homemade desserts. Dinner only. AE, CB, DC, MC, V.

The Winchester Inn. *Inexpensive–Moderate.* 513 Lafayette St.; 884–4358. Basic American food from old regional recipes. Three dining rooms with a restrained, plain Victorian feeling. Everything is freshly prepared—seafood, meats, and vegetables. Desserts are homemade. Lunch, Dinner. AE, CB, DC, MC, V.

Ocean City

No liquor is served in any Ocean City restaurant, and you cannot bring your own.

Dining Room of the Flanders Hotel. *Moderate.* 11th St. and the Boardwalk; 399–1000. Emphasis is on presenting quality food without dominant sauces. Nicely served in three elegant Victorian dining rooms. All meals served, including Sun. brunch. AE, MC, V.

The Portsider. *Inexpensive.* Port-O-Call Motor Hotel, 1510 Boardwalk; 399–8812. Classic Continental cuisine featuring seafood from around the world. Specialties include fresh regional seafoods, lobster Ste. Michelle, swordfish with avocado, *filet en croute* with brie, prime rib Oscar, steak stuffed with crab, and oyster imperial. Fresh garden vegetables. Dining room overlooks the boardwalk and the beach and ocean. Lunch, Dinner. AE, CB, DC, MC, V.

Sea Isle City

Canal 42 Restaurant. *Inexpensive.* Corner of 42nd Park Rd.; 263–2300. American seafood. Specialties include mussels with creamy white garlic wine sauce or marinara sauce. Clams on the half shell. Lunch, Dinner. No credit cards.

The Wildwoods

Wildwood

Groff's. *Moderate.* Magnolia at the Boardwalk; 522–5474. Old-fashioned roast meats, broiled and fried seafood, excellent gravies and sauces (from the Groff family). Desserts include black bottom pie, peach glaze, blueberry glaze, apple crumb, lemon meringue. Right on the boardwalk. Dinner only 4:30–8:30 P.M. AE, MC, V.

Seasons. *Moderate.* 222 East Schellenger Ave.; 522–4400. Specialties include seafood, prime rib, steak, veal. D, late supper until 1:30 A.M. AE, CB, DC, MC, V.

Urie's Fish Fry Restaurant. *Moderate.* 588 Rio Grande Ave. at the bridge; 522–4947. Seafood and steaks served on the Wildwood Yacht Basin with views of docks and marina, inland waterway and back bays. Hawaiian Revue, in season. Family atmosphere. Lunch, Dinner, late snacks until 2 A.M. AE, CB, DC, MC, V.

Urie's Reef & Beef Restaurant. *Moderate.* 448 Rio Grande Ave. near the bridge; 522–4947. Seafood and steaks. An exciting place to be—part of the Urie complex of food and fun. *Pegleg Parrot Lounge* with entertainment. Motel on premises. Dinner all year. AE, CB, DC, MC, V.

Ed Zaberer's Restaurant. *Moderate.* 400 Spruce Ave., N. Wildwood, NJ 08260; 522–1423. Famous family restaurant serving steaks, seafood, etc. Children's menu available. Open year-round. 11:30 A.M. to 9 P.M. AE, MC, V.

Johnson's Seafood Restaurant. *Inexpensive–Moderate.* Burk and Pacific; 522–1976. Serving seafood since 1946. Early-bird special. BYOB. Breakfast, dinner. AE, CB, DC, MC, V.

Kelly's Café Restaurant. *Inexpensive–Moderate.* 4400 Atlantic Ave.; 522–6817. Pub-style restaurant serving American food: flame-broiled chateaubriand, barbecued baby back ribs, roast prime beef, and fresh lobster and seafood. Open in season, Dinner only. AE, DC, MC, V.

Lobster Shack. *Inexpensive–Moderate.* Wildwood and Ocean Aves.; 522–4392. Seafood of all kinds. Open daily from 2 P.M. AE, MC, V.

Oak Avenue Seafood Restaurant. *Inexpensive–Moderate.* 220 East Oak Ave.; 729–4747. Features different seafood each day of week. All meals served. AE, CB, DC, MC, V.

Schellenger's Restaurant. *Inexpensive–Moderate.* 3516 Atlantic Ave. at Schellenger Ave.; 522–0433. American cuisine. Breakfast, Dinner, champagne breakfast. Early-bird special from 4:00–5:30 P.M. AE, CB, DC, MC, V.

Wildwood Crest

The Admiral's Quarters. *Inexpensive–Moderate.* Admiral West Motel, Ocean and Rambler aves.; 729–0031. Seafood and steak house. Specialties include spicy Italian-style mussels, homemade bread, salad bar. Dinner only. Children's, early-bird, and late-bird specials. BYOB. AE, CB, DC, MC, V.

Captain's Table. *Inexpensive–Moderate.* On the beach at Hollywood Ave.; 522–2939 Right on the beach. Seafood, with lobster the specialty. B (buffet breakfast from 9 A.M.), Dinner only. BYOB. AE, MC, V.

The Grand Hotel Restaurant. *Inexpensive–Moderate.* On the beach at Rochester Ave.; 729–6000 International cuisine in nautical surroundings. Seafood and steak specialties. Breakfast, Dinner. AE, MC, V.

Mariner Inn. *Inexpensive–Expensive.* 8100 Bayview Dr. on Sunset Lake; 522–1287 Overlooking the lovely Sunset Lake—get there in time to watch the sunset. Seafood. Dinner only; early-bird special 4:30–5:30 P.M. AE, CB, DC, MC, V.

TOURS. Unless noted, the following tours are held summers only. See also "Sports," below, for fishing boats that can take even nonfishing fans for pleasant cruises of the area. Trips to Atlantic City are under "Casinos," below.

Cape May

Cape May is, by far, the most enjoyable place on the New Jersey shore to take a tour, and fortunately, there are plenty from which to select. The following tours are sponsored by *The Mid-Atlantic Center for the Arts.* For information on any MAC activity, call 609–884–5404, or write P.O. Box 340, Cape May, NJ 08204.

Physick Estate Tours. This is a guided tour of the impressive Physick Estate (1048 Washington St.), featuring the 16–room house designed by renowned architect Frank Furness. Built in 1879 in the stick style, it is an authentically restored Victorian House Museum. Its interior contains many original furnishings, as well as collections of costumes, toys, and artifacts. The Estate Tour also includes the Carriage House, now home of the Cape May Art League. The Carriage House has rich wood paneling and horse stalls decorated with ornate grillwork. A small barn on the estate contains a display of antique tools. Time: 1¼ hours; $4 for adults, $1 for children. Tours run every 45 minutes starting at 10:30 A.M.; the last tour is at 3 P.M. Closed Fri. in summer. Open weekends only in spring and fall.

Walking Tours. This is great fun for those who like history close up and in detail. The best part is the enthusiastic, knowledgeable guides who provide amusing insights into the customs and traditions of the Victorians and their delightful and ornate architecture. Time: Approximately 1½ hours; $4 for adults, $1 for children.

Trolley Tours. Guided Trolley Tours go through the historic district of Cape May, with guides pointing out landmark buildings and telling stories of the heyday of Cape May as a Victorian seashore resort. There are three different Trolley Tours: The Historic East End Tour: includes the Physick Estate and two Victorian hotels—the Chalfonte (the oldest) and the Colonial (the newest)—picturesque Columbia Avenue, busy Ocean Street, and tree-lined Hughes Street, the oldest residential street in the city. The Historic West End Tour: includes the stately Congress Hall, the graceful Huntington House, the famous Pink House, quaint Congress Place, unique Perry Street, and the splendid aligned porches of Decatur Street. The Historic Beach Drive Tour: This is the tour for the architecture buffs. It features a century of the houses along the beach, from Victorian cottages to turn-of-the-century mansions, as well as the exotic revivals of the 1910s, and the best of contemporary design as well. Each trolley tour takes about half and hour. $3.50 for adults, $1.00 for children.

Mansions by Gaslight. This is on Wednesday evenings and holiday weekends only. Four of Cape May's finest Victorian interiors are opened for self-guided tours. Those shown are: The Emlen Physick House at 1048 Washington Street, The Abbey at Columbia Avenue and Gurney Street, The Mainstay Inn at 635 Columbia Avenue, and the Wilbraham Mansion at 133 Myrtle Avenue. $12 adults, $6 children.

To make it easy to go from one place to the other, the MAC trolley-bus runs a continuous transit loop. If you intend to take the trolley to all four houses, you should start at the Physick House no later than 8 P.M. Tickets are sold only at the Physick House, starting at 7:30 P.M. Total Tour Price (including trolley): $10 for adults, $5 for children.

Romantic Moonlight Trolley Tours. This is an hourlong ride in the MAC open-air trolley through gaslit streets in the historic district and along the beachfront. A delightful and memorable ride. Price: $3.

Children's Physick Estate and Trolley Tours. This is especially designed to delight children from the ages of six through 12 and is offered on Tuesday and Thursday mornings. Prices: $1 for children, $4 for adults.

Cape May Point Lighthouse Museum. This 1859 structure is one of the nation's most historic lighthouses. Guarding the vital shipping lanes where the Delaware Bay meets the Atlantic Ocean, it is still an active aid to navigation, visible up to 19 miles at sea. It is currently being restored as a quality maritime museum. View displays on the lighthouse's history, then climb the 218 stairs for the panoramic view at the top. For information, phone 609–884–8656.

Victorian Sampler Tours are offered on Saturdays in the spring and fall and on Fridays in the summer. Different houses are visited each week.

Pick up a copy of *This Week in Cape May* for the actual times of departures of all of the above MAC tours, and the departure points. In August, we advise getting at tour start points at least a half hour in advance of times given.

Other Cape May Tours

Inside Cape May. Tour of four of Cape May's authentic Victorian interiors: Duke of Windsor Inn, Alexander's Inn, Captain Mey's Inn, and Summer Cottage Inn (for descriptions, see section on Museums and Historic Sites). The tours are on Mon., Fri., and Sat., June and Sept. and also on Wed. in July and Aug. There are tours in October on Fri. and Sat. Prices: $8 for adults, $2 for children under 12. All are privately owned and run as Victorian inns; some offer bed and breakfast. For information on the tour call 609–884–4710.

There is also, during the Christmas holiday season, a seven-inn tour called *Cape May Inns at Christmas.* Admission tickets are: $10 for adults, $4 for children 12 and under.

Cape May Carriage Company (609–465–9854). This company provides a half-hour horse-and-carriage ride through Cape May. The tour leaves from Ocean Street and Washington Mall on weekends in the spring and the fall and every day in the summer. $5 adults; $2.50 children.

Dickens Christmas Extravaganza. 102 Ocean St.; contact Dane Wells, 609–884–8702. This annual event took place for the seventh time during Dec. 4, 5, and 6, 1988. Sponsored by the Dickens Disciples of America and the Victorian Society in America and assisted by the innkeepers of Cape May, it is a three-day event that is entertaining and highly informative. Especially interesting for lovers of Dickensiana and Victoriana. The Inns of Cape May have received national recognition for their yuletide decorations and festivities. Featured are hearty, old-fashioned breakfasts; fireside chats; strolls down the gaslit streets; and dynamic lectures. There are dramatic readings and costumed shows. Rates range from about $400 to $450 for two people, based on double occupancy, including inn accommodations for four days and three nights; full breakfasts and afternoon teas; six lectures; shows and readings; a trolley tour of the historic district; two progressive teas; tours of seven restored inns; a gala Dickens Feast at the Washington Inn; and a donation to either of the sponsoring societies. Contact the societies (see below) or Dane Wells for reservations and information on the 1989 festival. *The Dickens Disciples,* Box 50221, Raleigh, NC 27650; 919–787–9108. *Victorian Society in America,* East Washington Sq., Philadelphia, PA 19106; 215–627–4252.

Wildwood

Golden Age Festival. 9609 Pacific Ave.; 609–522–6316, outside of NJ 800–257–8920; within NJ 800–582–7618. Tours designed for those over 55. Golden Age offers Wildwood tour packages for five days and four nights ranging in cost from as low as $109 (for a budget tour, which doesn't include lunch) to as high as $149 (in the high season—July and Aug.). Among the features included in the tour are motel accommodations; dinners at the finest restaurants in Wildwood; full breakfast each day; lunch (except on budget tours); visits to such places as the Cape May historic area, Wildwood's boardwalk; and optional tours to the historic area of Philadelphia, the historic town of Smithville, the Renault Winery, Wheaton Village, or Longwood Gardens ($2 extra). Evening trips include a visit to Atlantic City casinos, a complimentary glass of wine, an evening of nightclub entertainment, an evening of music and dancing, and a cocktail party. Also included is a complimentary box of saltwater taffy, all baggage handling, and taxes and gratuities. Write or call for the Golden Festival catalog for 1987. Prices subject to change.

Trolley Car Sightseeing Tours. 609–729–9021, 609–884–1874. These open-air or air-conditioned trolley-car sightseeing tours originate in The Wildwoods. There is a daily trip, in season, from 11 A.M. until 2 P.M. The trolley will pick you up at your hotel, motel, or apartment. You'll see the old Cape May Lighthouse, historic Cold Spring Village, Cape May, and scenic coastal area.

Twilight Sightseeing Cruise. 609–522–3934. Aboard the Big Flamingo which sails daily at 7 P.M. for two hours. The trip goes through the wetlands and intercoastal waterway to the Atlantic Ocean. Passengers view the sunset over the beaches of Wildwood and see the boardwalk aglow with the riot of colored lights from the amusements. Bring your camera. There is a lecture, and snacks and sodas are available. Captain Sim's Dock, 6006 Park Blvd., Wildwood Crest.

ANNUAL EVENTS. Seasonal events draw visitors to the shore at times of the year other than the summer.

Cape May

April. *Tulip Festival.* This is the time Cape May celebrates its Dutch heritage with a spectacular display of vividly colored tulips, thousands of them blooming all over the historic village. There's a week of activities including Dutch folkdancing in native costumes and wooden shoes, foods, crafts; lots of music; and even a puppet theater.

May. *Great Cape May Footrace.* An annual event since 1979 called the 3K Run for Fun. The main event is the 10K (6.124–mile) run through the historic district and along the beachfront of Cape May. The route is fully paved; the event professionally timed; T-shirts are given to competitors; and medals, trophies, and prizes are awarded. There's a big party for the runners at a Friday night "carbohydrate Pre-Race Party" at the Convention Hall from 6–8 P.M.

June. *Cape May Victorian Fair.* An annual old-fashioned fair with crafts, collectibles, food, and much more. Held on the Physick Estate in mid-June.

September. *Founders' Day.* This is a special autumn celebration in honor of the founding of Cape May by Dutch explorer Cornelius Jacobsen Mey. Events include the Annual Beach Run, square dancing, music, lots of foods, and fun.

Ten days in the **Middle of October.** *Victorian Week.* This is a great time to be in Cape May, when it celebrates its Victorian heritage. The schedule includes a lot of special tours, lawn parties, and a fashion show. There's a spectacular grand dinner and a concert, as well as a fine antique show, among the many activities bringing back the charm of nearly a century ago.

December. *Christmas in Cape May.* This town celebrates Christmas the entire month of December. There are candlelight walks amid the gaily decorated Victorian shops, that invite browsers in for refreshments; carolers stroll on the malls and historic streets. There are the tours of the Christmas-decorated historic houses and a citywide Christmas lights competition. The Annual Christmas Ball is a major event.

On December 30 the annual Christmas Candlelight House Tour takes visitors to more than a dozen homes and churches that are magnificently decorated for the holiday. The tour is from 6 until 10 P.M. The cost is $13 for adults, $6 for children 15 and under. Funds used for restoration. Call Mid-Atlantic Center for the Arts for tickets and more information: 609–884–5404.

Ocean City

June. *Flower Show* on the Music Pier. *Annual Baseball Card & Sports Memorabilia Show.*

July. *Night in Venice.* A decorated boat parade on a Saturday late in July.

August. *Art Show* on the boardwalk featuring both local and international artists. The annual *Baby Parade.* The *Hermit Crab Race* and *Miss Crustacean Contest* at 12th St. Beach. *Sandsculpting Contest, Miss Ocean City Pageant.*

September. *Decoy Show, Rose Show, "Pops" Concert* on the Music Pier.

October. *Indian Summer Weekend,* early Oct.

Sea Isle City

July. *Little Miss Sea Isle City Pageant,* Townsends Inlet Civic Center, 85th St.

August. *Sea Isle City Baby Parade,* Promenade.

The Wildwoods

May. *Mid-Atlantic Music Festival.* Convention Hall, Wildwood. *Antique Custom Car Show* on the Boardwalk, Wildwood. *Chocolate Festival,* Pacific Ave. at Garfield, Wildwood. *East Coast Stunt Kite Flying Championship,* Beach at Wildwood Ave., Wildwood. *King Neptune Visit* on the beach, Wildwood.

June. *Pacific Avenue Merchants Sidewalk Sales* in Wildwood. *Best Dressed Bicycle Parade* on the boardwalk, Wildwood. *Model Airplane Show and Competition.* 16th Ave. and the beach, Wildwood. *North Wildwood Bowling Tournament.* Wildwood Bowl. *National Marbles Tournament* on the beach at Wildwood Ave., Wildwood. *Hoagie-Eating Contest.* Pacific Ave. at Maple, Wildwood. *Polka Spree by the Sea,* the boardwalk, Wildwood.

July. *Fireworks Display.* Wildwood Beach. *Golden Oldies Concert.* Convention Hall, Wildwood. *Clam Hunt for Treasures.* Beach and Pacific Aves., Wildwood. *Annual Regatta.* Greater Wildwood Yacht Club. *Lifeguard Races.* 15th Ave. and the beach, North Wildwood. *Canadian Weekend.* City of Wildwood. *Annual Art Show.* Kennedy Blvd., North Wildwood. *Strongest Man in New Jersey Contest,* Convention Hall, Wildwood.

August. *Mr. New Jersey Body-Building Contest.* Convention Hall, Wildwood. *Northeast Express Air Force Band Concerts.* Gazebo, Wildwood Crest. *Otten's Canal Boat Parade & Celebration,* 18th and Delaware,

North Wildwood. *Around the Island Row.* 15th Ave. and the beach, North Wildwood. *Baby Parade* on the boardwalk, Wildwood. *Annual Lakefront Art Show.* Sunset Lake, Wildwood Crest. *Family Kite Contest* on the beach at Wildwood Ave., Wildwood. *City's Jazz by the Sea,* Wildwood Bandstand, Boardwalk.

September. *Annual Surf-Fishing Tournament.* 2nd Ave. and Kennedy Blvd., North Wildwood. *Catamaran Classic* on the beach at Wildwood Crest. *Craft Show* and *Cat Show* at Convention Hall. *Antique and Classic Car Show* on the boardwalk, Wildwood. *Fine Arts Competition and Display* on the boardwalk, Wildwood. *Wildwood Photography Contest,* Wildwood.

October. *Frostbite Regatta.* Greater Wildwood Yacht Club. *N.J. Beach Buggy Assoc. Fishing Tournament.* 15th Ave. and the beach, North Wildwood. *N.J. Pops Champagne Gala* at the Wildwood Convention Hall. *Halloween Parade,* Wildwood. *William Penn Championship Cat Show* Convention Hall, Wildwood.

GARDENS, PARKS, AND PRESERVES. Cape May. *Topiary Hedge Gardens.* 158 Fishing Creek Rd.; 609–886–5148. Two and a half acres of hedges trimmed into various shapes, such as baseball players, ships, animals, Santa Claus and his reindeer, and biblical scenes. Some pieces, like that of the *Queen Mary* ocean liner, took 18 years to shape. There are 175 unique sculptures. To reach, follow signs to Cape May County Airport and turn right on Fishing Creek Road at a blinker light. This is the work of Gus Yearicks, a topiary artist, who spent over 60,000 hours, since 1928, in the Hedge Garden. Donations accepted.

Cape May Point State Park. Cape May Point; 609–884–2159. Site of the Cape May Point Lighthouse, one of the oldest functioning lighthouses on the East Coast. On the grounds are a bird observatory, nature trails, and a natural history museum. Open Mar.–Dec. The Cape May Point Lighthouse was built in 1859, and is still commissioned as a navigational aid by the U.S. Coast Guard. There's a beautiful beach here.

Leaming's Run Gardens and Colonial Farm. 1845 Rte. 9 North, Cape May Court House; 609–465–5871. A delightful walk along a sandy, winding path through twenty acres. Hidden around a bend, surrounding a pond, just over a bridge, or in a little nook along the way, there are twenty-five expertly designed gardens. Sometimes there is music played in the gazebo by the pond.

The Colonial Farm portrays life as faced by the whalers who first settled Cape May County. Tobacco and cotton are grown just as they were in 1695. There's a vegetable garden, laced with herbs, outside the one-room log cabin. Even the farm animals are historically correct.

At the end of the garden tour is the Cooperage, a charming gift shop in an antique barn. This shop can be visited separately from its own entrance on Route 9. There is an admission charge—$2, children under 12 free. Open May 15 until Oct. 20. Located on the west side of Rte. 9, Swainton, between Avalon (Exit 13 on the Garden State Pkwy.) and Sea Isle Boulevard.

Cape May County Park. On Rte. 9 at Crest Haven Rd., Cape May Court House; 609–465–5271. The park has a children's zoo with over 100 types of animals and birds. There is picnicking, a playground, a bike trail, and tennis courts. From June through September there are Sunday afternoon

band concerts. Handicapped facilities; Braille trail for visually impaired.
Free.

Stone Harbor. *Stone Harbor Bird Sanctuary.* 111th to 116th sts., on
Third Ave.; 609–368–5102. A nationally recognized nesting ground, this
21-acre sanctuary is home to a wide variety of birds, and is the only heronry sponsored by and located in a municipality in the United States. It's
a favorite for the American egret, the Louisiana heron, the black-crowned
and yellow-crowned night herons, the cattle egret, the glossy ibis, and the
green heron, the snowy egret, and the cattle ibis. The sanctuary is regis-
tered as a national landmark under the National Park Service. March
through October is the best time to view the birds in their nesting area,
and just before sunset is the best time to see the movement of the birds
from the sanctuary to the feeding grounds—thousands of birds fill the
skies.

Wetlands Institute and Museum. Stone Harbor Blvd.; 609–368–1211.
The museum includes an observation tower, salt-marsh trail, and the Wet-
landia Museum—on 6,000 acres of protected salt marsh and tidal creeks.
Birdlife observation is superb. Guided group tours are available. Free admission and parking.

Elsewhere in the Area

Pine Barrens. Off New Jersey Rte. 542; 609–561–3262. One million
acres of wilderness, featuring a famous dwarf forest. Known for hunting,
fishing, cycling, canoeing, hiking, swimming, and camping. Has forty-mile
Batona Hiking Trail—with scenic historic sites including Old Batsto, a
bog-iron village.

Belleplain State Forest. 609–861–2404. 11,270 acres. An ideal camping
site, open year-round, with boating, hiking, fresh water fishing, etc. Call
for information and directions. Northwest corner of Cape May County.

BEACHES. There are, of course, beaches all along the southern shore.
All are open to the public, although fees for beach badges vary—only
Wildwood beaches are free.

Avalon

There's a nice beach here, with a boardwalk.

Cape May

Along Beach Avenue, are the fifteen beaches of Cape May on the Atlantic Ocean. Between the beaches and Beach Avenue is the promenade; there
is virtually no boardwalk—except for a small stretch in front of the city's
Convention Hall.

At Cannone Beach are the Lifeguard Headquarters and First Aid. Rest
rooms are near the promenade at Broadway Beach and Grant Beach, on
the eastern side of the boardwalk in front of the Convention Hall; at Philadelphia Beach, and Wilmington and the beach, near the Cape May Cottag-
ers Beach Club at the east end.

The beaches, from west to east are: Second Avenue Beach, First Avenue
Beach, Broadway Beach, Colton Court Beach, Grant Beach, Cannone

Beach, Windsor Beach, Congress Beach, Steger Beach, Stockton Beach, Little Howard Beach, Queen Beach, and Philadelphia Beach.

Only Little Howard, Philadelphia, and Queen beaches, have lifeguards, and are not as wide as the beaches of the resorts north of Cape May. But they are clean. Most beach areas are very narrow and against the huge rocks supporting the combination seawall and promenade. Beach tags are required and cost $2 a day, $4 a week, and $9 for the season. Most hotels, motels, and inns lend guests beach tags at no charge.

If you get in your car, or feel like taking a long walk beside the sea, you can enjoy the beautiful beach at Cape May Point, about 2 miles southwest. The area is far less commercial than the Cape May beaches, and the views across the confluence of Delaware Bay and the Atlantic are magnificent.

Ocean City

There is a fee for a beach tag to permit you to use the fine, wide beach. The cost is $3 for a weekly tag, $5 for the season, if you buy it before June 1; after that date, it costs $7. You may purchase the beach tag at the Music Pier or from the City information booth on the causeway. There are bathhouses; picnicking is possible (permits are required for beach fires); you can surf at protected beaches before 9:30 A.M. and after 6 P.M. Surf all day at 7th St. and south of 59th St., scuba dive, raft. There's a large boardwalk.

Sea Isle City

Beach tags are required to use the five miles of beach. They are sold at the Dominic C. Raff Community Center, 127 John F. Kennedy Blvd. The beach fee is $5 per person for the season, if purchased before May 31. From June 1, it goes up to $7. Daily and weekly fee is $3 per person; children under 12 are free. There's a boardwalk; you can surf and scuba dive.

Stone Harbor

Stone Harbor maintains wonderful, safe beaches for swimming. The first lifeguard was assigned to the beach in 1912; now there are 48 guards and a beach doctor supervised by six officers. The modest beach fees help to cover the cost of preservation efforts and safety measures. There are bathhouses; surfing is permitted.

The Wildwoods

The only free beaches on the South Jersey Shore: no beach tags are required. Trained lifeguards are on duty. The beaches are especially fine and over 1,000 feet wide in some places. Boardwalk and bathhouses in North Wildwood and Wildwood.

SPORTS. Along the southern shore, water sports are most popular—especially fishing. Tennis courts are usually available, and bikes are often available to rent. To **rent horses,** contact *Hidden Valley Ranch,* 4010 Bayshore Rd., Cold Spring; 609–884–8205. Closed Sun. Open year-round.

Avalon

Fishing. *Avalon Sport Fishing Center,* 14th and Ocean Dr.; 609–465–9851, sponsors six-hour blue fishing trips, and two half-day trips aboard the *Miss Avalon II.* Every day from June 1 to the end of Sept.

Cape May

Competitions. The *Annual Hobie Cat Regatta,* Northeastern Regional Championship, has over 200 catamaran crews from 12 states competing. For exact 1989 dates, call Cape May, Department of Civic Affairs; 609–884–9565, Ext. 20 or 27.

The *Annual Jersey Cape Fishing Tournament,* now over fifty years old, is the oldest on the East Coast. Anglers who catch over minimum weights are recognized with bronze award pins and citations. There is no fee for entering the tournament and no advance registration is required. The tournament is sponsored by the Cape May County Board of Chosen Freeholders. For 1989 information, call 609–886–0901.

Bicycles. *Village Bike Shop.* Ocean St. at Washington Mall; 609–884–8500. Open 6:30 A.M.–8 P.M. Every type of bike available. Fee is $2.50 an hour or $7 a day; weekly fee $20. Free parking if you use their bikes.

Fishing. *Delta Lady.* Miss Chris Fishing Center, Schellenger's Landing; 609–884–1919. Has a three-hour cruise aboard a 65–foot schooner that sails at 10 A.M., 2 P.M., and 6 P.M.

South Jersey Fishing Center. Rte. 9, at the entrance to Cape May. Captain Bob Schumann's Sea Star fleet—*Sea Star II, Fiesta,* and *Miss Cape May*—offer four-, six-, and eight-hour deep-sea fishing charters. Rates: $14, $18, and $23 for adults and $8, $10, and $12 for children. Phone 609–884–4671 for times, reservations, and charter information.

Tennis. *William J. Moore Tennis Center.* Washington St.; 609–884–8986, has 13 clay courts. $4 an hour for a court; two-week rate is $45; other, longer-term arrangements possible.

Prices given subject to change.

Ocean City

Boating and water skiing. *Great Egg Bay Sailing Association,* 609–653–1750, has rentals and instruction for sunfishes, hobies, bay sailers, and sailboards. Call for current schedule and rates, which change often. Other establishments to contact: *Bayview Sailboats.* 312 Bay Ave.; 609–398–3049. *Blue Water Marina.* 600 Whelk Dr.; 609–398–9090. *Eastern Sailboards.* 202 Bay Ave.; 609–391–9650. *Jet Ski Rentals.* 2nd St. and Bay Ave.; 609–399–4017. *Speed & Ski.* 916 Palen Ave.; 609–398–0424. *The North Star.* On bay, between 9th and 10th Sts.; 609–398–0424.

Fishing. *Ocean City Marina and Fishing Center.* 3rd St. to Bay Ave.; 609–399–5011. Challenger Fleet: 4–hour fishing, 8 A.M. and 1 P.M.; 6–hour night bluefishing 7 P.M., Fri. and Sat. Sunset sightseeing cruises from 7–8:45 P.M. Mon.–Thurs.

The *Fishing Pier* is at 5th St. and the ocean.

The *Dockside Marina,* 10th St. on the bay, has 16–foot fishing boats for rent with rods, bait, etc.

Shuffleboard. 25 courts at 5th St. and the boardwalk; and eight courts at the 34th St. playground. There's also an Ocean City Shuffleboard Club.

Tennis. *Roger's Racquet Club;* 609–927–1089. $12 per hour non prime time, $14 per hour prime time (after 4 P.M. daily and weekends). Racquetball: $10 per hour non prime time, $12 per hour prime time. Open daily, 8 A.M.–midnight. Take 9th St. Bridge to Somers Point, last right off circle. Less than 10 minutes from Ocean City.

Ocean City Tennis Courts, located at 34th St. and Asbury Ave. and 6th St. and Atlantic Ave. Tournaments.

Sea Isle City

Fishing. *Capt. Robbins' Fish'n & Sightseeing Center,* 609–263–2020, Ludlam Landing Rd., one quarter mile west of the bridge, offers four-hour and eight-hour fishing trips. The half-day trip is from 8 A.M.–noon, with flounder fishing the speciality. The full-day fishing trip is from 8 A.M.–4 P.M., Apr. 1–Dec. 30. June 14–Sept. 14, nightly blue fishing trips, 7 P.M.–3 A.M., except Sunday.

Sea Isle Fishing Center. 42nd Pl.; 609–263–3800. 4–hour trips daily at 8 A.M. and 1 P.M. aboard the 70–foot *Starfish.* 8–hour night bluefishing sails at 7 P.M. Free bait, fish bags. Enclosed lounge, ladies' accommodations, refreshments, instructions for beginners.

Larsen's Marina. Old Sea Isle Blvd.; 609–263–1554.

Miss Townsend's Inlet Party Boat. 86th and Bay; 609–263–8174.

Tennis. Tennis courts in public playground at 63rd and Central Ave.

Somers Point

Sailing. *Great Egg Bay Sailing Marina,* Woodlawn Ave., off Rte. 559; 609–653–1198. Rentals, lessons, charters, sailing club.

Stone Harbor

Golf and tennis. *Stone Harbor Golf Club,* Rte. 9, 1½ miles north of Exit 10, Garden State Parkway, 609–465–9270. You must call in advance to obtain a guaranteed starting time. In season, daily green fees are $11 and, after 4 P.M., $7. Electric carts rent for $14.28 for 18 holes. There are two outdoor tennis courts available.

Water sports. *Stone Harbor Water Sport, Inc.,* 96th St. Bridge, Stone Harbor Marina; 609–368–3729. Jet skis sales and rentals; water-skiing boat rides by appointment. Fishing boats also available.

Strathmere

Boat rentals. *Frank's Boat Rentals,* Bayview and Whittier Rd.; 609–263–6913. *Strathmere Boat,* Bayview and Putnam Rd.; 609–263–7333.

The Wildwoods

Bicycling. Permitted on boardwalk until 11 A.M. weekdays, 10:30 A.M. Sat., Sun., and holidays. Many bike rental stations on and off the boardwalk.

Boating. *Aqua Ski Boat Rentals.* Boat leasing by hour, half day, or day; high-performance boats for pleasure cruising and water-skiing. Sea-sled rides can accommodate up to ten. 6th and New York Ave., North Wildwood; 609–522–5778.

Bocce. In Wildwood at Leaming Ave. and the boardwalk.

Bowling. Wildwood Bowl, 3400 New Jersey Ave.; 609–729–2695.

Exercise. At 10 A.M. every morning a Wildwood lifeguard leads an exercise class. Free to everyone at Lincoln Ave. beach.

Fishing. Over 100 party boats make daily trips to the ocean fishing grounds. Boats leave daily for a full day, starting at 8 A.M. and returning about 4 P.M.; for a half day, 8 A.M.–noon, and 1 P.M.–5 P.M. Fishing trips are available at most docks. Bait is furnished on all trips; rods and reels can be rented. Boats can be chartered for private parties or groups for sport fishing. They are also available for night fishing. Fishing docks: Wildwood: *Otten's Harbor,* Davis and Park Blvd. *Wildwood Yacht Basin,* Rio Grande and Susquehanna aves.; 609–522–1032. *Shawcrest Yacht Basin,* Shawcrest Rd. Wildwood Crest: Lake View Docks, Park Blvd. between Aster and Rosemary rds. Rentals, sailboats, fishing boats, motor boats, fishing equipment available.

Other fishing: *Wildwood Crest Fishing Pier.* For members and guests of members only. Heather and The Beach, Wildwood Crest. *Dad's Place.* Pier fishing or small rental boats, Stone Harbor Toll Bridge, Ocean Drive, just off North Wildwood Blvd., North Wildwood. *Canalside Boating & Crabbing.* Opens 6 A.M. Boat rentals by day, half-day, or hour. Bait and tackle shop, ice. Also hourly rates for sightseeing. 18th St. and Delaware Ave., North Wildwood; 609–522–7676.

Fishing boats: *The Royal Flush* is a 100–foot ship offering 4–hour daily trips sailing at 8 A.M. and 1 P.M., and 8–hour night blue fishing trips at 7 P.M. Enclosed separate lounge with ladies' accommodations; refreshments. 6100 Park Blvd., Wildwood Crest; 609–522–1395. The *Sea Raider* party boat sails at 10 A.M. for 6 hours of fishing. At 7 P.M. it goes fishing for "blues." *Wildwood Marine,* 560 W. Rio Grande Ave., Wildwood, 729–7777.

There are public boat ramps on New York Ave., between 4th and 6th aves., North Wildwood.

Golf. *Wildwood Golf and Country Club;* 609–465–7823. Located on the main seashore road about 10 minutes from the resort. There is an 18–hole championship course in excellent condition. Call for details.

Shuffleboard. At Ocean Ave., between Andrew and Taylor aves., Atlantic and Primrose aves., and 9th and Central aves. Wildwood.

Tennis. *Fox Park Tennis Courts,* Davis Ave. between Ocean and Atlantic, Wildwood, 609–522–2362. *Wildwood Crest Tennis Courts,* Columbine and Atlantic, Wildwood Crest, 609–522–0084. *Allen Recreation Park,* 22nd and Delaware aves., North Wildwood, 609–729–6734.

Volleyball. On the beach in Wildwood at Lincoln Ave. and Taylor Ave.

CASINOS. All of the gambling casinos are in hotels in Atlantic City, about 20 minutes from Ocean City. It is easy to get there by bus or by limousine. There are a variety of services for a day's—or a few hours'—excursion to the tinsel-land of gambling "up north" in Atlantic City. See the chapter on Atlantic City for details.

Ocean City

Casino Tours, 1320 Boardwalk; 609–646–5555. For only $12.00 you can purchase package tours to either Resorts International or Harrah's Marina from Ocean City (with pickups at Somers Point, Linwood, and Northfield). They are good deals. The Resorts trip, if taken before 4 P.M. Sun.–Thurs. or all day Fri., includes $7.50 in coins, $2.50 in food coupons, and $5 deferred (a deferred coupon is redeemable on a return trip if used before the expiration date). If you go after 4 P.M., it's even better—you get $12.50 in coins as well as the other coupons. For Harrah's Marina, the details vary, but there are times when you get from $7.50 to $12.50 in coins and other benefits. They also have a $10 Bally's charter which provides $5 in coin and $5 deferred. These prices and packages change from time to time. The trips begin about 9 A.M., with the last trip leaving Atlantic City at 2 A.M. the next day.

Casino Challenger; 609–399–5011. Cruise to the Harrah's Marina Hotel Casino on the 85-foot *Casino Challenger* from the Ocean City Marina and Fishing Center, 3rd St. and Bay Ave. Price is $20 per person, which includes at least $10 in coins and $5 in a coupon good for food, beverage, or both. Call for rates, current bonus package, and other information. The cruise is an hour and a half with four hours at the casino. Available year-round.

The Wildwoods

Holiday Tours Casino Bus; 609–729–5810. Offers packages to Caesars and the Atlantis in Atlantic City for $13.95. The various packages change from time to time and include as much as $12.50 in coins, and $3 to $5 in coupons exchangeable for food, drink, gifts, etc. The deferred tickets range from $5 to $7.50. Tickets delivered free in Wildwood, Wildwood Crest, and Cape May. Tickets can be purchased in a dozen places on the South Jersey Shore—call to find place nearest you. Prices all subject to change.

Adventure Trails, 5501 Ocean Ave., Wildwood Crest; 609–886–4100. Offers daily door-to-door limousine and bus tour service to eight of the Atlantic City casinos, all for $13.95. Some of the packages offer as much as $17 in coins. There are 12 daily departures starting at 8:30 A.M., with the last at 9 P.M. Call to find the nearest place to purchase tickets. Prices all subject to change.

Lion Limousine and Bus Tour Service, 6000 New Jersey Ave., Wildwood Crest; 609–522–3734. Door-to-door service to casinos in Atlantic City from Cape May, Avalon, Sea Isle City, and Ocean City. Call for information on current packages, prices, and departure times. Eight casinos.

Luxury Casino Limousine, 6700 New Jersey Ave., Wildwood Crest; 609–729–4800. Door-to-door casino tours seven days a week. Buses have color TV, reserved seats. Packages with various contents at $13.95. Price subject to change. Tickets can be picked up at 10 locations in The Wildwoods. Call for details.

MUSEUMS AND HISTORIC SITES. *Cape May.* Much of Cape May is a museum and a historic site. In fact, in the Bicentennial Year of 1976 the City of Cape May was officially designated a National Historic Landmark City, only one of five such towns in the nation. That designation requires that the community must retain all structures in their original form and design, and this assures that Cape May will remain within the architectural concept of the Victorian period. In the last decade, there was a major renaissance in this city. Around 600 Victorian structures, adorned with carved barge boards, ornate verandas, and crowned dormers, have been restored. Most of the homes, hotels, shops, and other buildings were constructed in the late 1800s at the height of the Victorian era. Today a number of small gingerbread houses stand beside magnificent Victorian showplaces. Since its founding in 1970, the Mid-Atlantic Center for the Arts (MAC) has played a leading role in Cape May's revival through a year-round schedule of activities, such as tours. Its events do much to establish the rich and warm ambience of this unique resort. See also Tours, above. Following are the outstanding historical spots in Cape May:

The Abbey (John B. McCreary House), Columbia Ave. and Gurney St., 1869. A final example of the popular Gothic style as built in Cape May. Notable is the vertical emphasis in the structure, with the Gothic arch repeated in windows, doors, and the porch brackets.

Church of the Advent. Franklin and Washington sts., 1867. This Gothic church has vertical siding over a fieldstone foundation. Most of the church's furnishings have survived, including the stained glass of the windows.

Alexander's Inn (Joseph Hughes House). 653 Washington St., 1883. Built in the Second Empire architectural style for Joseph and Emma Hughes as their year-round home. Their daughters lived in the house until 1969. This 20-room Victorian home has been authentically restored and now is a bed-and-breakfast inn with an elegant dining room.

The George Allen House. 720 Washington St., 1863. Designed by architect Samuel Sloan, this fine Italianate villa has a wide veranda, extended eaves with heavy brackets, rounded top windows, and delightful cupolas, all of which were popular in the buildings of the Victorian era.

The Baldt House. 26 Gurney St., 1871. Considered to be the original of the seven identical cottages called the Stockton Hotel, and rented for the summer. They were designed by Stephen D. Button, and this cottage is distinguished by the wealth of wooden ornamentation.

Cape May Country House. 726 Corgie St. One of the few remaining examples of a small, private Victorian home. Originally summer retreat of Dr. Augustus Bourneville of Philadelphia. Still under restoration but interior is about completed.

The Cape May County Historical and Genealogical Society Museum. John Holmes House, Rte. 9, Cape May Court House, NJ 08210; 609–465–3535. This museum features exhibits of artifacts, objects, and documents significant to the history and culture of Cape May County and is the operation of the Cape May County Historical and Genealogical Society, founded in 1927. The John Holmes House, which holds the museum, is a pre-Revolutionary structure listed on both state and national registers of historical places. It was constructed by Robert Cresse in the mid-eighteenth century. The rear portion of the present house may date to as early as 1751. There are a variety of interesting historical displays of china, furniture, and glass from the late seventeenth to the early twentieth centuries. Admission: adults $2; 12 to 18 years old, $.75; under 12, free.

Carriage House. 1050 Washington St., 1876. Built two years before the Physick House. Operated by the Cape May Art League.

Chalfonte Hotel. 301 Howard St., 1876. This is a fine old hotel which has been open every summer since it was built in 1876 by Colonel Henry Sawyer. Sawyer, a prisoner of the Confederacy, was later exchanged for Colonel R. E. Lee, Jr., son of General Robert E. Lee.

The Colonial Hotel. Beach Ave. and Ocean St., 1894. The Colonial was considered ultramodern in its time because it had the first elevator in town and electric bells from the rooms to the front desk. Wallis Warfield, later Duchess of Windsor, held her first coming-out party in this popular hotel.

Colonial House. 653 Washington St., 1775. Now under restoration by the Greater Cape May Historical Society, this home is believed to be the oldest in Cape May.

Congress Hall. This was one of the earlier hotels, built in 1812 and called "The Big House." The name was changed to Congress Hall when Tom Hughes, the owner, decided to run for Congress. What is now standing is actually the third hotel, built after the disastrous fire of 1878 which wiped out thirty acres of the city. This building served as the summer White House for President Harrison, one of five presidents who came to Cape May for their summer holidays.

Damback House. 651 Hughes St., 1865. The second-floor addition to the right was the typical way of adding indoor plumbing at the time.

The Delsea. 621 Columbia, 1867. Good example of the sawed ornamentation today called "gingerbread," an important folk art of the nineteenth century.

Franklin Street Methodist Church. Franklin and Lafayette sts., 1879. Large wood corner buttresses and elaborate frames around the windows and doors of this unique Gothic church create a feeling of massiveness usually associated with masonry buildings.

Gibson House. Jackson and Carpenter. This is a good example of the mansard style. Four or five colors of exterior paint were used to create the shadows and highlights so popular in the nineteenth century.

Hall House. 645 Hughes St., 1868. Multi-colored exteriors were thought to enhance the originality of gingerbread trim. At the time, white was the one color considered most unoriginal and actually in bad taste. The colors of Hall House are splendid.

Dr. Henry Hunt House. 209 Congress Pl., 1881. This house is typical of the eclectic styles of the 1870s and 1880s, showing a collection of elements of the most popular of the Victorian architectural styles.

Huntington House. Grant St. near Branch, 1878. Built by John Kromer of Baltimore as the Arlington Hotel. This is one of the few buildings to escape the destructive fire of 1878.

Kiwanis Clubhouse. 1111 Beach Dr., 1870. First used by the Coast Guard as a lookout for the small craft that fought the dangerous riptides of the Point.

Annie Knight and Joseph Evans Houses. 203 and 207 Congress Pl., 1878 and 1881. These show the Southern influence in the architecture of Cape May. They are two-story veranda homes with French doors placed to take advantage of the cool ocean breezes. Iron captain's walks are featured on the roofs of both of these homes.

Joseph Leedham House. Corner of Congress St. and So. Lafayette. This is a good example of the Queen Anne style, with its textured surfaces, rounded corners, towers, and complex shapes—reflecting hallmarks of the late medieval-revival style.

The Mainstay. 635 Columbia Ave., 1872. This was originally a gambling house and club for gentlemen, called "Jackson's Clubhouse." It is a truly elegant villa with original furnishings and gas chandeliers.

Captain Mey's Inn. 202 Ocean St., 1890. Built by Dr. Walter H. Philips, a homeopathic physician. The inn is named after Dutch explorer Captain Cornelius Jacobsen Mey who founded Cape May in 1621. Highlights include a Delft Blue collection, magnificent oak staircase, and Tiffany stained glass.

Octagonal House. 1284 Lafayette, 1875. Popular style of house construction in the mid-nineteenth century, but now a rare sight.

The Emlen Physick House and Estate. 1048 Washington St., 1881. This is an impressive stick-style building designed by Frank Furness, the famous Philadelphia architect. Highlights include elaborate chimneys, dormers, and trim. The building has been extensively restored and is open to the public every day except Fri. in summer, weekends only in spring and fall. This house contains Cape May's extensive museum of Victorian furniture, clothing, toys, tools, and artifacts.

The Pink House. 33 Perry St., 1880. The interesting sawed ornamentation which is called "gingerbread" today, was an important folk art of the nineteenth century. Patterns were unique to individual houses, and it was considered important to show originality. This is an especially good example. Now a gift shop.

Rotary Bandstand. Lyle La. This bandstand, copied from the English Bandstand in Sefton Park, was designed with the structural pieces of wood, in keeping with the Victorian taste for woodwork, rather than with the usual English iron pieces.

Schellenger House. 1219 Lafayette St. Construction date not certain but was built before 1837. Features hand-hewn oak beams and the original window glass.

Joseph and John Steiner Cottages. 22 and 24 Congress St., 1881. Two of the earliest summer cottages built in Cape May.

Summer Cottage Inn. 613 Columbia Ave., 1867. The wealthy Harrison family of Philadelphia built this as their summer cottage. The architect designed wraparound verandas and floor-to-ceiling windows to welcome the cool sea breezes. Delightful ornate Victorian wallpapers, furnishings, and tall mirrors combine with wicker, crazy quilts, and lots of collections to add to the period elegance. The fireplace is unusual.

William Townsend House. 1037 Lafayette St., 1883. Has three fireplaces and a steep staircase with ornate hand-carvings.

Ware House. 653 Hughes St. Beautifully restored Victorian home. Elaborate trim along roof edges, with ornate dormers.

Daniel Ware House. 1142 Lafayette St., 1846. This is a rare example of the pre-Victorian cottages of Cape May, most of which were destroyed in one of the great fires of the resort.

Washington Inn. Washington and Jefferson, 1843. Building was moved several times on this property, and the facade changed to reflect changes in architectural tastes. It once had columns reaching to the third floor.

Welcome Center. 405 Lafayette St., 1853. Once a church, the building features an unusual onion dome on the tower, reflecting Victorian fascination with the Oriental.

Wilbraham Mansion. 133 Myrtle Ave., 1840. Built by Judith Hughes, one of many local Mayflower descendents, as a farmhouse. In 1900 it was bought by John W. Wilbraham who "Victorianized" it by adding a wing, rooms, bay windows. Now a private home on the gaslight tour. Plans are afoot to make it a bed-and-breakfast inn.

Duke of Windsor Inn. 817 Washington St., 1896. Built as the year-round residence of Mr. and Mrs. Harry Hazelhurst; he was a Delaware River pilot. The classic Queen Anne architectural style is dominated by a 45-foot tower, which holds some of this inn's unique rooms. There is also a dramatic, 3-story "floating" oak staircase, surrounded by natural paneling and wainscoting.

Ocean City

Discovery Seashell Museum and The Shell Yard. 2721 Asbury Ave.; 609–398–2316. Run by the owner, Larry Strange. Here he shows his worldwide collection of shells and coral, and also his live marine tanks of local sea life. Open May–Sept., Mon.–Sat., 8 A.M.–8 P.M. Free.

Ocean City Historical Museum. 409 Wesley Ave.; 609–399–1801. Shows nineteenth-century furnishings, marine and wildlife exhibits, and Indian artifacts. Open June–Aug., daily except Sun., 10 A.M.–4 P.M.; Sept.–June, Tues.–Sat., 1–4 P.M. Donations invited.

The Wreck of the Sindia. Beach at 16th St. The remnants of the sailing merchant ship *Sindia* were declared a historic site by the State of New Jersey. The *Sindia* ran aground and sank in 1901. Rumors of untold wealth left aboard the ship attract diving teams; it is believed that about a quarter of the cargo is still in the ship's hold, buried in the deep sand. Relics from the ship are in the Ocean City Museum.

Somers Point

Atlantic County Historical Society. 907 Shore Rd.; 609–927–5218. The Victorian Museum now offers a short slide show of early Atlantic City. There is also a genealogical research library and a maritime museum. Open year-round, Wed.–Sat., 10 A.M.–noon, 1–4 P.M. Free.

Somers Mansion. Shore Rd.; 609–927–2212. The oldest house in Atlantic County. Built around 1725 it is partially furnished with original pieces from that era. Open year-round, Wed.–Fri. 9 A.M.–noon, 1–6 P.M.; Sat. 10 A.M.–noon, 1–6 P.M.; Sun. 1–6 P.M. Free.

The Wildwoods

Hereford Lighthouse. First and Central Aves., North Wildwood; 609–729–1714. Hereford Lighthouse has been here since the 1800s. Steven R. MacDonald, the local historian, may be there to talk with you. Mon.–Fri., 9 A.M. to 4 P.M. free.

The George Boyer Historical Museum. In the City Hall, New Jersey and Montgomery, Wildwood. Here the Wildwood Historical Society tells the story of the Wildwoods. Open Mon. through Fri., 10 A.M.–3 P.M., in rooms 212–216. Free.

SHOPPING. The southern shore has an intriguing variety of shops that offer some unusual handcrafted items. If it's souvenirs you're looking for, though, you may choose to take the classic route—a T-shirt from one of the myriad souvenir stands on the boardwalk.

Cape May

There are a few shopping squares and malls in Cape May. Some of the shops listed below are in these fun complexes: *The Washington Street Mall* has a collection of shops open year-round. *The Merry Widow* is an 1879 Victorian family residence, with four apartments and several interesting shops. *Carpenter's Square* surrounds the Pink House at Perry Street and Carpenter's Lane. This complex has shops and restaurants. You reach it by the Sawyer Walk from the Washington Street Mall.

All Irish Imports. 401 Lafayette St.; 609–884–4484. The place to find gift items from Ireland, including fashions, Waterford crystal, and fine Belleek china.

The Baileywicke. 656 Washington St.; 609–884–2761. This interesting leather and crafts shop features handcrafted leather goods—handbags, briefcases, and more, and custom-designed 14K, sterling, and scrimshaw jewelry. If you buy a leather product here, they'll condition it for you annually, free of charge; your leather can last a lifetime. John Bailey is a member of the Guild of Master Craftsmen, Sussex, England. Ask for their catalog.

Barry Clothes, Ltd. On the mall at Jackson St.; 609–884–8693. Featuring classic apparel for men and women, including quality brands and traditional sportswear and outerwear.

Christmas Island. 400 Madison Ave., between Beach Dr. and Washington St., 609–884–4342. A fun place in the Christmas spirit.

Country Store. 731 Seashore Rd., in Cold Spring; 609–884–1810. A real country store in historic Cold Spring Village. There's a country restaurant there, too.

Crystal Persuasion. 510 Carpenter's La.; 609–884–2112. Selected handcrafted crystal and gem jewelry, Austrian crystal prisms, figurines, gifts.

Finer Finds. 664 Washington St.; 609–884–0494. A shop with nineteenth-century antiques, Colonial and Victorian lighting a specialty. Other collectibles.

Flim Flam Candles. 106 Jackson St.; 609–884–0081. You can see the candles being made here, both cast and carved. They have antique tapers, feather jewelry, and a selection of unusual gift items.

The Gingerbread Angel. Ocean and Hughes sts.; 609–884–6431. An original shop from 1843, featuring Cape May commemorative pottery, clay dream houses, basketry, bears, and other soft creatures—fun, witty, elegant objects.

Imported From Portugal. 324 Carpenter's La.; 609–884–6399. Featuring a wide variety of interesting gifts from Portugal. A great display of that country's handicrafts.

Keltie News. 518 Washington St. Mall; 609–884–7797. This is the place to buy books, periodicals, tobacco, stationery, etc.; the largest bookseller in the county.

Klothes Kove. 517 Washington St. Mall; 609–884–2444. Women's fashions.

McDowell's Gallery of Gifts. 526 Washington St.; 609–884–0430. This fine gift shop is in an old bank, built about 1895. Featured are the works of America's leading glass-blowers, jewelers, potters, and wood-workers.

Midsummer's Night's Dream. 668 Washington St.; 609–884–1309. Features Victorian furniture and vintage clothing in a romantic setting. Antiques, collectibles, gift items.

Morrow's Nut House. The Promenade; 609–884–4966; Washington St. Mall; 609–884–3300. An old-time, family-run shop filled with home-made candies, nuts, and gift items.

The Original Fudge Kitchen. 513 Washington St. Mall; 609–884–4287; 728 Beach Drive. Fudge, saltwater taffy, fine chocolates, and other good things.

Patricia Jackson. 611 Jefferson; 609–884–0323. Handcrafted jewelry. Open year-round.

The Pink House. Perry St.; 609–884–2253. Collectibles and antiques from Victorian era through art deco. Victorian-style cards and prints.

Sandpiper. 308 Carpenter's La.; 609–884–0600. Featuring unique clothing and gifts for all members of the family. A large selection of embroidered Cape May designs.

Treasure Cove. 512 Washington St. Mall; 609–884–3669. The place for all kinds of fun souvenirs, including the famous "Cape May Diamonds," T-shirts, miniature dollhouse furniture, collectible dolls, etc.

Tussie Mussie. Lobby of historic Congress Hall; 609–884–8421. A distinctive shop just off the Washington Street Mall featuring country and Victorian items. Hand-made gifts from Cape May.

The Victorian Look. 1159 Washington St.; 609–884–5360. A very interesting place for fabrics and wall coverings. Many of the designs are documented for use in restorations.

The Victorian Sampler. On the mall; 609–884–3138. Counted cross-stitch and needlepoint designs of Cape May. A large selection of books, fabrics, and kits.

Village Woodcrafter. 678 Washington St.; 609–465–2197. Restored antique furniture and a large selection of antiques and collectibles. Also a good place to get old-fashioned Christmas cards and ornaments.

Whale's Tale. 312 Washington St. Mall; 609–884–4808. A fun-to-browse-in shop with imported glass, pottery, dolls, novelties, gifts. Great selection of paper items in upstairs shop.

Ocean City

Accent Gallery. 956 Asbury Ave.; 609–398–3577. Interesting original art.

Central Square, Linwood; 609–926–1000. One of the really nice shopping centers, not far from Ocean City; across the 9th Street Bridge on to the mainland, then Rte. 9 to Linwood. If you go, plan to have a snack at the Cheese Board. Not only does this gourmet shop sell fine cheeses, coffees, etc., but it has about forty different combination sandwiches listed on a blackboard, selling for $1.75 to about $3.75. They are fantastic and delicious and a real bargain. Even the iced tea is special—freshly brewed with a touch of spice.

The Connoisseur, Ltd. 1112–22 Boardwalk; 609–399–4603. Plan to spend a lot of time browsing in what is really four shops that feature a delightful variety of things, ranging from seashore fashions and necessities to fine art glass and porcelain. Too many kinds of things to list here, and lots of them most interesting and original. Nice place for better or modest-priced gifts.

Discovery Seashell Museum and Shell Yard. 2721 Asbury Ave.; 609–398–2316. Here you can see a tenth of the hundred thousand varieties of seashells on this earth. All kinds of shells for sale. Open Memorial Day–Sept.

Donna/Gay Dillon Fashions. 733 Asbury Ave.; 609–399–0082. A nice seasonal collection of women's fashions.

Heritage Shoppe. 976–978 Boardwalk; 609–399–0025. One of the nicest shops to browse in on the boardwalk. It has a wonderful collection of early-American reproductions, a lovely collection of dolls, and an exciting Christmas shop on the second floor. Don and Lynn Claghorn also are involved in religious pilgrimage arrangements to France and elsewhere.

Lifestyle. 762 Boardwalk and 1212 Boardwalk; 609–399–5710 and 399–7646. Popularly priced beachwear, footwear, hats, sportswear, etc.

Lillian Albus. 846 Boardwalk; 609–399–9129. One of the real fashion shops on the boardwalk and one of the few offering high fashion in the South Jersey resorts. They have lunch fashion shows at the Portsider restaurant in the Port-O-Call Motor Inn at 1510 Boardwalk.

Sew What? 1340 Boardwalk; 609–398–8201. Handpainted skirts, shorts, sweaters, and shirts. Hawaiian prints, duffle bags, garment bags, etc. Original art and monogramming while you wait.

Shell Cove. 1008 Boardwalk; 609–398–6102. 500 shells and corals from around the world.

The Ship's Store. 34th St. and Bridge; 609–399–1707. All kinds of things nautical.

Stainton's. 810 Asbury Ave.; 609–399–5511. This is Cape May County's largest department store. Accepts a number of credit cards and has a gift shop as well as the usual department store goods, such as furniture, appliances, carpets, TVs, bedding, clothing, toys, etc. Closed Sun.; open daily 9 A.M.–5 P.M., to 9 P.M. Fri.

The Sweater Outlet. 618 8th St.; 609–399–4001. Women's designer sweaters at bargain prices.

Uranus. 808 Boardwalk; 609–398–5305. Clothing boutique; unique and unusual things.

Young's Ltd. 1010 Boardwalk; 609–399–9515. A gift shop with a fair-sized collection of Lladro pieces, dolls, jewelry, porcelains, and gifts of all sorts.

Stone Harbor

96th Street has a collection of shops and restaurants. *The Bread & Cheese Cupboard.* 246 96th St.; 609–368–1135, is one of the most interesting shops here. About 30 varieties of freshly baked breads and lots of other freshly baked items; gourmet foods as well. To enter is to be overcome by the aroma! Buy a batch of bread to take home.

The Wildwoods

Paula Aaronson's Miracles. 501 W. Spruce St., North Wildwood; 609–522–8516. Unusual items for home and gifts, including porcelain dolls, wall-decor items, bears, wreaths, sterling silver jewelry, French country and Victorian home accessories. Open 10 A.M.–9 P.M. weekdays, 10 A.M.–3 P.M. Sun.

Winterwood Gift & Christmas Shoppe. 3137 Rte. 9 S., Rio Grande; 609–465–3641. The area's largest and most complete gift shop, featuring Christmas items from around the world. It is in the historic Hildrith House (circa 1722).

BOARDWALKS AND AMUSEMENTS. As in other parts of the Jersey Shore, along the southern shore, the presence of a boardwalk (or lack thereof) can dictate the atmosphere of a town: brassy, noisy, and brightly lit, filled with teenagers holding hands, or serene and more sparsely populated.

Cape May

Cape May doesn't have much of a boardwalk: there is a short piece of one—about two blocks long—in front of the Convention Hall with a row of candy and miscellaneous shops and an amusement arcade of modest proportions. There is a delightful beachside promenade and a fisherman's wharf.

Ocean City

Ocean City has a delightful, well-kept boardwalk. The busy area is around the Music Pier. There are several movie houses and lots of fast-food shops selling everything from fresh lemonade to candies and all sorts of pizzas. There are amusement arcades, but none of the big amusement parks of the sort that color Wildwood. There are some miniature golf courses with strange and gigantic creatures adorning them.

Up until 11 A.M. bikes are the popular thing on the boardwalk. Not only regular bikes and bikes for two, but "buggy bikes," which can hold up to six passengers (usually the two youngest sit in a sort of basket in front), and have an awning to keep off the sun. Fees for the buggy bikes range from $5 per half hour on up, depending upon the size.

Sea Isle City

Fun City. 32nd and Boardwalk. Rides. Also arcade and amusements at 63rd and Landis Ave.

Stone Harbor

There is a non-mechanical children's play park at 9505 Third Ave., which also has a puppet theater.

The Wildwoods

This is one of the biggest boardwalks on the entire shore: three miles of amusements, rides, games, shops, and restaurants, and seven "world-famous" amusement piers. This is a paradise for teenagers of all ages, with a glitzy, honky-tonk feel that puts the "wild" in Wildwood.

Morey's Pier, 25th and Boardwalk, and *Mariner's Landing,* Schellenger Ave. and Boardwalk. These amusement centers have over sixty of the most outlandish and delightful entertainments for children of all ages. The legendary Sea Serpent, considered the best ride on the Jersey shore is at Mariner's Landing. You may purchase individual "passports" to the piers: the Gold Passport costs $11.95 per person and is usable day and night, 1 P.M.–closing. The Silver Passport is for nighttime, 5 P.M.–closing, and costs $9.95 per person. The Bronze Passport is for the daytime, 1–6 P.M., and costs $7.50 per person. The passports are good for all rides, and are available Tues.–Fri. from June 24 until Labor Day.

Raging Waters at Mariner's Landing. Schellenger Ave. and Boardwalk. A delightful water park featuring a cruise down the Lazy River, a slip down the wildest water and speed slides, the Shotgun Falls, the White Water Tube ride, and the Activity Pool. All for $7.50 per person.

Wildwood Go-Kart Rides. Wildwood Blvd.

Roaring Rapids Waterslide. Wildwood Blvd.

ENTERTAINMENT AND NIGHTLIFE. Days of fun in the sun can be completed any way you wish. In addition to strolling along the boardwalk (and maybe enjoying that beloved family sport, miniature golf), there's a wide range of entertainment. Whether your idea of fun is an old-time vaudeville show or a rock-and-roll bar, you can find it along the southern Jersey shore.

Cape May

Film. *The Mid-Atlantic Center for the Arts Vintage Film Festival.* Popular films from the 1930s and 1940s. To find the hours and what's showing call 609–884–5404.

Stage. *Victorian Revues.* Old-time vaudeville shows presented on the outdoor stage at the Emlen Physick Estates on Sun. evenings at 8:30 during July and August. For details call 609–884–5404.

MidAtlantic Stage: Theatre by the Sea. The MidAtlantic Stage offers a summer of professional theater on the outdoor stage at the Physick Estate during July and August. For the name of the show, information, and tickets call 609–884–5404. Adults, $6; children, $3. 1987 is the theater's fifth season.

Concerts. *Band Concert Series.* At the Rotary Bandshell, Wed. and Sat. evenings during the summer, beginning at 8 P.M. There are as many as 20 concerts during the summer, under the direction of Art Doran, Band Concert Coordinator for Historic Cape May.

Concerts by Candlelight at the Chalfonte Hotel. Every Thurs. night, mid-June–Sept., at 8:30 P.M. (or at 6:30 if you choose the dinner-concert package), the Chalfonte features informal evenings of chamber music. Single tickets, $4. Dinner and concert, $17.95. Purchase tickets at door or call 609–884–8409 for reservations. Everything from baroque to American spirituals.

Bars and Lounges with Music. *Carney's.* Beach Dr. and Decatur St.; 884–4425. A crowded rock club in season, on the beach. *Carney's Other Room,* next door, attracts an older crowd, with lots of ethnic songs and lively sing-alongs.

Crystal Room. Atlas Motor Inn, Beach Drive near Madison Ave.; 884–7000. Music for dining and dancing every night.

Old Shire Tavern. Washington St. Mall; 884–4700. Features everything from swing to jazz from the '30s up to and including the '80s. Lots of sing-alongs.

Pilot House. 142 Decatur St.; 884–3449. After 9 P.M. Western and blue-grass are featured. It's a tavern with a nautical decor.

Rusty Nail. Coachman Motor Inn, 205 Beach Dr.; 609–884–0220. Music for dining and dancing nightly except Monday.

Top of the Marq. Marquis de Lafayette Motor Hotel; 884–3431. This is the rooftop restaurant of this motor hotel. Dinner and dancing to piano music nightly from about 8:30 P.M. In the spring and fall, only on weekends.

Ugly Mug. Mall at Decatur St.; 884–3459. Features a duo starting at about 10 P.M. Decor features drinking mugs hanging from the ceiling beams to remind visitors of the days of the "famous" Ugly Mug Club whose purpose was to see who could blow the most foam out of a beer glass.

Bars. *The King Edward Bar* in the Chalfonte, 301 Howard St., is an intimate spot for a nightcap. The turn-of-the-century decor will complete the Victorian mood of a day in Cape May.

Ocean City

Concerts. *Ocean City Music Pier.* Boardwalk at Moorlyn Terr., between 8th and 9th sts. There's usually a free concert on Sun. nights by the Ocean City Pops orchestra. On other nights, there may be a string band, a brass group, or a choral group entertaining. The big event is the Fourth of July show when the pier is illuminated as part of the excitement. The pier is also the center for summer events including dances, flower exhibits, flea markets, antique shows, and crafts shows. The "Pops" Concerts, which run from late June through early September, are the longest running concerts of their type in the nation.

Sea Isle City

Concerts. The city provides free concerts on the Promenade every Wed. at 7:30 P.M. during July and August.

Bars. *Dead Dog Saloon.* 39th and Landis Ave.; 609–263–1500.
Shenanigans. 3815 Landis Ave.; 609–263–6430.
Springfield Inn. 12 43rd St.; 609–263–4951.

Somers Point

Discos. *Egos.* 939 Bay Ave.; 609–653–4141. Favorite spot with locals as well as tourists. Large, two-story club has DJ and light show. No jeans. Cover charge. Open 9 P.M.–3 A.M. "Under 21" night every Mon., 8 P.M.–midnight.

Bars. *Harbor Lights.* 520 Bay Ave.; 609–653–0900. A favorite of local professionals; right off the marina. Open until 2 A.M. nightly.

The Waterfront. Somers Point Circle; 653–0099. A romantic bar over-looking the bay. This large club's main attraction is its patio, where you can sip a drink and enjoy a nice view of the water. Open until 3 A.M.

The Wildwoods

Concerts. *The Gazebo Park.* Rambler Rd. and beach, Wildwood Crest. Free municipal concerts throughout the week, May–Sept.

Music Cruises. *The Delta Lady.* Wildwood Marina, 609–522–1919. The *Delta Lady* paddlewheel sails daily at 10:30 A.M., 2 P.M., and 7 P.M. Provides a relaxing inland and harbor tour with banjos and dixieland sounds. There is also a special 10 P.M. cruise as well. Refreshments on board. Call for current cruise rates and reservations.

Bars with Music. This is the nightlife famous all over the shore. Most of these clubs get very crowded in season and are no place for intimate conversation. Crowds tend to be under 30. (But don't let that stop you—everyone should experience these legendary nightspots!)

North Wildwood

Antler's Cafe. 119 East 17th Ave.; 522–8950. Sounds from the '50s to the '80s on Thurs., Fri., and Sat. Mon. night is all-you-can-eat-crab-night for $5, 7 P.M.–midnight, when a DJ comes on. Tues. is Motown Night with dancing from 9 P.M. until the wee. Wed. from 9 P.M. until 2 A.M. is ladies' night, and there is an afternoon jam, 4–8 P.M. Sun.

Club Avalon. Spruce and New Jersey aves.; 729–2210. Features show-time at 10 P.M., doors open at 9 P.M. Shows every night except Sun. Jam sessions, 3–8 P.M. Sat. and Sun. in the Bulkhead Bar. Singers and orchestras.

Harry the Hat's Club. 113 New Jersey Ave.; 522–9377. Has the largest dance floor in North Wildwood—features entertainment by singing groups; tropical drinks, sandwiches. Favors the oldies as well as top sounds of the '40s, '50s, and '60s, with, on the weekend, the hot '80s sounds.

Kitty's. Corner Walnut and Old New Jersey; 522–5071. Features continuous live music from 9 P.M. with dance bands and groups. On Sun. night there is the Gong Show with prizes and $1 schnapps.

Moore's Inlet. Spruce and New Jersey aves.; 522–6348. Features live entertainment, groups, soloists, and has music day and night, seven days a week. Ladies' night is at 9 P.M. on Thurs. Tropical drinks and a seafood bar. Sandwiches (including cheesesteaks) available during lunch, along with pizza.

Red Garter. Spruce and New Jersey aves.; 522–7414. Features cold beer, hot music, hard stuff, and dancing too. Everybody sings and there is "provocative rendezvous entertainment." Open every night.

Talk of the Town Lounge & Restaurant. Walnut and New Jersey aves.; 522–8570. Live musical entertainment. Mon. night is amateur night.

Wildwood

Club Cheers. Cedar and Pacific; 729–3900. Dancing in a smart informal atmosphere. Tues. is oldies night; Wed. is ladies' night; Sun. there is an "Under-21" dance with a dance contest.

Club Quo Vadis. Roberts and Pacific aves.; 522–4949. On Super Sunday the Great Buffet is offered, compliments of the house. Thurs. is ladies' night. Features "QV's All Nite Barbeque with Baby-back ribs." Music with a DJ.

The Fairview. Lincoln and Pacific aves.; 729–1477. Dancing with modest prices for drinks—draft beer is 25¢, drinks are $1, Fri. and Sat. until midnight. And Wed.–Sat. snack at bargains—jumbo shrimps at 25¢ each; hot dogs, 35¢; and hamburgers, 45¢. Ladies' night on Tues.; Ladies' Nite Out on Thurs.

Playpen. 9900 Atlantic Ave.; 729–3566. Claims to be the largest nightclub in South Jersey. Four clubs in one—the Rock Room, the Game Room, Club Malibu Dance Room, and Sir Winston's Pub & Deli. Open until 5 A.M., but entry stops at 3 A.M. Two live rock bands featured Wed.–Sat.

Rainbow Club. Spicer and Pacific aves.; 522–0515. On weeknights the doors open at 9 P.M. On Fri. opens at 10:30 P.M.; Saturday, at 9:30 P.M. and again at 11:30 P.M.; and Sunday, at 10:30 P.M. Features a male review on weeknights and comedy shows on weekends. Liquor store on premises.

7 Seas Cafe. 4601 New Jersey Ave.; 522–3583. Opens at 10 A.M., Wed.–Sun. Jam sessions Sat. and Sun. 5–9 P.M. Continuous live music seven days. No cover. Jumbo sandwiches, package goods, draft beer, and homemade soups and chowders.

Urie's Dockside Bar and Urie's Port Hole Lounge. Rio Grande Ave.; 522–4947. The bar features hula girls and Hawaiian music and a revue. The Port Hole Lounge has big-band sounds 9 P.M.–2 A.M. nightly, except Tues.

Wildwood Crest

Grand Hotel. Oceanfront at Rochester; 609–729–6000. Features "fine nightclub entertainment" in *Cheers,* the hotel's nightclub. Sophisticated dance music for discriminating adults: oldies, Motown, and the top 40s. Live music every night during the summer.

West Wildwood

Fun Spot. 557 W. Glenwood Ave.; 609–522–3580. Features female impersonators in the show Fantasy Follies: Barbra Streisand, Liza Minnelli, Gypsy Rose Lee. Closed Mon. Shows at 8:30 P.M. and 11 P.M. except Sun., when the show is at 8:30 P.M. only.

Index

Index

Stage shows, 49, 96, 150
Steel Pier, 20
Stone Harbor, 105–106, 124, 136, 137, 148
Storybook Land, 25, 47
Strathmere, 121
Student discounts, 3–4
Sunset Lake, 107, 119
Surf City, 16, 67, 84, 97
  sing-along bar in, 12–13
Surf-fishing tournament, 135
Surfing, 9, 41, 43, 88
Swimming, 9. *See also* Beaches
  on North Shore, 88–89

Taj Mahal (casino), 7
Taxis
  in Atlantic City, 26, 27
  to North Shore, 61
  on Southern Shore, 113
Telephones, 10
Tennis, 9, 43–44, 105, 137–140
  on North Shore, 89
Theater, 49, 96, 150
  puppet, 149
3K Run for Fun, 133
Tourist information, 2, 27–28, 62, 107, 113–114
Tours of the Northern Shore, 92
Tours of the Southern Shore, 130–132
Train rides, 59, 95
Train travel, 4, 25, 61
Trolleys and trams, 20, 26, 27, 61–62
  Cape May and Wildwood tours by, 131, 132, 133
TropWorld (casino), 22
  description of, 30
  nightlife at, 51
Trump Plaza (casino), 22
  description of, 30
  nightlife at, 51
Trump's Castle (casino), 6, 18
  description of, 30
  nightlife at, 51

Tuckerton, 53, 98
Tulip festival, 133
Twilight sightseeing cruise, 133

Vaudeville, 150
Ventnor, 18, 24
  beach and boardwalk at, 40, 41
  house rentals in, 32–33
Volleyball, 140

Walking tours, Cape May, 131
Wall, 78, 99
Walsh Offshore Grand Prix, 91
War of 1812, 109
Waretown, 96
Water skiing, 89, 138, 139
West Creek, 99
Wharton State Forest, 35, 40, 83
Wheaton Village, 92
Wheel of Fortune, 45
When to go, 2–3
Wildlife management areas, 40
Wildlife refuges, 25, 46, 60, 82, 105
Wildwood, 16, 106–107, 121, 129–130
  tours of and from, 132–133
Wildwood Crest, 107, 114, 122–123, 130
Wildwoods, 106–107, 114
  accommodations in, 121–123
  beaches at, 5, 106–107, 137
  calendar of events for, 134–135
  casino tours from, 133, 140–141
  house rentals in, 125
  restaurants in, 129–130
Winemaking, 25, 47, 92
World Wildlife Fund, 105

Zoos, 40, 46, 47
  children's, 135

Fodor's Travel Guides

U.S. Guides

Alaska
American Cities
The American South
Arizona
Atlantic City & the
  New Jersey Shore
Boston
California
Cape Cod
Carolinas & the
  Georgia Coast
Chesapeake
Chicago
Colorado
Dallas & Fort Worth
Disney World & the
  Orlando Area

The Far West
Florida
Greater Miami,
  Fort Lauderdale,
  Palm Beach
Hawaii
Hawaii (Great Travel
  Values)
Houston & Galveston
I-10: California to
  Florida
I-55: Chicago to New
  Orleans
I-75: Michigan to
  Florida
I-80: San Francisco to
  New York

I-95: Maine to Miami
Las Vegas
Los Angeles, Orange
  County, Palm Springs
Maui
New England
New Mexico
New Orleans
New Orleans (Pocket
  Guide)
New York City
New York City (Pocket
  Guide)
New York State
Pacific North Coast
Philadelphia
Puerto Rico (Fun in)

Rockies
San Diego
San Francisco
San Francisco (Pocket
  Guide)
Texas
United States of
  America
Virgin Islands
  (U.S. & British)
Virginia
Waikiki
Washington, DC
Williamsburg,
  Jamestown &
  Yorktown

Foreign Guides

Acapulco
Amsterdam
Australia, New Zealand
  & the South Pacific
Austria
The Bahamas
The Bahamas (Pocket
  Guide)
Barbados (Fun in)
Beijing, Guangzhou &
  Shanghai
Belgium & Luxembourg
Bermuda
Brazil
Britain (Great Travel
  Values)
Canada
Canada (Great Travel
  Values)
Canada's Maritime
  Provinces
Cancún, Cozumel,
  Mérida, The
  Yucatán
Caribbean
Caribbean (Great
  Travel Values)

Central America
Copenhagen,
  Stockholm, Oslo,
  Helsinki, Reykjavik
Eastern Europe
Egypt
Europe
Europe (Budget)
Florence & Venice
France
France (Great Travel
  Values)
Germany
Germany (Great Travel
  Values)
Great Britain
Greece
Holland
Hong Kong & Macau
Hungary
India
Ireland
Israel
Italy
Italy (Great Travel
  Values)
Jamaica (Fun in)

Japan
Japan (Great Travel
  Values)
Jordan & the Holy Land
Kenya
Korea
Lisbon
Loire Valley
London
London (Pocket Guide)
London (Great Travel
  Values)
Madrid
Mexico
Mexico (Great Travel
  Values)
Mexico City & Acapulco
Mexico's Baja & Puerto
  Vallarta, Mazatlán,
  Manzanillo, Copper
  Canyon
Montreal
Munich
New Zealand
North Africa
Paris
Paris (Pocket Guide)

People's Republic of
  China
Portugal
Province of Quebec
Rio de Janeiro
The Riviera (Fun on)
Rome
St. Martin/St. Maarten
Scandinavia
Scotland
Singapore
South America
South Pacific
Southeast Asia
Soviet Union
Spain
Spain (Great Travel
  Values)
Sweden
Switzerland
Sydney
Tokyo
Toronto
Turkey
Vienna
Yugoslavia

Special-Interest Guides

Bed & Breakfast
  Guide: North America
1936...On the
  Continent

Royalty Watching
Selected Hotels of
  Europe

Selected Resorts
  and Hotels of the U.S.
Ski Resorts of North
  America

Views to Dine by
  around the World